Dispute Resolution in Islamic Finance

Dispute Resolution in Islamic Finance addresses how best to handle disputes within Islamic finance. It examines how they can be resolved in a less confrontational manner and ensure such disagreements are settled in a just and fair way.

There has been little focus on how disputes within Islamic finance are resolved. As a result, many of these disputes are resolved through litigation, notwithstanding that the various jurisdictions and court systems are generally poorly equipped to handle such matters. This book addresses this gap in our knowledge by focusing on five centres of Islamic finance: the United Kingdom, the United States of America, Malaysia, the Kingdom of Saudi Arabia and the United Arab Emirates. Before exploring these countries in detail, the book considers the issues of the choice of law within Islamic finance as well the prevailing forms of dispute resolution in this form of finance.

The book brings together a group of leading scholars who are all specialists on the subject in the countries they examine. It is a key resource for students and researchers of Islamic finance, and aimed at lawyers, finance professionals, industry practitioners, consultancy firms, and academics.

Adnan Trakic is a Senior Lecturer with the School of Business, Monash University Malaysia. He is the Director of Undergraduate Studies for the School of Business and a Course Director for Bachelor of Business and Commerce. He has taught and researched in the fields of conventional and Islamic finance law, business law, and dispute resolution. The co-author of Law for Business (2nd ed, Sweet and Maxwell 2018) other published works include numerous articles, book chapters and other contributions.

John Benson is Professor and Head of the School of Business at Monash University Malaysia and an Adjunct Professor in the Department of Management, Monash Business School at Monash University Australia. His major research interests are Japanese management and unions, the restructuring of Chinese industry, employee voice, outsourcing, and dispute resolution in its various forms. John has published numerous papers and monographs.

Pervaiz K Ahmed is Professor of Management at the School of Business, Monash University Malaysia. He is the Deputy Head of School (Research), Director of Entrepreneurship Innovation Hub (eiHub) and Director of Global Asia in the 21st Century (GA21). His research interests cut across entrepreneurship, religion, ethics, and social responsibility. He has held a number of senior editorial roles and published extensively. He is a strong advocate of bringing to bear multidisciplinary perspectives to address modern-day issues.

Routledge Islamic Studies Series

This broad ranging series includes books on Islamic issues from all parts of the globe and is not simply confined to the Middle East.

24 **Refashioning Secularism in France and Turkey**
The Case of the Headscarf Ban
Amélie Barras

25 **Islam, Context, Pluralism and Democracy**
Classical and Modern Interpretations
Yaser Ellethy

26 **Young Muslim Change-Makers**
Grassroots Charities Rethinking Modern Societies
William Barylo

27 ***Da'wa* and Other Religions**
Indian Muslims and the Modern Resurgence of Global Islamic Activism
Matthew J. Kuiper

28 **A Genealogy of Islamic Feminism**
Pattern and Change in Indonesia
Etin Anwar

29 **The Idea of European Islam**
Religion, Ethics, Politics and Perpetual Modernity
Mohammed Hashas

30 **Dispute Resolution in Islamic Finance**
Alternatives to Litigation?
Adnan Trakic, John Benson and Pervaiz K Ahmed

For more information about this series, please visit: www.routledge.com/middle eaststudies/series/SE0516

Dispute Resolution in Islamic Finance

Alternatives to Litigation?

Edited by Adnan Trakic, John Benson and Pervaiz K Ahmed

LONDON AND NEW YORK

First published 2019
by Routledge
2 Park Square, Milton Park, Abingdon, Oxon OX14 4RN

and by Routledge
52 Vanderbilt Avenue, New York, NY 10017

First issued in paperback 2020

Routledge is an imprint of the Taylor & Francis Group, an informa business

British Library Cataloguing-in-Publication Data
A catalogue record for this book is available from the British Library

Library of Congress Cataloging-in-Publication Data
Names: Trakic, Adnan, editor. | Benson, John, 1945 September 6- editor. | Ahmed, Pervaiz K., editor.
Title: Dispute resolution in Islamic finance : alternatives to litigation? / edited by Adnan Trakic, John Benson, and Pervaiz K. Ahmed.
Description: Abingdon, Oxon [UK] ; New York, NY : Routledge, 2019. | Includes bibliographical references and index. |
Identifiers: LCCN 2018048223 (print) | LCCN 2018050698 (ebook) | ISBN 9781351188913 (master) | ISBN 9781351188906 (Adobe Reader) | ISBN 9781351188890 (Epub) | ISBN 9781351188883 (Mobipocket) | ISBN 9780815393313 (hardback) | ISBN 9781351188913 (ebook)
Subjects: LCSH: Finance (Islamic law) | Finance-Religious aspects-Islam. | Finance-Law and legislation-Islamic countries. | Dispute resolution (Islamic law)
Classification: LCC KBP940.2 (ebook) | LCC KBP940.2 .D57 2019 (print) | DDC 347/.16709-dc23
LC record available at https://lccn.loc.gov/2018048223

ISBN 13: 978-0-367-66222-6 (pbk)
ISBN 13: 978-0-8153-9331-3 (hbk)

Typeset in Times New Roman
by Wearset Ltd, Boldon, Tyne and Wear

Contents

List of tables vii
Notes on contributors viii
Preface xii

1 **In search of an effective dispute resolution mechanism in Islamic finance** 1
ADNAN TRAKIC, JOHN BENSON AND PERVAIZ K AHMED

2 **Choice of law in Islamic finance** 8
JULIO C COLÓN

3 **Prevailing dispute resolution mechanisms in Islamic finance** 30
SITI FARIDAH ABDUL JABBAR, SUZANA MUHAMAD SAID AND ASMA HAKIMAH AB HALIM

4 **Islamic dispute resolution in the United Kingdom** 54
MARIA BHATTI

5 **Settlement of Islamic finance disputes in the United States of America** 68
JULIO C COLÓN

6 **Settlement of Islamic finance disputes in Malaysia** 95
ADNAN TRAKIC

7 **Settlement of Islamic finance disputes in the Kingdom of Saudi Arabia** 120
AISHATH MUNEEZA AND ZAKARIYA MUSTAPHA

8 Settlement of Islamic finance disputes in the United Arab Emirates 136
NOR RAZINAH BINTI MOHD ZAIN AND RUSNI HASSAN

9 Dispute resolution in Islamic finance: the way forward 158
JOHN BENSON, ADNAN TRAKIC AND PERVAIZ K AHMED

List of statutes and regulations 168
List of cases 171
Bibliography 173
Index 186

Tables

1.1 Selected data for case study countries 4
8.1 List of treaties entered into by the UAE for the enforcement of judgments or awards 152

Contributors

Pervaiz K Ahmed joined Monash University Malaysia in 2007. He is Professor and Deputy Head of School (Research), Director of the Global Asia in the 21st Century (G21) and also Director of the Enterprise and Innovation Hub (eiHub). Before coming to Malaysia, Pervaiz held a number of senior academic positions in the UK. Pervaiz has published extensively in international journals. He is a regular keynote speaker and won numerous academic awards for his research. He has served as editor and sat on the editorial boards of several international journals. His research interests cut across entrepreneurship, religion, ethics, and social responsibility. He has extensive experience working with and advising blue chip companies and public sector organizations such as Unilever, Ford, AT&T, NCR, BT, and the NHS in Europe. He has also been involved with corporate clients in Asia such as Malaysia Airlines, CELCOM, as well as government agencies such as the Singapore National Productivity Council. Recently, he has been involved with the Islamic Development Bank as well as the Government of Dubai's Public Sector Innovation and Improvement Initiative.

John Benson is Professor and Head of the School of Business at Monash University Malaysia and an Adjunct Professor in the Department of Management, Monash Business School at Monash University Australia. He is a Fellow of the Academy of Social Sciences in Australia, a Senior Associate of St Antony's College at Oxford University, and has held visiting professorships at Oxford University and the London School of Economics in the United Kingdom; University College Dublin, Ireland; Université Jean Moulin, Lyon 3 in France; and Osaka and Hiroshima national universities in Japan. John has been a frequent consultant to government, business and trade unions in Australia, Japan and Europe. John has published 13 books and over 120 academic journal articles and book chapters. His research has focused on employment relations with a special interest in alternate dispute resolution processes, and the links between HRM practices and employee and firm performance.

Maria Bhatti is an Australian lawyer, and a lecturer at the University of Western Sydney. She completed her master of laws from the University of

Melbourne, and her thesis focused on the taxation implications of Islamic finance for which she received a prestigious National Australia Bank scholarship. Dr Bhatti's PhD thesis examined the implication of Islamic law on international commercial arbitration. She has previously taught at Monash University and University of Technology Sydney in the departments of law. Her areas of interest include corporate governance, commercial arbitration, corporate social responsibility, and ethics in business and finance.

Julio C Colón began his legal career at the University of Texas School of Law where he was conferred a Juris Doctor. During law school, he was active in the international law society and published an article in the *Texas International Law Journal*, which was well-received by scholars internationally. Following law school, Mr Colón began his legal practice assisting non-profit organizations and advising on immigration law. He later shifted to practicing full-time in civil law while serving as an adjunct professor at his alma mater. During this time, he published articles in several Islamic finance trade magazines and presented at various venues, including the 2017 International Conference on Dispute Resolution at the International Islamic University in Kuala Lumpur, Malaysia. He currently resides in San Juan, Puerto Rico where he continues to write and develop his practice while exploring the Caribbean in his free time.

Asma Hakimah Ab Halim is a lecturer at the Faculty of Law, Universiti Kebangsaan Malaysia (UKM). She obtained a Bachelor of Law (LBB) degree and completed her second degree, a Bachelor of Syariah (LLB.S) degree at International Islamic University Malaysia (IIUM). Throughout the course of study, she also took a Certificate of Company Administration (CiCA) within the same institution. After graduating she undertook a nine-month chambering under Messrs Elida, Imran & Partners in Kajang. She then obtained an LL.M degree at Faculty of Law, UKM and served as a temporary tutor at several institutions of higher learning in Malaysia. She became a lecturer at Multimedia University, before being admitted as a temporary lecturer at the Law Faculty, UKM. She was awarded a PhD from Glasgow Caledonian University in May 2015 with her research entitled 'Sukuk in Malaysia and Dubai: Selected Legal and Shari'ah Issues'.

Rusni Hassan is a Professor at the Institute of Islamic Banking and Finance, International Islamic University of Malaysia. She graduated with LLB (Honours), LLB (Shari'ah) (First Class), Master of Comparative Laws (MCL) and PhD in Law. She is actively involved in various Islamic Financial Institutions as the Shari'ah Committee locally and internationally. She has spoken extensively in conferences, workshops and trainings on various Islamic finance issues. She has published books on Islamic banking and Takaful, Islamic banking under Malaysian law, Islamic banking cases and commentaries, corporate governance of Islamic financial institutions, and remedies for default in Islamic banking. She has more than 100 articles in local and international journals. She has received several awards for her contribution to Islamic finance such as Top 10 Women in Islamic Finance (2013); Most Talented Women Professional in Islamic Banking (2014); Women of Distinction in Islamic Finance and Law (2016); Distinguished Woman in Management (2017); 100 Influential Women in Islamic Finance (2017) and recently as The Top 50 Most Influential Women in Islamic Finance (2018).

Siti Faridah Abdul Jabbar (PhD, London), (LLM, Cambridge), (LLB, UKM) is Associate Professor in Law at the Faculty of Economics and Management, Universiti Kebangsaan Malaysia. She was a Guest Lecturer at the London BPP School of Law from 2008 until 2010 lecturing on Islamic finance and financial regulation. Faridah has presented at conferences and published in journals relating to the legal aspects of Islamic finance. She was an invited panelist in a roundtable discussion on Islamic finance organized by the UK Centre for the Study of Financial Innovation and is a regular invited speaker at the Cambridge International Symposium on Economic Crime. To date, Faridah has received three Outstanding Paper Awards from the Emerald Literati Network of Excellence for her work on financial regulation and Islamic finance.

Aishath Muneeza is an Associate Professor at the International Centre for Education in Islamic Finance. She is the first female Deputy Minister of Ministry of Islamic Affairs and is the Deputy Minister of Ministry of Finance and Treasury of Republic of Maldives. She is also the chairwoman of Maldives Center for Islamic Finance and is considered the founder of Islamic finance in Maldives. Her contribution to Islamic finance include the structuring of the corporate *sukuks* and sovereign private *sukuk* of the country including the Islamic treasury instruments. She also drafted the Islamic Capital Market framework for the Maldives and is the only registered Shari'ah adviser for Islamic capital market in the country since 2013. She played a key role in setting up of the Tabung Haji of Maldives, Maldives Hajj Corporation and was the first chairperson of it. She sits in various Shari'ah advisory bodies nationally and internationally and is chairman for many of these Shari'ah advisory bodies including the apex Shari'ah Advisory Council for capital market in Maldives. She holds a doctorate in law from International Islamic University of Malaysia.

Zakariya Mustapha practices law in Nigeria where he has been an advocate and solicitor of Nigeria's Supreme Court since 2008. In 2010, he joined Faculty of Law, Bayero University Kano, Nigeria, as a lecturer where he taught conventional and Islamic banking and finance law, alongside other Islamic law courses until 2017. He specialises on legal and Shari'ah issues in Islamic banking and finance and offers legal and Islamic financial advisory services about legal framework, dispute resolution and Shari'ah-compliant product development in Islamic banking and finance. He has published numerous articles and he has presented research papers in national and international conferences. He holds a LL.B, LL.M, BL with membership of Nigerian Bar Association and Nigerian Institute of Management (Chartered).

He is currently pursuing his PhD in Islamic finance law at the Faculty of Law, University of Malaya, Kuala Lumpur.

Suzana Muhamad Said is a Senior Fellow of Law at the Faculty of Economics and Management, Universiti Kebangsaan Malaysia. Throughout her 25 years of professional working experience, she has served both the private and public sectors. She was a practicing advocate and solicitor specializing in banking litigation and commercial matters prior to her appointment in the Judicial and Legal Service attached to the Attorney General's Chambers (AGC) of Malaysia. She was assigned to various government departments including the Ministry of Finance, The Insolvency Department, Ministry of Housing and Local Government, Ministry of Rural and Regional Development and the Judicial and Legal Training Centre (ILKAP), just to name a few. She is an advocate and solicitor (Malaysia)(non-practising), Syarie Counsel for the State of Perak (non-practising), Certified Translator, Associate Mediator under Singapore Mediation Centre and panel of reviewers for two SCOPUS publications. She was also the alumni fellow in Advocacy Skill (Civil Litigation), Faculty of Law, Universiti Kebangsaan Malaysia. Her PhD was on the conflict of laws focusing on family and child law.

Adnan Trakic is a Senior Lecturer with the School of Business, Monash University Malaysia. He is the Director of Undergraduate Studies for the School of Business and a Course Director for Bachelor of Business and Commerce. He obtained his LLB (Hons) degree, Master of Comparative Laws (*with Distinction*) (MCL), PhD in Law from International Islamic University Malaysia, and Graduate Certificate in Higher Education from Monash University. He has taught and researched in the fields of conventional and Islamic finance law, business law, and dispute resolution. The co-author of *Law for Business* (2nd edn, Sweet and Maxwell 2018) and contributing co-editor of *Islamic Banking and Finance: Principles Instruments and Operations* (2nd edn, Current Law Journal 2016), his published work extends to numerous articles, book chapters and other contributions.

Nor Razinah Binti Mohd Zain is currently an Assistant Professor at the IIUM Institute of Islamic Banking and Finance (IIiBF), International Islamic University Malaysia (IIUM). She has published on dispute resolution, Islamic banking, and Islamisation of knowledge. She was trained in mediation for conflict solution and trauma conciliation (2014) by Prof. Dr Johan Galtung, the Founder of Peace Research Institute, Oslo, Norway. Prior to joining IIUM, she was an Advocate and Solicitor of the High Court of Malaya (Non-Practising). She is an active researcher of religion, politics, history, and law. She is also a member of International Council of Islamic Finance Educators (ICIFE). Recently, she and her team successfully made proposals pertaining to dispute resolution to the Malaysian Government, which lead to the establishment of the National Unity and Reconciliation Council in overcoming interfaith and interracial disputes.

Preface

Islamic finance has developed rapidly over the past half century and has increasingly captured the attention of financial organizations, governments and academic scholars. While there is a growing body of research on Islamic finance, there has been little focus on how disputes within Islamic finance are resolved. As a result, many of these disputes are resolved through litigation, notwithstanding that the various jurisdictions and court systems are generally poorly equipped to handle such matters. However, this means that we know little about dispute resolution within Islamic finance and how disputes may be resolved in a less confrontational manner and one which is more attuned to the interests of both parties.

The aim of this book is to address this gap in our knowledge by focusing on five centres of Islamic finance; the United Kingdom, the United States of America, Malaysia, the Kingdom of Saudi Arabia and the United Arab Emirates. Before exploring these countries in detail, the book considers the issues of the choice of law within Islamic finance as well the prevailing forms of dispute resolution in this form of finance. These are complex questions that are contested and open to various interpretations. By addressing questions concerning choices of law and legal mechanisms, we hope to be able to draw some conclusions on how best to resolve disputes in Islamic finance that inevitably arise from time but to also point to the direction that shows most promise in resolving such disputes in a just and fair way.

To address these issues in depth, we have drawn together a group of leading scholars who are all specialists in the legal issues or countries they examine. They have access to both English and domestic literature, as well as a long standing interest in Islamic finance. We thank them for their important and original contributions to this book. It is also important for us to point out that this book had its origins in a symposium held in Kuala Lumpur in September 2017 titled 'Dispute Resolution in Islamic Finance: Litigation or Arbitration'. This event was jointly organized by the Faculty of Law of the International Islamic University of Malaysia and the School of Business at Monash University Malaysia, in collaboration with the Malaysia Current Law Journal and with the support of the Kuala Lumpur Regional Centre for Arbitration. We would like to put on record our sincere thanks to our partners in that event as well as our thanks to the participants who provided insightful comments and analysis of the current state of dispute resolution in Islamic finance. Finally, we are grateful for the ongoing support we have received from Routledge and for their willingness to publish on this important issue. We hope that this volume will create further interest in exploring dispute resolution in Islamic finance and will contribute to a greater understanding of the complexities involved.

Adnan Trakic, John Benson and Pervaiz K Ahmed
September 2018

1 In search of an effective dispute resolution mechanism in Islamic finance

Adnan Trakic, John Benson and Pervaiz K Ahmed

Introduction

Islamic finance has grown rapidly since the beginning of the new millennium. In 2003 Islamic financial assets were approximately US$200 million; by 2013 these assets had grown to an estimated US$1.8 trillion.[1] By the end of 2017 total Islamic assets were valued in excess of US$2 trillion.[2] This growth has outperformed conventional finance in this period with much of this growth occurring in the Gulf Cooperation Council (GCC) countries, Iran and Malaysia. In these countries Islamic finance has increased the penetration rate to above 15 per cent of all financial assets.[3] Whilst still a minor share of the global financial assets the recent growth has been due to a desire of many people and institutions to have a more ethical form of banking as well as a significant growth in the number of Islamic compliant financial products being offered.

Islamic or Shari'ah compliant products offered by Islamic banks are tailored by Islamic financial institutions (IFIs) to comply with both Shari'ah (Islamic law principles) and laws of the jurisdictions in which they operate. Shari'ah compliance is an important governance layer in IFIs, which not only ensures that products offered are in compliance with Islamic principles but also ensures that all processes and dispute resolution mechanisms adopted by the IFIs are consistent with Shari'ah. Islamic financial transactions are, in many cases, intra-national but increasingly involve parties originating from different countries. In practice, parties in cross-border Islamic financial transactions normally choose English law as the basis to their contractual documents, or the law of another country like Malaysia, instead of Shari'ah.[4]

As a consequence, when disputes occur and parties choose litigation (resolution of disputes through the courts), the courts of those countries are more likely to treat the Islamic finance transaction as a conventional contract and apply domestic conventional law thereby neglecting the Shari'ah underlying nature of the transaction.[5] An examination of English and Malaysian cases involving Islamic finance matters shows that the courts are not well-equipped to adjudicate Shari'ah aspects of the Islamic finance contracts.

This deficiency in litigation has led to debate about whether litigation through the court system or some form of alternative dispute resolution (ADRs) mechanism should be the preferred process for dispute settlement in Islamic finance.[6] A number of studies have shown that Islamic financial institutions have generally favoured litigation over ADRs when attempting to resolve disputes.[7] In recent years, however, there has been a move in Islamic finance towards the use of alternative dispute resolution mechanisms, especially arbitration. It has been claimed that arbitration and mediation, which have a strong basis in Islamic jurisprudence, have an advantage over litigation as they promote settlement of disputes speedily and discreetly.[8] Some proponents of arbitrations have gone further and suggested that arbitration clauses should be made mandatory in Islamic finance agreements.[9]

This recent trend raises an important question: are there viable alternatives that can be used to resolve disputes in Islamic finance whilst maintaining the fundamental basis of Shari'ah both in principle and contract? This volume addresses this weakness in the literature and key research gap by exploring alternative dispute resolution mechanisms that could serve to resolve disputes in Islamic finance in a more appropriate way.

Alternative dispute resolution mechanisms

As with all forms of contractual agreements disputes between the parties will, from time to time, occur. There are a number of mechanisms that can be used to resolve such disputes which lead to the question: can products offered by the IFIs withstand the test of time and remain Shari'ah compliant even after the disputes have been resolved? If the contracting parties have chosen an appropriate Shari'ah compliant dispute resolution mechanism, an Islamic finance product is likely to remain Shari'ah compliant. Therefore, it is important to have an effective and appropriate dispute resolution mechanism in Islamic finance, which not only upholds the intentions of the parties as evidenced by their agreement but also recognizes and enforces the Shari'ah underlying nature of the Islamic finance transaction.

There is at present an on-going debate as to whether litigation or alternative dispute resolution mechanisms, such as arbitration or mediation, is more effective in the settlement of Islamic finance disputes. A variety of ADRs are available, although the most common are conciliation, mediation and arbitration. Conciliation involves an impartial third party directing negotiations to assist the parties to reach a mutually acceptable agreement. Mediation is a similar dispute settling method to conciliation (often used interchangeably) and involves an impartial and independent third party facilitating dialogue to assist the parties to reach a mutually acceptable agreement. Both these approaches are less adversarial than litigation or arbitration and have a clear focus on the actual outcomes. Mediation is different to conciliation in that whilst it has a similar aim its focus is on process and encouraging the parties to articulate their own interests, priorities, needs and wishes to each other.

Arbitration is a more formal process than conciliation or mediation and aims to settle the dispute through the parties presenting their case to an independent, qualified third party (or a panel). The arbitrator can be chosen by the parties. This ADR has many variants, such a final-offer arbitration, and involves the arbitrator or panel of arbitrators handing down a decision (often referred to as an award), which can be binding or non-binding. The dispute is considered settled with the final decision, although in some cases, depending on the particular system or prior agreement between the parties, a decision can be appealed. Arbitration decisions usually remain private and conciliation or mediation can serve as a useful prelude to arbitration.

In contrast to these mechanisms, litigation is a contested proceeding where a party files a lawsuit against another party. It can be costly, usually slower and often with the power balance between the parties unequal. The general aim of litigation is to declare a winner rather than to resolve the disputes or address what is perceived as an inequity. Litigation does however, allow for full discovery, gaining and/or enforcing interlocutory measures against a party, legal enforcement of the decision, and a formal appeals process. Litigation also leads to a public body of consistent decisions that can be used as precedence in future similar disputes.

Key objectives and research approach

The book has four major objectives that underpin the analysis of the questions and the countries explored. First, to increase the awareness of dispute resolution mechanisms and infrastructure available for effective resolution of Islamic finance disputes. Second, to enable proponents and opponents of litigation and ADRs in Islamic finance to present their arguments in an appropriate manner. Third, to enable the participants from industry, the judiciary, and academia to learn from the presented views. Fourth, to suggest to the related bodies and government agencies reform of the existing laws and policies, where considered necessary.

These objectives lead to the following questions:

- What are the appropriate ways to settle disputes in Islamic finance and do such approaches vary depending on context and issue?
- What basis in Islamic law exists to support the various dispute settling processes and what are the arguments against the adoption of such processes?
- How ready are Islamic financial institutions to reconsider the ways they currently use to resolve disputes?
- Is there a strong argument, based on Islamic law, for the reform of existing laws and policies governing the way disputes can be, or should be, settled?

Further questions that the book will address are provided in the discussion of the case study countries in the following section.

The case study jurisdictions

To answer these questions the monograph will focus on five countries specifically chosen to provide a contrast in context and in the significance of Islamic finance. The first two countries, the United Kingdom (UK) and the United States of America (US), are large, industrialized economies. They are both secular societies and have a legal framework that represents such secularity. Islamic finance is not a major financial actor at the present time in either of these countries. They have been included, however, due to the large number of international Islamic financial transactions taking place in both jurisdictions and that many financial contracts have a clause relating to settlement under the prevailing secular laws of these countries. The last three countries, Malaysia, Saudi Arabia and the United Arab Emirates (UAE), are smaller and developing economies, although they have some of the largest Islamic financial providers. All three are Islamic countries[10] that subscribe to Islamic law and have strong Islamic banking institutions as can be seen by their top five rating on the Islamic Finance development Index. This is particularly the case with Malaysia which is arguably the most advanced jurisdiction in Islamic finance. Details are presented in Table 1.1.

The UK's and US's laws and courts tend to be the most popular choice among the parties in international Islamic transactions. The Islamic finance cases decided in both jurisdictions lead to the conclusion that the courts are not prepared or well equipped to recognize and enforce Shari'ah aspects of an Islamic finance agreement. As a result, the courts, through the adjudication process, inadvertently transform an Islamic finance transaction into a conventional one.

Table 1.1 Selected data for case study countries

Country	*Population 2017 (millions)*[1]	*GDP (US$) 2016 (trillions)*[2]	*Islamic vs Secular State*[3]	*Penetration of Islamic Finance (%)*[4]	*IFDI Index Score*[5]
UK	66.2	2,650.9	Secular	1.0	13.54
USA	324.5	18,624.5	Secular	<1.0	3.21
Malaysia	31.6	296.5	Islamic	23.8	128.87
Saudi Arabia	32.9	646.4	Islamic	51.1	50.43
UAE	9.4	348.7	Islamic	19.6	64.18

Sources: 1 United Nations, 'World Population Prospects (2017 Revision), 2017' https://esa.un.org/unpd/wpp/publications/Files/WPP2017_KeyFindings.pdf accessed 16 June 2018. 2 World Bank, World Bank National Accounts data and OECD National Accounts data files, 2016 https://data.worldbank.org/indicator/NY.GDP.MKTP.CD accessed 16 June 2018. 3 A secular state is a country whose laws and institutions are not connected to any particular spiritual or religious doctrine (for further details see the Oxford Dictionary). 4 Islamic Financial Services Board, 'Islamic Financial Services Industry Stability Report 2017', Islamic Financial Services Board, Kuala Lumpur, pp. 8–9. 5 ICD-Thomson Reuters, 'Islamic Finance Development Report 2017, Thomson Reuters and Islamic Corporation for the Development of the Private Sector, available at https://islamicbankers.files.wordpress.com/2017/12/icd-thomson-reuters-islamic-finance-development-report-2017.pdf accessed 17 June 2018. This index covers five criteria: Quantitative development, knowledge, governance, corporate social responsibility, awareness. Malaysia is currently ranked number 1, whilst Saudi Arabia and UAE are in the top five globally.

The situation seems to be different in arbitration. Arbitration legislations in both countries are accommodative of Shari'ah principles involved in Islamic finance transactions. This monograph will investigate the above claims and will address the question as to whether the above jurisdictions are appropriate forums for the settlement of Islamic finance disputes.

Malaysia has, arguably, the most advanced laws on Islamic finance anywhere in the world. Malaysian courts are experienced in dealing with Islamic finance cases. The Malaysian dispute resolution mechanism for Islamic finance cases is unique in the sense that the courts are obliged to refer Shari'ah aspects of the agreement to the Shari'ah Advisory Council of either the Central Bank or the Securities Commission for ascertainment and ruling.[11] The legislative provisions allowing for this, however, have been under attack recently. The Federal Court decision, in 2017, in *Semenyih Jaya Sdn Bhd v Pentadbir Tanah Daerah Hulu Langat* emphasized that the judicial power of the court can only reside in the judiciary and provision of a federal law which usurp the judicial power of the court are unconstitutional. This monograph will assess the suitability and effectiveness of the Malaysian dispute resolution mechanism for Islamic finance. It will also investigate the constitutionality of the impugned legislative provisions in the light of the recent Federal Court decision. Malaysia is home to the Asian International Arbitration Centre (AIAC),[12] which has recently passed AIAC i-Arbitration Rules 2017, which is the first of its kind anywhere in the world. The monograph will thus explore the rules and prospects of AIAC being used in local and international Islamic finance disputes.

The Middle East, in this case represented by Saudi Arabia and the United Arab Emirates, being a key centre and the main generator for Islamic finance, is the final part of the analysis of alternative dispute resolution mechanisms in Islamic finance. In most of international Islamic finance disputes, either both or at least one of the parties involved is based in the Middle East. Interestingly, the parties originating from these countries rarely submit their disputes for adjudication to the courts of their respective states. Neither do they have the law of their states identified as the governing law of their contracts. Are their national legal systems, which often comply with Shari'ah and, in some cases based on Shari'ah, inferior to the English common law legal system? This monograph investigates if and why is this the case? These two countries also host a number of international arbitration centres for Islamic finance disputes. The take-up rate by the disputing parties, however, appears to be low. The reasons for that being so will also be considered in this monograph.

Structure and framework

The monograph is broken into nine chapters. The introductory chapter provides a framework for the book and the key questions to be addressed. This chapter is followed by two underpinning chapters that discuss the choice of law (national versus Shari'ah) and the prevailing dispute resolution mechanisms that are currently used in Islamic finance. These chapters are then followed by the five country specific chapters that follow a standard format that is designed to assist the reader to compare and contrast the approach adopted in each country. Each of these chapters will outline the legal framework in the particular country, the approach of the courts, the use of arbitration and other forms of ADRs, as well as addressing the particular questions relating to individual countries referred to in the previous section. A short conclusion, presenting the overall findings and answers to the core questions completes the monograph. In doing so the chapter will make an assessment of the role and effectiveness of the available dispute resolutions mechanisms available to settle Islamic finance disputes.

Conclusion

This book will explore the strengths and weaknesses of both litigation and alternative disputes resolution mechanisms and assess their appropriateness in the context of Islamic finance. Resolving disputes arising in Islamic finance can present major challenges to the parties especially when litigation is utilized. Whilst this may present fewer difficulties in Islamic countries, even then differences in the application of Shari'ah, in maintaining the intention of the parties and various approaches of national laws can create major obstacles. This monograph explores the various approaches currently adopted and suggests that one possibility is to move away from a reliance on litigation and adopt alternative dispute resolution procedures such as mediation and arbitration. This contention is discussed in relation to five jurisdictions namely the UK, USA, Malaysia, Saudi Arabia and the UAE.

Each of the five case study chapters will address the four key questions listed earlier in this chapter as well as the questions raised concerning each particular country. Whilst there will be unique characteristics underpinning dispute resolution in the various countries, there will also be some common characteristics which will inform explanations of the way Islamic finance disputes can be resolved. Generally, disputes in Islamic finance are more difficult to resolve due to the need to ensure Shari'ah principles are maintained and given due recognition by secular courts. Nevertheless, the aim of the book is to openly discuss the advantages and disadvantages of various forms of dispute resolution, and by so doing raise awareness of the key issues that serve to achieve or prevent effective dispute resolution. By understanding the problem more clearly and raising awareness of these issues among the key stakeholders will, we hope, lead to appropriate suggestions for the reform of existing laws and policies.

Notes

1 International Monetary Fund, 'Islamic Finance and the Role of the IMF' (International Monetary Fund, February 2017 www.imf.org/external/themes/islamicfnance accessed 14 June 2018.

2 Islamic Financial Services Board, 'Islamic Financial Services Industry Stability Report' (Islamic Financial Services Board, 2018) www.ifsb.org/docs/IFSI%20Stability%20Report%202016%20(final).pdf accessed 15 June 2018.

3 Ibid, International Monetary Fund [1].

4 J C Colón, 'Choice of Law and Islamic Finance' (2011) 46 *Texas International Law Journal* 412; T A Hamid and A Trakic, 'Enforceability of Islamic Financial Contracts in Secular Jurisdictions: Malaysian Law as the Law of Reference and Malaysian Courts as the Forum for Settlement of Disputes' (ISRA Research Paper, no. 33, 2012); A Trakic, 'The Adjudication of Shari'ah Issues in Islamic Financial Contracts: Is Malaysian Islamic Finance Litigation a Solution?' (2013) 29 *Humanomics* 260.

5 Z Hasan and M Asutay, 'An Analysis of the Courts' Decisions on Islamic Finance Disputes' (2011) 3 *ISRA International Journal of Islamic Finance* 41; C Paldi, 'The Dubai World Islamic Finance Arbitration Center and the Dubai World Islamic Finance Arbitration Center Jurisprudence Office as the Dispute Resolution Center and Mechanism for the Islamic Finance Industry: Issues and a Proposed Framework', *Master Dissertation in Islamic Finance*, Durham University, 2013, 1–57.

6 NHD Foster, 'Encounters Between Legal Systems: Recent Cases Concerning Islamic Commercial Law in Secular Courts' (2006) 68 *Amicus Curiae* 2; UA Oseni, 'Islamic Finance Arbitration: Integrating Classical and Modern Legal Frameworks' in Adnan Trakic and Hanifah Haydar Ali Tajuddin (eds), *Islamic Banking and Finance: Principles, Instruments and Operations* (2nd edn, Malaysian Current Law Journal 2016) 549–568; L C Thomas, 'Developing Commercial Law Through the Courts: Rebalancing the Relationship Between the Courts and Arbitration' (The Bailli Lecture, 9 March 2016) https://aberdeenunilaw.files.wordpress.com/2016/05/lcj-speech-bailli-lecture-201603091.pdf accessed 24 July 2018.

7 H Yacoob, M Muhammad and E Smolo, *International Convention for Islamic Finance: Towards Standardization* (ISRA Research Paper, no. 29, 2011); J Lawrence, P Morton and H Khan, 'Dispute Resolution in Islamic Finance', (Global Islamic Finance Report, April 2012) http://klgates.com/files/Publication/0b2f56b0-d738-4217-85ee-6670f2101659/Presentation/PublicationAttachment/3e2c3cd0-43fd-4ef4-ac96-700e33340e6a/Dispute_Resolution_in_Islamic_Finance.pdf accessed 20 February 2018.

8 A Othman, 'Islamic Finance Dispute Resolution in Malaysia', Workshop on Dispute Resolution and Insolvency in Islamic Finance: Problems and Solutions, 19 September 2013, National University of Singapore, 13–26.

9 SAB Hamid, *International Arbitration with Commentary to Malaysian Arbitration Act 2005* (Janab (M) Sdn Bhd 2016) 443–467.

10 By referring to these countries as 'Islamic', it is not our intention to designate them as constitutionally Islamic countries or otherwise. We refer to them as 'Islamic' as all three are Muslim majority countries with large Muslim populations, their legal systems are either based or strongly influenced and shaped by Islamic law, and, in the context of our book, they are world leaders in Islamic finance.

11 See ss 56 and 57 of the Central Bank of Malaysia Act 2009 and ss 316A(1), 316F and 316G of the Capital Markets and Services Act 2007 (Malaysia).

12 Formally known as Kuala Lumpur Regional Centre for Arbitration (KLRCA).

2 Choice of law in Islamic finance

Julio C Colón

Introduction

Shari'ah is international law. There are billions of individuals in dozens of national jurisdictions where Shari'ah underlies their business dealings. When such individuals negotiate and sign contracts referencing Shari'ah as governing the contract or stating that all duties shall be interpreted with regard for Islamic principles, it also follows that when a dispute occurs that the parties to the agreement will also derive arguments from Shari'ah. The question is, how can they?

Shari'ah is international in character. It has happened that a United Kingdom company came into a contractual dispute with a company from Bahrain and argued Shari'ah matters during the course of litigation in London.[1] Why is that? Today, a Qatar-based company specializing in Shari'ah-compliant investment products is going through restructuring at a New York bankruptcy court.[2] How is that working out? This chapter is dedicated to exploring the means by which Shari'ah is implemented as a choice of law in the litigation of contracts governing the execution of Islamic finance-related business.

The choice of law clause, of course, refers to the jurisdiction whose laws will govern the contract. However, if Shari'ah is a body of legal principles, and Islamic finance is interpreted by reference to those principles, then what shall parties write in their choice of law clause as their jurisdiction of reference? Shari'ah, the laws of a particular jurisdiction, or something else?

Shari'ah as a choice of law

Within any agreement, naming the law that will govern the contract in the case of a dispute puts parties on notice as to each other's expectations in terms of the agreement, and tells the decision maker presiding over the litigants – whether a judge or arbitrator – by what law to judge. Even more importantly, in a world where the majority of people live outside of Shari'ah jurisdictions and Islamic law influenced jurisdictions,[3] it is necessary for a party to base the agreement and its execution on the condition of Shari'ah-compliance in order to avoid it being interpreted according to conventional practices.

Furthermore, the term 'Shari'ah-compliant' may have a temporal limitation which does not extend towards litigation. After all, consider the financial and time premiums paid by parties in the following hypothetical situation:

> Two companies negotiate a financial arrangement. They ensure the hiring of attorneys familiar with drafting agreements derived from classic contractual forms from Shari'ah jurisdictions.[4] Before signing the agreement, the contract is given to a board of Shari'ah experts in order to obtain a certification of Shari'ah compliance or suggestions in order to remedy the contract and make it Shari'ah compliant. At the bottom of the contract, before the signatures, one final clause written in beautiful calligraphy reads, 'This contract shall be governed according to the Shari'ah'.

In such a case, did the two contracting parties go through trouble of hiring specialist lawyers and academics to review their contract only to govern the function of the agreement but not anticipating that Shari'ah would influence legal analysis during the adjudication of disputes? If it later turned out that a party sought enforcement of a contractual provision that both litigants undisputedly state is not Shari'ah-compliant, should a judge in a non-Shari'ah jurisdiction give way to one party's argument that the provision is unenforceable due to illegality (under the Shari'ah)? What if a cause of action existed in Shari'ah, should either of the parties be able to sue and obtain a judgment against the other while they both choose to litigate in a common law jurisdiction?

These and other questions arise in the case of a contract which purports to elect Shari'ah as a choice of law.

Case study: Shamil Bank of Bahrain EC v Beximco Pharmaceuticals Ltd

In *Shamil Bank of Bahrain EC v Beximco Pharmaceuticals Ltd*,[5] the Court of Appeals was asked to consider whether a particular contract was invalid under the Shari'ah. In that case, Beximco Pharmaceuticals entered into a *murabaha*[6] agreement with Shamil Bank of Bahrain, a financial institution holding itself out to be a bank which conducts its business within the limits of the Shari'ah.[7] The agreement was signed by the parties and resulted in the acquisition of nearly US$47 million in assets.[8] The agreement contained a choice of law clause which read, 'Subject to the principles of the Glorious Sharia'a, this agreement shall be governed by and construed in accordance with the laws of England'.[9] When Beximco failed to make payments under the agreement, Shamil Bank claimed the amount outstanding under the agreement.[10] Beximco claimed that the agreement was invalid because it contained a hidden form of *riba*.[11] The Appellate Court acknowledged that if the phrase '[s]ubject to the principles of the Glorious Sharia'a' was a valid choice of law clause, then Beximco would succeed under the agreement.[12] The Appellate Court found this statement to be invalid, because the 1980 Rome Convention on the Law Applicable to Contractual Obligations

('Rome Convention') allows only one system of law to govern a contract and requires that the chosen law be that of a particular country.[13] According to the court, if the intention of the parties was to incorporate the Shari'ah into the contract, then they did not do so effectively. To so do effectively, they would have had to specifically identify a foreign law or code and to which part of the contract the clause applied.[14] The Appellate Court, in strict application of this principle, stated, 'It is plainly insufficient for the defendants to contend that the basic rules of the Sharia applicable in this case are not controversial. Such "basic rules" are neither referred to nor identified'.[15]

At the core of the court's inability to accept Shari'ah as the governing law was a principle that if followed consistently would also prevent the same court from applying the law of 'the civil code'. Ultimately, the judge in *Shamil Bank* needed the parties to identify an actual jurisdiction.

Shari'ah as non-state law

The English Appellate Court prohibited the use of a combined-law clause based on the principle that a contract cannot be governed by two systems of law and the statement in the Rome Convention on the Law Applicable to Contractual Obligations that '[a] contract shall be governed by the law chosen by the parties';[16] i.e. that 'law' being in the singular form means that two laws cannot govern the same part of the contract.[17] Though, legal scholars within continental Europe and various jurisdictions in the western hemisphere have argued for the permissibility that a non-state law govern a contract.[18] Such arguments continue to be denied by courts and standard-setting organizations.

A comparison of the Rome Convention and Rome I Regulation reveals that there may be some future argument against the reasoning of the court in *Shamil Bank*.[19] Paragraph 13 of the preamble of Rome I states, 'This Regulation does not preclude parties from incorporating by reference into their contract a non-State body of law or an international convention'. However, Article 3(3) of the regulation provides essentially the same language as the Rome Convention which was relied upon in *Shamil Bank:*

> Where all other elements relevant to the situation at the time of the choice are located in a country other than the country whose law has been chosen, the choice of the parties shall not prejudice the application of provisions of the law of that other country which cannot be derogated from by agreement.[20]

Therefore, most commentators agree that courts will interpret this to restrict the law applicable to the contract as necessarily belonging to a specific jurisdiction.[21] As for reconciling the difference between Article (3)(1) of Rome I ('A contract shall be governed by the law chosen by the parties') and Paragraph 13 of its preamble ('[...] incorporating by reference into their contract a non-State body of law [...]'), the incorporation of a non-state body of law by reference merely makes the incorporated text a provision of the agreement itself, while the law governing the contract still prevails substantively in litigation.

At best, Rome I gives the parties an opportunity to instruct the future judge or arbitrator to take into account the *lex mercatoria* of Islamic finance,[22] such as the classic contractual forms commentated on by Shari'ah scholars. However, it is still inadvisable to reference an entire jurisprudential system for the purposes of incorporating the traditions of the Islamic finance industry, given the availability of standards, codes, and treatises that comment and expound on Islamic finance and even on Shari'ah standards of evidence, burdens of proof, causes of action, and defences.

The desire to include non-state law as an option in regard to choice of law in national court is not a novel idea, generally. In his article, *Non-State Law in the Hague Principles*, Ralf Michaels explains that this principle was debated among members of the Hague Academy.[23] The Hague Principles are a form of soft law,[24] a body of commentary similar to the Restatement of Law in the US, or the Accounting and Auditing Organization for Islamic Financial Institutions (AAOIFI) standards. The idea that a contract could be governed without resort to law other than what was mentioned within the contract seems to have come up in discussions before, the so-called *contrat sans loi*, or self-sufficient contract.[25] This notion still envisioned the inclusion of transactional customary law, i.e. *lex mercatoria*.[26] Bearing this in mind, the Hague Conference's 'Principles on Choice of Law in International Contracts' (hereinafter called Hague Principles) chose an interesting definition of the word 'law' in Article 3, which reads:

> Article 3 – Rules of Law: Under these Principles, the law chosen by the parties may be rules of law that are generally accepted on an international, supranational or regional level as a neutral and balanced set of rules, unless the law of the forum provides otherwise.[27]

Ralf Michaels points out that this is not the mere incorporation of industry principles, but allows for the choice of those standards as the law itself.[28] In support of his thesis, Michaels points out that non-state law in commercial arbitration has long been possible, and its use was the most controversial issue at the convention.[29]

In regard to Shari'ah as a choice of law in jurisdictions outside of Islamic law-influenced jurisdictions, the Hague Principles are not altogether reassuring. On one hand, the commentary states that the criterion of '[...] the "rules of law" chosen by the parties [is that it] must have garnered general recognition beyond a national level [...]',[30] which surely applies to Shari'ah. On the other hand, the commentary at 3.15 explains that the choice of law clause should address the necessity of 'gap-filling' to cover matters which the parties' chosen 'rules of law' do not cover.[31] The commentary gives as an illustration:

> A choice of law agreement provides that: 'This contract shall be governed by the UNIDROIT Principles of International Commercial Contracts and, with respect to issues not covered by those principles, by the law of State X.'.[32]

Though, a similar choice of law clause in Islamic finance would better be described as a 'gatekeeping' more than a 'gap-filling' provision, such as this modified version of the illustration above:

> A choice of law agreement provides that: 'This contract shall be governed by the UNIDROIT Principles of International Commercial Contracts ~~and~~, except with respect to issues ~~not covered~~ in contradiction to ~~by those~~ the principles of Shari'ah, ~~by the law of State X~~ in which case Shari'ah will govern.'.

Thus, it would seem like the Hague Principles, approved on 19 March 2015, create as many counter-arguments as arguments regarding use of Shari'ah as a choice of law in non-Islamic law influenced jurisdictions.[33]

Finally, it is worth mentioning that neither *lex mercatoria* nor religious law likely applies within the scope of its Article 3 of the Hague Principles, as '[m] ere principles of law are not rules'.[34] Though, it must be noted that the Hague Principles seek to offer guidance to jurists in general, including state courts which have never allowed the use of *lex mercatoria* and are uncomfortable with interpreting religious law.[35] Thus, regarding the use of non-state law in courts, I conclude alongside Ralf Michaels when he writes, '[… A]llowing the choice of non-state law responds to few existing needs, while necessarily running into a number of practical problems'.[36]

Shari'ah in common law courts

There are written opinions from common law jurisdictions in which the court elaborates its reasoning with reference to Shari'ah sources. These stand as practical examples that Shari'ah as a body of law is (1) comprehensive in its rules; (2) impartial in its application; and (3) balanced towards people in its benefits and drawbacks.[37]

But generally, you will not find such a scenario because of all of the reasons henceforth discussed. However, because courts in the US will typically apply a given choice of law as long as it is that of a particular jurisdiction, the law of the Kingdom of Saudi Arabia presents a quirky situation for a common law judge uncomfortable with the application of religious law.

Saudi Arabia's Basic Law of the Government states that '[t]he Kingdom of Saudi Arabia is a sovereign Arab Islamic state with Islam as its religion; God's Book and the Sunnah of His Prophet, God's prayers and peace be upon him, are its constitution […]'.[38] These Nizam, or supplementary Saudi laws, exists as necessary regulations and are regarded as valid only to the extent that they are consistent with the Shari'ah.[39]

In *National Group for Communications & Computers v Lucent Technologies International*, National Group filed suit against Lucent Technologies in a US district court for breach of contract.[40] National Group, a Saudi Arabia-based company, contracted Lucent Technologies to assist in a lavish project to design and install emergency and pay telephones throughout Saudi Arabia.[41] Lucent Technologies terminated its subcontract, and National Group was forced to liquidate its Project Department, which it had created specifically to implement the telecommunications contract.[42] National Group then brought suit against Lucent Technologies seeking actual and expectation damages.[43] Both National Group and Lucent Technologies acknowledged that Saudi Arabian law governed the terms of the dispute, and the district court judge agreed that in order to judge the case it would have to understand how a Saudi Arabian judge would decide the claim for loss of the plaintiff's Projects Department.[44] In doing so, the court analysed tenets of Shari'ah, which it understood as the Islamic 'divine law' based on the 'Qur'an, the Sunnah, and fiqh [...]'.[45]

Turning to the parties' dispute, the district court began to analyse the issue of whether expectation damages would be allowable against Lucent Technologies under Saudi Arabian law. In fact, it went on to state, 'Several historical [...] statements of the Prophet Muhammed [...] are instructive on this issue', and then it proceeded to quote the Prophet Muhammed's prohibition of *gharar* transactions.[46] Thus, the district court found a principle, which worked in favour of the defendant – that expectation damages constitute a form of *gharar*.[47] The district court elaborated, explaining that book value is an accounting convention that would not produce an accurate picture of actual losses as defined under Islamic law.[48]

The value of *National Group for Communications & Computers v Lucent Technologies Intl*, is its persuasive impact in terms of *gharar* transactions and its application to book value as an accounting method. But more importantly, as the body of US jurisprudence relating to Shari'ah grows, it is incumbent upon our legal practitioners to analyse and predict how these decisions affect the Islamic finance industry. If we compare *National Group for Communications & Computers v Lucent Technologies Intl* to another case involving Saudi Arabia law, we see the court reject a viable Shari'ah defence, whilst acknowledging that the law of Saudi Arabia applies and will necessitate the reference of Shari'ah.

In *Saudi Basic Industries Corp v Mobil Yanbu Petrochemical Co*, Saudi Basic Industries Corporation, a company organized under the laws of Saudi Arabia, entered into a joint venture with Mobil Yanbu Petroleum Company and Exxon Chemical Arabia, Inc.[49] Saudi Basic Industries then sued in Delaware court seeking a declaratory judgment that payments made to it by the joint venture partners were not overcharges that violated any applicable provision of the contract. Mobil and Exxon made counterclaims on the basis that Saudi Basic Industries had been overcharging them for technology that it had licensed from another company.[50] The dispute was governed by Saudi Arabian law.[51]

On appeal from the trial court decision, Saudi Basic Industries argued the point that the trial judge's use of the ijtihad legal methodology 'employed to determine Saudi law was "free wheeling," "standardless," and a "bare 'guess" as to the correct content of Saudi law'.[52] In reality, this trial judge was presented with over nine reports from experts on Saudi law, as well as over 1,000 pages of their deposition testimony.[53] However, after Saudi Basic Industries received the adverse verdict, it attacked the American trial judge's *ijtihad* on the basis of a post-trial affidavit of an influential expert witness (Dr Vogel), claiming that the trial judge 'was simply not qualified to practice ijtihad'.[54] But, in denying that the trial court engaged in a standardless determination of Saudi Arabian law, the Delaware supreme court mentioned that the expert of Saudi Basic Industries Corporation (SABIC) stated that no US court possesses the qualifications to engage in legal analysis under Saudi Arabian law.[55] The appellate court proceeded to point out the strange timing of the appellant's argument as it quoted the words of the trial judge, 'It is remarkable that SABIC, having [purposefully] selected this forum [...] comes forward after a verdict against it to claim that no American judge is qualified to interpret and apply Saudi law [...]'.[56]

The decisions of both the trial and appellate courts support the safety of the contract by diminishing the 'Shari'ah risk'. Because a seemingly valid defence pointing to a US judge's lack of capacity to decide under the laws of Saudi Arabia or other Shari'ah-influenced jurisdiction is rejected when the law of the contract and location of litigation are chosen by freely consenting parties, the purpose of the contract is protected from litigation-related considerations.

These US decisions indicate that the courts are protective of the financial aims of the contract and do not accept Shari'ah-based defences that undermine the validity of the agreement. However, Shari'ah-based defences are acceptable when within bounds of the contract, and courts are willing to engage in independent reasoning using Shari'ah-based sources of jurisprudence.

Jurisdictional options for the law governing Islamic finance contracts

There are as many options for choice of law as there are jurisdictions. Given that, I shall conduct this discussion by describing examples of choices of law from two broad categories: (1) non-Islamic law influenced jurisdictions and (2) Islamic law influenced jurisdictions.

Non-Islamic law influenced jurisdictions

It is not strange to select the law of a jurisdiction with no Shari'ah tradition to govern disputes arising from Islamic financial arrangements; in fact, the laws of New York and of England are popular choices. However, in order for the contract to retain its character beyond merely utilizing the nominal forms of traditional contracts from Shari'ah jurisdictions, it is necessary for parties to define boundaries, incorporate standards, and assent to procedures. If these considerations are not made, then the character of the agreements is in danger of changing to that of a conventional interest-based arrangement when a non-Islamic law influenced jurisdiction's law is selected.

Defining boundaries

In a jurisdiction which accepts the collection of interest or forms of *riba*, an Islamic financial arrangement should seek to be Shari'ah-compliant within the four corners of the document. It is irrelevant if traditional forms from commentary on Islamic law are selected, as many forms of 'alternative finance' are acceptable in a Shari'ah sense of the word. In fact, the principal criticism of the modern Islamic finance industry is that the use of traditional forms is a mere marketing ploy and that substantively the agreement promotes the charging and collection of interest.[57] Therefore if such a situation is to be avoided, then at minimum the parties must clearly state that the contract prohibits the collection of interest regarding its execution or in the awarding of judgments in the case of disputes. Similarly, the parties may agree that in the case of litigation, speculative damages will not be awarded. Lacking such provisions, the contract is likely to be interpreted in the context of a given jurisdiction's tradition.

For example, after the Appellate Court in *Shamil Bank v Beximco* decided that the only law that applied to the contract was that of England,[58] it proceeded to analyse the contract in light of the commercial goals that it served to accomplish, as English law requires,[59] and decided that the goal of Beximco was but to acquire working capital through an agreement couched in Islamic terms.[60] The court proceeded to affirm the decision of the lower court which arguably permitted the recovery of monies that were effectively interest.[61] Had the choice of law clause omitted reference to Shari'ah, then it would have been upon the defendants to take a greater role in structuring the agreement in such a way that it would be acceptable according to Shari'ah.

However, in defining boundaries, it is important for purposes of clarity that the extent of the use of Shari'ah defences be decided. After all, it is possible that two jurists from the Shari'ah tradition have a difference as to the permissiveness of a contractual form. Is it therefore advisable for parties to agree to abandon the use of attacks on the Shari'ah-compliance of their very own arrangement?[62] By doing so, parties mitigate against the use of Shari'ah-related defences being used during litigation in non-Islamic law influenced jurisdictions. Again, this should in turn incentivize parties that truly seek to avoid *riba* and its variants to draft their agreements accordingly. In the absence of such a clause, the court may or may not consider such defences.

For example, the lawyers in *Investment Dar Company K.S.C.C v Blom Developments Bank S.A.L* made a Shari'ah-inspired defence, while couched in common law terms, and successfully defended against a motion for summary judgment.[63] In that case, the defendant argued that the master *wakala* contract effectively required it to pay interest and that such an arrangement was not Shari'ah-compliant, and hence it was not permitted by its Articles of Association, which stated, 'None of the objectives shall be construed and interpreted as permitting the company to practice directly or indirectly any usury or non-Sharia compliant activities'.[64] As such, the defendant reasoned that the contract was void under the doctrine of *ultra vires*.[65] Ultimately, the court concluded that there was at least a triable issue in this regard.[66] This was in spite of a provision in the master *wakala* contract which stated, '[Defendant] will not at any time assert that any provision thereof or any transaction effected pursuant hereto contravenes the Sharia'.[67]

Alternatively, there are foreseeable cases in which parties would elect to govern the agreement according to the law of a non-Islamic law influenced jurisdiction while still accepting the use of Shari'ah-related defences in litigation. However, the court may prohibit such tactics on the basis of the laws of that specific jurisdiction. For example, in the case of *Bank Kerjasama Malaysia Rakyat Bhd v PSC Naval Dockyard*, the presiding judge applied the doctrine of *estoppel* to the defendant's raising of issues concerning the Shari'ah-compliant features of the bank, because 'the customer had [already] agreed to the terms of the financing and documentation at time of execution [...]'.[68]

Incorporating standards

In order to compensate for a jurisdiction's lack of laws dealing with Islamic finance, standards – such as those published by the Accounting and Auditing Organization for Islamic Financial Institutions ('AAOIFI') – may be incorporated into the contract, as suggested in the Hague Principles.[69]

However, standards such as those published by the AAOIFI 'do not provide "secondary rules" for unforeseen circumstances or non-performance of either party to the transaction'.[70] And finally, standards incorporated by reference do become part and parcel of the contract itself, though to varying degrees.[71]

Assenting to procedures

Last, it is possible that a court may be excluded from adjudicating Shari'ah issues. This does not in essence destroy the character of a company and its agreements if it continues to acknowledge Shari'ah standards within its non-litigation concerns.

For example, Arcapita, a Shari'ah-compliant investment company, was undergoing reorganization under Chapter 11 of the US Bankruptcy Code in the federal court for the Southern District of New York.[72] Seeking more funds to assist in its reorganization efforts, Arcapita moved the bankruptcy court to approve its plan to seek $150 million of debtor-in-possession financing, which it structured as a *murabaha* financing package, including findings in its motion for debtor-in-possession financing regarding the transactions within the *murabaha* deal, such as the sale of metals and other Shari'ah-compliant commodities.[73] When some parties-in-interest questioned whether the *murabaha* financing was actually Shari'ah-compliant, the bankruptcy court ultimately concluded that the Shari'ah-compliance of the debtor-in-possession financing could not be before court, and that the standards for approval of debtor-in-possession financing are to be taken solely in the US Bankruptcy Code.[74]

Ultimately, when litigating disputes arising from Islamic finance agreements utilizing the laws of non-Islamic law influenced jurisdictions such as the US, it is important to understand the limitations of the courts in addressing matters according to parties' intentions. And while the incorporation of standards is key and partially addresses ambiguities, it is still possible that courts will make analogies towards the system of loans and interest in the same way that Islamic finance professionals make analogies to partnerships and profits.[75]

Islamic law influenced jurisdictions

The matter that I put forth for consideration in this section is to glimpse at what choosing the law of an Islamic law influenced jurisdiction[76] looks like within the context of dispute resolution within Islamic finance by analysing statutes and illustrations from case law.

The regulatory environment in regard to Islamic finance is minimal in some countries; therefore, in such a jurisdiction the judge may need to apply law from the primary sources of Shari'ah in order to judge a dispute in Islamic finance. Compounding the issue of predictability, many court systems do not publish decisions in periodic reporters, as judicial opinions in such jurisdictions do not hold precedent. That stated, it is still possible that such a jurisdiction will suit the juristic requirements necessary for a finder of law to adjudicate a dispute in Islamic finance as it is at its root bounded by Shari'ah principles and defined by custom and written agreements.

Such was the case in *National Group for Communications & Computers v Lucent Technologies International*. Though that case did not arise from a dispute in Islamic finance per se, the issue whether the damages sought by the appellant were a form of *gharar*, and hence prohibited by Shari'ah, is exemplative of a dispute involving Islamic finance. Recall that in that case, a US federal judge was called on to judge the dispute according to Saudi Arabia law, determining whether it would permit the recovery of expectation damages.[77] Compounding the issue, Saudi Arabia judges are not required to follow the precedent of a higher court in regard to analogous cases and judicial decisions are rarely published; therefore, the US federal judge in *National Group for Communications & Computers v Lucent Technologies International* had no case on point to follow in order to assist him in acting as Saudi Arabia judge.[78] Taking note that Article of 48 of the 'Basic Regulation of the Kingdom of Saudi Arabia' stated that

> [t]he courts shall apply in cases brought before them the rules of the Islamic shari'a in agreement with the indications in the Book [The Qur'an] and the Sunna and the regulations issued by the ruler that do not contradict the Book or the Sunna,[79]

the court considered the briefs of both parties and the testimony of their experts in order to derive the necessary juridical foundation by which to judge the dispute.[80] Ultimately, the court concluded that expectation damages were indeed a form of *gharar*.[81] The trial court in *Saudi Basic Industries Corp v Mobil Yanbu Petrochemical Co*, discussed above, followed a similar process by which it was presented by the litigants with over nine reports from experts on Saudi law, as well as over 1,000 pages of deposition testimony.[82]

Perhaps entirely on the other side of the spectrum in terms of regulation and judicial precedent in Islamic finance is the jurisdiction of Malaysia. Several commentators have hinted at the idea of Malaysian law, or its jurisdiction, as being adaptable towards the adjudication of Islamic finance-related issues outside of the country.[83]

As Islamic banking accounts for nearly a quarter of Malaysia's banking sector, comprising 17 Islamic banks, and 11 Islamic banking windows,[84] the country's regulations are analysed in courts whose decisions will be criticized at various stages of appeal; thus, lending academic commentators fuel for scholarly discourse. Furthermore, much of Malaysia's case law is published in English, allowing a great many people trained and practicing in non-Islamic law influenced jurisdictions (such as myself) the opportunity to grasp its tenets. That having been stated, what is being chosen when the law of Malaysia is governing a contract in Islamic finance? What are its sources of jurisprudence that the practitioner must be aware of?

As indicated above, there is a growing amount of commentary which advocates the use of Malaysian law to govern contracts in Islamic finance. The sources of jurisprudence implicated when Malaysian law is chosen as controlling in Islamic finance agreements are (1) regulation; (2) Shari'ah Advisory Council decisions; and (3) case law.

Islamic Financial Services Act of 2013

In regard to regulation, the current law in Malaysia governing Islamic financial arrangements is the Islamic Financial Services Act of 2013 ('IFSA').[85] This law replaced several previous acts, including the Islamic Banking Act of 1983, Takaful Act of 1984, and the Payment Systems Control Act of 2003. Among some interesting points in the law are: (1) The duty of ensuring the institution's compliance with the Shari'ah;[86] (2) Empowering Bank Negara Malaysia with regulatory authority;[87] (3) Shari'ah Advisory Council decisions are binding authority;[88] and (4) prohibited conduct is defined—the statute extensively lists prohibited conduct in business, going as far as defining inchoate crimes relating to the act.[89]

While the IFSA provides rules for compliance and governance in the Islamic finance sectors, it is important to point out that the governance of organizations is implicated within the act. Therefore, it may be necessary for the practitioner to opt out of provisions dealing with the licensing of Islamic financial institutions and carrying on of business, such as the requirement of establishing a Shari'ah committee.[90]

Bank Negara Malaysia Shari'ah Advisory Council

The Central Bank of Malaysia Act of 2009 requires judges and arbitrators to take into consideration any published rulings of the Bank Negara Malaysia Shari'ah

Advisory Council ('BNM SAC') or refer to the BNM SAC for rulings relating to Sharia issues arising from disputes before them.[91] The BNM SAC publishes its opinions in its book *Shari'ah Resolutions in Islamic Finance*,[92] which is something of a combination of a reporter and legal treatise because on one hand, the resolutions are (1) binding upon courts and some arbitrators; (2) the resolutions are based on actual disputes; and (3) novel issues may be referred to the BNM SAC which may ultimately appear in an updated version of the its book; however on the other hand, the styles of cases are not reported and background facts and procedural matters are not always mentioned.

It must be noted that the BNM SAC resolutions touch upon five principal areas of Islamic finance; to wit: (1) Shari'ah contracts; (2) supporting Islamic concepts [regarding Shari'ah contracts]; (3) Islamic financial products, (4) Shari'ah issues in relation to the operations of supporting institutions in Islamic finance; (5) Shari'ah issues in Islamic finance [regarding accounting and miscellaneous matters].[93] Thus, *Shari'ah Resolutions in Islamic Finance*, which is binding in Malaysia, is similar in scope to the AAOIFI standards in that it addresses the business of Islamic finance but does not elaborate on secondary concepts which arise in litigation such as causes of action, defences, damages, etc.[94] This is beneficial in that *Shari'ah Resolutions in Islamic Finance* may be incorporated by reference without involving other aspects of Malaysian law where it may be contrary to parties' intentions.

Malaysian case law

The legal system of Malaysia is in many respects based on common law. The doctrine of *stare decisis* applies in Malaysia, and decisions are published in reporters such as the Current Law Journal (CLJ), Malayan Law Journal (MLJ), All Malaysia Reports (AMR), Malaysian Law Review High Court (MLRH), Malaysian Law Review Appellate Courts (MLRA), and various specialty journals. Many of these decisions are available through LexisNexis and other online databases.

Though the Central Bank of Malaysia Act of 2009 provides that judges and arbitrators consider published rulings of the BNM SAC or refer Shari'ah issues to the BNM SAC,[95] case law describes the application of the BNM SAC rulings to real facts. At the same time, some novel issues are contained within the case law itself.

For example, in *Bank Kerjasama Malaysia Rakyat Bhd v PSC Naval Dockyard*,[96] the judge applied the common law doctrine of *estoppel* in the face of the customer's argument that the agreement was not Shari'ah-compliant due to a level of uncertainty within the terms of the agreement.[97] Noting that the evidence at trial did not suggest that the defendant was uncertain as to any terms, and mentioning that defence counsel did not demonstrate how the level of certainty should be different for an Islamic banking agreement, then given that the parties' conduct demonstrated a meeting of the minds, the 'law of estoppel [... was] obviously applicable to the defendant in raising such arguments'.[98] However, it should be noted that this case was decided before the passage of the Central Bank of Malaysia Act of 2009.

Given that each judge in Malaysian has a varying degree of knowledge in the field of Shari'ah generally, or Islamic finance specifically, I find the Malaysian judiciary to represent a microcosm of dispute resolution in Islamic finance. Taking into account the above-three categories of jurisprudence, their publication, and availability in English, one could argue that the law of Malaysia is sufficient as a governing law for international Islamic finance transactions. I am inclined to agree, with the following caveat. As mentioned previously, Malaysian Islamic finance regulation is comprehensive and extends to the very inception and day-to-day operations of financiers; therefore, the scope of the law's incorporation must be clear in the agreement.

Choice of law in arbitration

The law applicable to contracts in regard to arbitration is characterized by freedom; just as is the choice of opting out of national courts, the choice of arbitrators, the choice of forum, etc. In fact, arbitration is specifically excluded from Rome I;[99] therefore, an Islamic finance agreement referencing first principles in the form of the primary sources of Shari'ah is plausible because parties are so free in regard to tailoring their choice of law within agreements to arbitrate that they may well choose Shari'ah as the governing law of their agreements, or even the 'Code of Hammurabi or rules of Monopoly' for that matter.[100]

The basic arbitration clause requires four elements: (1) the place of arbitration; (2) applicable law; (3) composition of the arbitral tribunal; and (4) language of the arbitration. However basic, the arbitration clause requires negotiators to know what is essential to the parties of interest—which in the case of this book would be those who are engaged in the industry of Shari'ah-compliant finance. Given that one basis of drafting a dispute resolution clause is to deter either party from breach of contract, the more effectively the arbitration clause is drafted 'the less likely it is that it will ever be used'.[101]

Place of arbitration

Regarding the place of arbitration, the law of the *situs* state is important for several reasons. First, is the *situs* state a signatory to international conventions for the recognition and enforcement of arbitral awards?

For example, until 1994, Saudi Arabia was not a member of the New York Convention.[102] And, some signatory states require reciprocity, and will only enforce awards inasmuch as the arbitration occurred at a forum located within another signatory state.[103]

The law of the *situs* state also is important due to the procedural versus substantive law dichotomy, which in some cases can result in the complete dismissal of some claims. For example, in an ICC arbitration initiated in 1982 between a Finnish corporation and Australian corporation, London was selected as the place of arbitration in the contract's arbitration clause.[104] Dealing with an alleged missed royalty payment prior to 1976, Finnish law applied substantively; however, the arbitrator found that as the arbitration was taking place in England, the English Limitation Act must have applied.[105] Therefore, all claims prior to 1976 were barred.[106]

Therefore, it is worth the same effort researching the law of the *situs* state's law as it is the law applicable to the contract.

Applicable law

The choice of law applicable to the arbitration is not necessary to create a binding arbitration clause; however, leaving this decision to the arbitrators can create an undesirable result for at least one of the parties.[107] Several important considerations apply to choosing the applicable law of the arbitration of disputes in Islamic finance, and these do not differ from any other arbitration.

First, the jurisdiction relied upon should be chosen based on the ability of its law to resolve the matter.[108] Second, you may wish to limit the application of the chosen law to 'substantive law', excluding both procedural and jurisdictional questions.[109] Third, consider whether the chosen law permits the resolution of the matter by arbitration.[110] For example, Saudi Arabia's Law of Arbitration states that the law applies '[w]ithout prejudice to provisions of Islamic Sharia'[111] and 'shall not apply to personal status disputes or matters not subject to reconciliation'.[112]

One interesting point regarding the applicable law in the context of international arbitration and Islamic finance is the possibility of using combined-law approach, meaning that a national law would be selected (or for that matter a non-national, secular law such as '*ex aequo et bono*'[113,114]), and that law itself would be subject to objections based on the parameters of Shari'ah.[115] For example, in *Sanghi Polyesters Ltd. (India) v The International Investor KCFC (Kuwait)*, the parties came into a dispute concerning an *istina'a* agreement.[116] The parties agreed to arbitrate the dispute at the ICC, and Mr Samir Saleh, a qualified attorney and scholar of Shari'ah, was appointed arbitrator.[117] The contract contained a choice of law clause which stipulated that any dispute should be 'governed by the Law of England except to the extent it may conflict with Islamic Shari'ah, which shall prevail'.[118] The entire dispute in the arbitration proceedings was whether the application of the Shari'ah would serve to invalidate the contract and prevent the defendant from a return of its investment capital.[119] The losing party challenged the judgment in English Court, and the judge recognized that there was no issue regarding the Law of England and Wales, and that the only issue was whether the contract was 'invalidated under the manner claimed […] under Shari'a law'.[120] The judge ruled that there had been no serious irregularity or injustice and that the award would stand.[121,122]

In fact, non-state law is occasionally the only law applicable in the context of arbitration. For example, *lex mercatoria* is occasionally applied to the contract in the context of arbitration, but it is rare.[123]

Composition and language of the arbitral tribunal

The language of the arbitration can relate to the qualifications of the arbitrators and the applicable law. For example, if the law of the Saudi Arabia is chosen, then perhaps Arabic would be the recommended language as to dispense with the necessity of expensive translations, of which the quality may leave either party dissatisfied.[124]

In the past, it was more difficult to find an arbitrator experienced in international dispute resolution and accepted as a fair and trusted decision-maker and who would also have sufficient insight into the general goals of Shari'ah-compliant business. Some early decisions demonstrate an opinion from the arbitrator that Shari'ah-based sources – though necessary and legitimate given the applicable law – were too primitive to use to properly adjudicate a sophisticated business dispute.[125] However, as is apparent from the discussions in the previous sections, times appear to have moved towards a more moderate view of the incorporation of Shari'ah principles into business and law.

Some thoughts concerning public policy

At its core, Islamic finance is one method of alternative finance. However, because of the methodology, it is inescapably a religiously inspired form of business. Stemming from that, arbitration in the context of Islamic finance may at times be considered religious arbitration. Therefore, before the arbitration occurs, thought should be given to the public policy of the jurisdiction where the decision may be enforced. The New York Convention provides that signatory states need not enforce arbitral awards if doing so would be against public policy.[126] This is a stipulation with broad ranging consequences, and awards have been denied for reasons ranging from the failure to comply with procedural requirements of the *situs* state to the awarding of interest.[127]

One question is whether the state of enforcement of the award would consider religious-based arbitration as against public policy. For example in the US, the state of Texas enacted the law HB 45, which require[s] the Texas Supreme Court to 'adopt rules of evidence and procedure to implement the limitations on the granting of comity to a foreign judgment or an arbitration award involving a marriage relationship or a parent-child relationship [...]'.[128] While HB 45 addresses choice of law in regard to family law cases, movements against international law cannot entirely be written off given the stakes involved and costs of litigation.[129]

In the US at least, the Federal Arbitration Act and several state-level variants on arbitration law favour enforcing agreements to arbitrate, and religious arbitration is not unique to Islamic finance. However, if the arbitration is expected to expound on Shari'ah matters, then in order to best ensure enforcement within non-ILIJ countries,[130] it is best to include some simple standards to the arbitration in case the forum does not have such requirements within its own law. At minimum, an arbitration occurring in a non-IJIL, which incorporates Shari'ah into the applicable law should (1) occur within a panel that has adopted written procedural and evidentiary rules; (2) consider publication of its factual and legal findings in the form of a reasoned decision; and (3) include a trained attorney on the arbitration panel.[131] By doing so, courts would be more inclined to take into account all published rules of procedure and evidence when making a decision to confirm an arbitration award, and given an otherwise impartial arbitration, that court would also be more likely to confirm the award, finding fewer public policy considerations to deny its confirmation.[132]

Final thoughts

Shari'ah as a governing law is indeed possible, but only whereas the forum itself is located within a Shari'ah influenced jurisdiction. Thus, it seems out of place to discuss whether Shari'ah as a choice of law or gap-filler provision should apply in a traditionally common law or civil law jurisdiction. Why is this even a topic of discussion? It would seem that there are two considerations that make this topic relevant.

First, there are in fact private individuals who choose to negotiate based on Shari'ah terms and prefer to settle disputes according to those same terms, and it may be beyond their capacity to either arbitrate or seek adjudication outside of their home jurisdiction (i.e. non-Shari'ah influenced system). Second, due to the international flows of capital, investors from Shari'ah jurisdictions invest elsewhere and *vice versa*, and these disputes are contractually stipulated to be resolved in non-Shari'ah forums, which perhaps is due to the magnitude of international offerings originating in those place (e.g. New York and London).

Therefore, research regarding choice of law will continue to be relevant in order to increase the predictability of dispute resolution within the field. In doing so, specializations within this field could include inquiries into the jurisprudence of contracts, torts, and securities within Islamic law influenced jurisdictions such as Saudi Arabia, Malaysia, etc., as well as surveys on choice of law rules within popular forums for dispute resolutions in jurisdictions without Shari'ah traditions. In-depth research should also be published analysing the feasibility of incorporating by reference documents such as AAOIFI standards, or in-depth research regarding the efficacy of documents such as 'ISDA/IIFM Ta'Hawwut Master Agreement' as an integral agreement despite provisions which rule out the possibility of reference to Shari'ah in the case of future disputes.[133]

Notes

1 See *Shamil Bank of Bahrain EC v Beximco Pharm Ltd* [2004] EWCA Civ 19, [1]; [2004] 1 WLR 1784, 1787.
2 See *In Re Arcapita Bank BSC (C)*, Bankruptcy Case No 12-11076 (SDNY 6 January 2014).
3 Term borrowed from João Ribeiro and Jin Lee, 'Overview of UNCITRAL Texts on International Commercial Arbitration in Islamic Law Influenced Jurisdictions (ILIJ)' [2015] 46 VUWLR 139.

4 Greg Jehle, 'Innovation, Arbitrage, and Ethics: The Role of Lawyers in the Development of a New Transnational Islamic Finance Law' [2016] 104 Georgetown LJ 1345.
5 [2004] EWCA Civ 19, [1]; [2004] 1 WLR 1784, 1787.
6 *Murabaha*, often called 'cost-plus', is an agreement in which one party acquires an asset with the promise that the other party will purchase it, usually in installments. As in retail transactions, the original purchaser makes a profit by selling the product at a higher price. The difference between this type of transaction and a traditional mortgage is that the original purchaser, most often a bank, acts much like a middleman by retaining an ownership interest in the product until the goods are completely paid for. See HM Kabir Hassan and Mervyn K. Lewis (eds), *Handbook of Islamic Banking*, (Elgar Original Reference 2007) xvii, 52 (defining *murabaha*).
7 *Shamil Bank*, [2004] EWCA (Civ) 19, [1], [6], [2004] 1 WLR 1787–89.
8 Ibid. [15]–[17], 1 WLR 1790–91.
9 Ibid. [1], 1 WLR 1787.
10 Ibid. [21], 1 WLR 1791–92.
11 Ibid. [27], 1 WLR 1793. Riba, often translated as 'interest', literally means 'an excess' in Arabic. An important fact to consider in Shamil Bank is that there was no explicit interest in the agreement, compound or simple. Riba often arises due to the way the transaction is carried out, where interest is in effect charged on the borrower.

> [Riba] is defined as "any unjustifiable increase of capital whether in loans or sales." It is essentially any unlawful or unjustified gain. Any contracts which include an excessive profit margin will also be considered as a form of riba if it is exploitative, oppressive, or unconscionable.
> Faisal Kutty, 'Shari'a Factor in International Commercial Arbitration' [2006] 28 Loyola Intl & Comparative L Review 565, 604

12 *Shamil Bank*, [2004] EWCA (Civ) 19, [55], 1 WLR 1801.
13 Ibid. [40], 1 WLR 1795–96.
14 Ibid. [52], 1 WLR 1800.
15 Ibid.
16 1980 Rome Convention on the law applicable to contractual obligations [1998] OJ (L 177) 34, art 3 (1).
17 See also Jason Chuah, 'Recent Case, *Shamil Bank of Bahrain EC v Beximco*' [2004] 10 J Intl Maritme L 126.
18 For an excellent history of this discussion, see Ralf Michaels, 'Non-State Law in the Hague Principles on Choice of Law in International Contracts' https://ssrn.com/abstract=2386186 accessed 7 July 2017 (forthcoming).
19 Anowar Zahid and Hasani Mohd Ali, 'Shariah as a Choice of Law in International Islamic Finance Contracts: Shamil Bank of Bahrain Case Revisited' [2013] 27 US–China L Review 10.
20 Compare with 1980 Rome Convention on the Law Applicable to Contractual Obligations, (n 16), at article 3(3)

> Where all other elements relevant to the situation at the time of the choice are located in a country other than the country whose law has been chosen, the choice of the parties shall not prejudice the application of provisions of the law of that other country which cannot be derogated from by agreement.

21 Michaels (n 18) 23.
22 Zahid and Ali (n 19) 31.
23 Michaels (n 18).
24 Ibid. 1.
25 Ibid. 3.

26 Ibid.
27 Hague Principles on Choice of Law in International Contracts Text and Commentary, (approved 19 March 2015, HCCH) www.hcch.net/en/instruments/conventions/full-text/?cid=135#text accessed 7 July 2017.
28 Michaels (n 18) 2.
29 Ibid. 13.
30 Hague Principles (n 27) comment 3.4.
31 Ibid. at comment 3.15, Illustration 3–1.
32 Ibid.
33 Term borrowed from Ribeiro and Lee (n 3).
34 Hague Principles (n 27).
35 Michaels, (n 18) 15.
36 Ibid. 23.
37 Here I make reference to the Hague Principles (n 27) comment 3.9 (requiring a 'neutral and balanced set of rules').
38 Arthur J Gemmell, 'Commercial Arbitration in the Islamic Middle East' [2006] 5 Santa Clara J Intl L 169, 172.
39 Basic Law of Government (1992), art 1, quoted in Gemmell (n 38) 172.
40 *National Group for Communications & Computers v Lucent Technologies Intl*, 331 F Supp 2d 290, 292 (DNJ 2004).
41 Ibid.
42 Ibid.
43 Ibid.
44 Ibid. 293–294.
45 Ibid. 295.
46 Ibid. 296.
47 Ibid. 297–300.
48 Ibid. 301.
49 *Saudi Basic Industries Corp v Mobil Yanbu Petrochemical Co*, 866 A2d 1, 7 (Del 2005).
50 Ibid. 6.
51 Ibid. 11.
52 Ibid. 30.
53 Ibid. 32.
54 Ibid. 32.
55 *Saudi Basic Industries Corp*, 866 A2d at 32.
56 Ibid.
57 James Garner, 'A Critical Perspective on the Principles of Islamic Finance Focusing on Sharia Compliance and Arbitrage' (2016) *The New Jurist* 6, available at http://thenewjurist.com/islamic-finance-principles.html.
58 *Shamil Bank*, [2004] EWCA (Civ) 19, [55], 1 WLR 1801.
59 Ibid.
60 Ibid.
61 Ibid.
62 Such stipulations attempt to rectify what has become known in the industry as the 'Sharia risk', a term associated with the risk that one party will fail under its contract obligations and then state the entire agreement is void for being invalid under Islamic law. Kilian Bälz, 'Sharia Risk?: How Islamic Finance Has Transformed Islamic Contract Law' (2008) Islamic Legal Studies Program Harvard Law School. However, even such a provision is not guaranteed to have the desired effect.
63 *The Investment Dar Company KSCC v Blom Developments Bank SAL*, [2009] All ER (D) 145, 2009 WL 5386898.
64 Ibid. 1.
65 Ibid. 4.

66 Ibid.
67 Ibid.
68 Aida Othman and Zaid Ibrahim, 'Islamic Finance Dispute Resolution in Malaysia, Dispute Resolution and Insolvency in Islamic Finance: Problems and Solutions A Workshop at the Faculty of Law' (2013) Report of Proceedings, National University of Singapore 17 (citing *Bank Kerjasama Malaysia Rakyat Bhd v PSC Naval Dockyard* [2008] 1 CLJ 784 (HC (KL)).
69 Hague Principles (n 27) introductory paragraph 18. ('Some regimes have allowed parties to incorporate by reference in their contract "rules of law" or trade usages. Incorporation by reference, however, is different from allowing parties to choose 'rules of law' as the law applicable to their contract').
70 K Bälz, 'Sharia Risk?: How Islamic Finance Has Transformed Islamic Contract Law' (2008) Islamic Legal Studies Program Harvard Law School, 14.
71 Robert Whitman, 'Incorporation by Reference in Commercial Contracts' [1961] 21 Maryland L Review 1, 2–12.
72 *In re Arcapita Bank BSC (C)*, 529 BR 57, (Bankr SDNY 2015).
73 David Griffiths, 'Sharia Compliant DIP Financing: Coming Soon, to a Bankruptcy Court Near You, Bankruptcy Blog' (2013) https://business-finance-restructuring.weil.com/dip-financing/sharia-compliant-dip-financing-coming-soon-to-a-bankruptcy-court-near-you/ accessed 7 July 2017.
74 Ibid.
75 See Jehl (n 4) 1354 ('Although it naturally draws upon the classical sources of Shari'ah for inspiration and legitimization, this new body of law is distinctly separate from the classical schools of jurisprudence and has arisen in response to a completely different set of historical, political, and economic circumstances'), and note 59 at 1358 ('IFIs may also use an undisclosed joint venture (sharikat muhassa) or other form of partnership such as mudarabah or musharikah, in combination with a murabahah agreement').
76 Term borrowed from Ribeiro (n 3).
77 *National Group for Communications & Computers v Lucent Technologies Intl*, 331 F Supp 2d 290.
78 Ibid. 295.
79 Ibid. 294 (quoting the Basic Regulation of the Kingdom of Saudi Arabia art 48 (1992)).
80 Ibid. 297–300.
81 Ibid. 297, 300.
82 *Saudi Basic Industries Corp*, 866 A2d 32.
83 See for example Abdul Hamid Mohamad and Adnan Trakic, 'The adjudication of Shari'ah issues in Islamic finance contracts: Guidance from Malaysia' [2015] 26 J of Banking & Islamic Finance 39, 40. (Authors propose that Malaysia as a forum for Islamic finance dispute resolution is desirable precisely because its legal framework, acknowledging that court will at times confront Shari'ah issues.)
84 Vineeta Tain, 'Malaysia: Undisputed Leader?' http://islamicfinancenews.com/glossary/tawarruq 7 July 2017.
85 Othman (n 68) 23.
86 Islamic Financial Services Act 2013, ss 30–38.
87 Ibid. ss 43, 57, 152.
88 Ibid. at s 28 ('[C]ompliance with any ruling of the Shari'ah Advisory Council in respect of any particular aim and operation, business, affair or activity shall be deemed to be a compliance with Shari'ah' regarding business governed by IFSA).
89 Ibid. ss 136, 158, 225, 265.
90 Ibid. s 30.
91 Central Bank of Malaysia Act 2009, s 56.

92 Ibid. *Bank Negara Malaysia Shariah Resolutions in Islamic Finance* (2nd ed, Bank Negara Malaysia 2010) www.bnm.gov.my/microsite/fs/sac/shariah_resolutions_2nd_edition_EN.pdf accessed 7 July 2017.
93 Ibid.
94 Bälz, (n 70) 14.
95 Central Bank of Malaysia Act of 2009, s 5.
96 [2008] 1 CLJ 784.
97 *Bank Kerjasama Malaysia Rakyat Bhd v PSC Naval Dockyard* [2008] 1 CLJ 784, 790–92 (HC (KL)). Also see Othman (n 68) 17. ('In Bank Kerjasama Malaysia Rakyat Bhd v PSC Naval Dockyard [...] Rohana Yusuf J found [...]. The doctrine of estoppel is applied; the customer, because of its conduct, cannot raise these issues later in court.')
98 *Bank Kerjasama* [2008] 1 CLJ 784, 790–92 (HC (KL)).
99 Council Regulation (EC) No 593/2008 of the European Parliament and of the Council of 17 June 2008 on the law applicable to contractual obligations (Rome I) [2008] OJ (L 177) 6, 10 (EC), art 1 (2) e.
100 Alan Scott Rau, 'The Agreement to Arbitrate and the "Applicable Law"' [2017] University of Texas Law Public Law Research Paper No 644 (Professor Alan Rau was my law school arbitration seminar professor and one of those to whom I credit with developing my interest in the subject of international arbitration).
101 Stephen R Bond, 'How to Draft an Arbitration Clause' [1989] 6(2) J of Intl Arb 65, 66.
102 www.newyorkconvention.org/countries accessed 21 September 2017.
103 Ibid. ('Declaration: On the Basis of reciprocity, the Kingdom declares that it shall restrict the application of the Convention to the recognition and enforcement of arbitral awards made in the territory of a Contracting State').
104 Bond (n 101) 72.
105 Ibid. (citing [1985] 2 J of Intl Arb 4491).
106 Ibid.
107 Ibid. 74.
108 Ibid.
109 Ibid.
110 Ibid.
111 Royal Decree No M/34, Law of Arbitration art 2, April 4, 2012, available at www.idc.gov.sa/en-us/RulesandRegulations1/Arbitration%20Law.pdf.
112 Ibid.
113 Bond (n 101) 74.
114 Latin for 'according to the right and good'.
115 For a general discussion of a theoretical 'combined-law approach', see my previous article Julio C Colón, 'Choice of law and Islamic Finance' [2011] 46 Texas Intl LJ 412.
116 *Sanghi Polyesters Ltd. (India) v Int'l Investor KCFC (Kuwait)*, [2000] 1 Lloyd's Rep 480, 480 (2000). *Istina'a* is a form of contract where one party, paid in advance, is contracted to manufacture something. The practice is widely accepted as valid under Shari'ah, although there has been and continues to be debate among Muslim scholars on the contract's legality due to the Islamic prohibition of selling items which you either do not yet own or whose possession is uncertain.
117 Alan Redfern *et al.*, *Law and Practice of International Commercial Arbitration* (4th edn, Sweet & Maxwell 2004) 115.
118 Ibid.
119 *Sanghi Polyesters Ltd*, [2000] 1 Lloyd's Rep 480.
120 Ibid.
121 Ibid.

122 Is this approach falling out favour within the world of arbitration? The inoperative KLRCA Rules for Islamic Banking and Financial Services Arbitration Rules r 39(1) (2007) concerning the applicable law states, '[t]he arbitral tribunal shall apply Shariah principles and the law designated by the parties as applicable to the substance of the dispute'. However, the current KLRCA I-Arbitration Rules. art 35 (2017), provides, 'The arbitral tribunal shall apply the rules of law designated by the parties as applicable to the substance of the dispute'. No mention of Shari'ah occurs in art 35 of the prevailing KLRCA I-Arbitration Rules.

123 See Michaels (n 18) 4 ('Indeed, in arbitration, lex mercatoria and other non-state law have occasionally been selected, though not frequently'); Bond (n 101) 74 ('No clause in 1987 or 1989 mentioned lex mercatoria. [...] [T]he parties appear to desire a resolution based on a specified, predictable legal system').

124 Bond (n 101) 74.

125 For example, in the case of *Petroleum Development (Trucial Coasts) Ltd v Sheikh of Abu Dhabi*, Lord Asquith acted as an arbitrator in a dispute arising out of a contract executed in Abu Dhabi. He acknowledged that Abu Dhabi's law, which was based on Islamic law, should be applied. He subsequently refused to apply the law because, according to him, 'it would be fanciful to suggest that in this very primitive region there is any settled body of legal principles applicable to the construction of modern commercial instruments'. He described the ruler of Abu Dhabi as an absolute monarch who administers a 'purely discretionary form of justice with some assistance from the Koran'. After analysing the choice of law issue, the arbitrator relied instead on principles of English law. *In re Arbitration Between Petroleum Dev (Trucial Coast) Ltd v Sheikh of Abu Dhabi*, 1 Intl & Comp L Q 247, 250–251 (September 1951); Gemmell (n 49) 179.

126

> Recognition and enforcement of an arbitral award may also be refused if the competent authority in the country where recognition and enforcement is sought finds that: [...] (b) The recognition or enforcement of the award would be contrary to the public policy of that country.

Convention on the Recognition and Enforcement of Foreign Arbitral Awards art V 2(b), June 10, 1958, 21 UST 2517, 330 UNTS 38 [hereinafter New York Convention].

127 Mark Hoyle, 'Topic in Focus: Demystifying UAE Arbitration Law' [2013] www.lexology.com/library/detail.aspx?g=fc4ff6d6-cafb-4063-8dc1-f20fc1544c9e accessed 25 September 2017 ('For example, a failure to ensure that a witness is sworn by reciting the mandatory oath renders the arbitration null and void').

128 Texas HB 45, 85th Legislature (2017).

129 More extreme measures in other states have not passed. See for example C Brougher, 'Application of Religious Law in US Courts: Selected Legal Issues' (2011) Congressional Research Service, 19 (In the US, a law was introduced in the state of Tennessee which would have made it an offence to provide 'material support or resources to a designated sharia organization' and defining 'Sharia' and 'Sharia organization' expansively:

> 'Sharia' means the set of rules, precepts, instructions, or edicts which are said to emanate directly or indirectly from the god of Allah or the prophet Mohammed and which include directly or indirectly the encouragement of any person to support the abrogation, destruction, or violation of the United States or Tennessee Constitutions, or the destruction of the national existence of the United States or the sovereignty of this state, and which includes among other methods to achieve these ends, the likely use of imminent violence. Any rule, precept, instruction, or edict arising directly from the extant rulings of any of the authoritative schools of Islamic jurisprudence of Hanafi, Maliki, Shafi'I, Hanbali, Ja'afariya, or Salafi, as those terms are used by sharia adherents, is prima facie sharia without any further evidentiary showing.

'Sharia organization' means any two (2) or more persons conspiring to support, or acting in concert in support of, sharia or in furtherance of the imposition of sharia within any state or territory of the United States.

130 Term borrowed from Ribeiro (n 3).

131 Julio C Colón, 'Improving Dispute Resolution for Muslims in the United States', (International Conference on Dispute Resolution 2017: Modern Trends in Effective Dispute Resolution, International Islamic University of Malaysia, August 2017) 15 https://ssrn.com/abstract=3007811 accessed 7 July 2017.

132 Ibid.

133 See 'ISDA/IIFM Ta'Hawwut Master Agreement' sec (1)(d) ('Laws. For the purposes of this Agreement, any reference to any "law" or "laws" in this Agreement does not include reference to principles of the Shari'ah').

3 Prevailing dispute resolution mechanisms in Islamic finance

Siti Faridah Abdul Jabbar, Suzana Muhamad Said and Asma Hakimah Ab Halim

Introduction

Among the essentials of a sound and dynamic Islamic financial services industry are sophisticated financial products and services, strong financial infrastructure, robust regulatory framework and a suitable dispute resolution mechanism. While Islamic finance has demonstrated progress in product innovations and in various other aspects, the same cannot be said of its dispute resolution mechanisms. The Islamic financial services industry is still searching for a suitable dispute resolution forum. This chapter discusses the prevailing dispute resolution mechanisms in Islamic finance, namely litigation, arbitration and mediation, as well as the attendant problems in resorting to the dispute resolution fora.

Litigation

Key features and foundations of litigation

Litigation refers to the proceeding related to a 'civil action brought by a claimant against a defendant based on legal principles, asserting some right or legal entitlement'.[1] It is conducted in a court of law by at least one neutral decision maker who is typically called a judge. The judge hears evidence from the disputing parties' lawyers and determines the parties' legal rights by rendering a binding decision based on the law and legal precedents.[2] The court of law in which the litigation is conducted is established by the State which renders the initiation of the litigation process, the litigation process itself and the resulting decision binding.[3] In other words, the procedures in a litigation are formal and structured with a set of court rules to be followed and shall be strictly adhered to by the parties involved.[4]

The main advantage of litigation is that it is the most binding form of dispute resolution.[5] Although it is intended to achieve finality, litigation, however, has its drawbacks. Litigation focuses on the facts and is past oriented.[6] It is insensitive to indigenous problems, needs and political processes.[7] Litigation is adversarial,[8] acrimonious,[9] hostile, alienating[10] and competitive.[11] A decision is normally 'all or nothing' where the disputing parties are either the winner or the loser[12] and where one party's gain is another party's loss.[13] Further, the most well-known disadvantages of litigation are costliness, time-consuming[14] and delays,[15] thus, the pressure for creation of alternative dispute resolutions such as, arbitration and mediation.[16]

Litigation in Islamic law

The administration of Islamic law (Shari'ah) recognizes the process of litigation, known as *qada*, as one of the mechanisms for dispute resolution. Litigation from the Shari'ah perspective literally means 'the judgment between the people'.[17] It is about disputes and their resolution.[18] The judge in a litigation is called *Qadhi* or *Hakim*. The appointment of a *Qadhi* is an obligation of the Ruler and a communal obligation (*fard kifayah*) in the Muslim legal doctrine.[19] Islam emphasises the act of doing justice to all the parties involved when resolving disputes. This is evidenced in the Qur'an (Holy Book for Muslims) where Allah (God) said, as translated thus: 'Verily, Allah commands you to render trusts to whom they are due and when you judge between people to judge with justice. Excellent is that which Allah instructs you. Verily, Allah is ever Hearing and Seeing'.[20]

Meanwhile, the tasks of a *Qadhi* may be understood clearly from the letter of Caliphate Umar to Abu Musa Al-Ashari where Umar stated that a trial shall be conducted according to the Qur'an and *Sunnah*.[21] Umar further emphasized that it is important to listen to both parties before any decision is made regarding their dispute and that they shall be treated equally regardless of their position.[22] A similar text was sent by Umar to *Qadi* Shurayh where Umar stated that if a case was presented to Shurayh and the matter was treated in the Qur'an, Shurayh was to decide accordingly and not go against the Qur'anic injunctions. Umar stated further that if the matter was not treated in the Qur'an, Shurayh was to then follow the *Hadith* and decide accordingly, but if the matter had no provision in the Qur'an and *Hadith*, Shurayh was to then look for the solution in the *Ijma ul' umat* (consensus of the Islamic jurists) and follow it. Umar went on further to say that if the matter had no precedent in the Qur'an and *Hadith* and had not been decided by anyone before, Shurayh was to then decide according to his own judgment after due care and caution.[23]

The instructions from Umar to both Abu Musa and Shurayh augur well with the *Sunnah* of the Prophet Muhammad. When the Prophet sent Mu'adh ibn Jabal to be the *Qadhi* in Yemen, the Prophet asked Mu'adh what the latter would base his judicial decisions on. Mu'adh replied that he would first refer to the Qur'an, then to the *Sunnah* of the Messenger of Allah (the Prophet) and if the answer to an issue could not be found between the two sources, he would then use *ijtihad*.[24] Prophet Muhammad was pleased upon hearing the reply given by Mu'adh.[25] Thus, it is understood that in making a decision, a *Qadhi* is required to refer to the Qur'an, *Sunnah*, *Ijma'*, *Qiyas* and other sources approved by the jurists. During the life of the Prophet Muhammad and his Great Companions, the decisions that were made also took into consideration the aspects of *maqasid* (higher objectives of the Shari'ah) and *maslahah*, namely the exigencies of the situation at that particular time. This is an important aspect for a *Qadhi* in deliberating a case to ensure that the rights of those involved are not oppressed and that the beauty of Islam as the religion of justice is truly materialised.

With regard to the criteria to be appointed as a *Qadhi* (judge), the individual must have *'aqidah* (creed) and *akhlaq* (good morals). In other words, he must be a person who has faith in the oneness of Allah (Muslim) and possesses good attributes. Islamic jurists also agree that the individual to be appointed as a *Qadhi* shall have reached the age of puberty; shall be just, wise, a free man, free from any deficiency in terms of sight or speaking capability; and shall have knowledge in Shari'ah ruling.[26] The office of a *Qadhi* shall be independent from the Ruler so that the decision of the *Qadhi* is not influenced by the latter. If a case involves the Ruler himself, the *Qadhi* shall remain impartial and decide with justice, regardless of the status of the disputing parties. During the time of Caliphate Umar, a separation was made between the *Qadhi* and the Ruler for the whole Islamic territory. As for the litigation process, the disputing parties are to give their evidence to the *Qadhi*. Upon listening to both parties, the *Qadhi* is to give his decision based on the principles of justice and fairness. Where the decision made by the *Qadhi* is in accordance with the principles of Shari'ah, it shall be binding on the parties involved[27] and the matter shall not be brought to the court again for reconsideration or rehearing of claims.[28]

This, however, does not mean that a dissatisfied losing party may not challenge the *Qadhi*'s decision. The losing party may do so but the process does not involve an appeal mechanism as widely practiced in the contemporary world. As explained by Shapiro, 'initially, no distinct appeal mechanism was necessary in Islam because of a constitutional theory of delegation apparently inherited by the Arabs from the Byzantines'. All political, legal, and religious authority adhered to the Caliph. He might delegate portions of that authority to subordinates. They in turn might redelegate it. But, the delegator retained full and complete jurisdiction and authority over all matters delegated. Thus, the Caliph and his governors retained full judicial authority even when delegating judicial tasks to the Qadhi. The notion of a level of appeals courts superior to the Qadhi did not develop due to the fact that a litigant dissatisfied with the Qadhi's decision or initial reluctance to seek a Qadhi's judgment could place his case directly before the highest political authority. A system of appeal by 'trial de novo' conducted by the delegating authority therefore implicitly existed. There are scattered recorded instances of Caliphs reversing the decisions of a Qadhi or sending a case back to him with new instructions. Because initially the political authorities retained such complete judicial jurisdiction, they had no need for special appellate courts'.[29] Nonetheless, in the contemporary Muslim world, for example in Malaysia, it is common to find a hierarchy of Shari'ah courts with a structured appeal mechanism.[30]

Litigation in Islamic finance

The majority of disputes relating to Islamic finance are litigated in the courts.[31] This holds true in cross-border as well as in domestic Islamic financial transactions.[32] The adoption of a standard contract in Islamic financial transactions as well as familiarity with the court process are the contributing factors to litigation being the chosen forum albeit it is not the most suitable mechanism for dispute resolution in Islamic finance. A consideration of several court decided cases demonstrates this difficulty.[33] In *Islamic Investment Company of the Gulf (Bahamas) Ltd v Symphony Gems NV & Ors*,[34] a dispute relating to an Islamic *murabahah* (mark-up sale)[35] contract was litigated in the English court since the contract between the parties stipulated that the English courts would have jurisdiction over the contract with English law being the governing law. An expert witness who was called to testify in court gave his opinion that the supposedly *murabahah* contract was not Shari'ah-compliant since the contract did not fulfil the prerequisites of a *murabahah* contract. Despite the expert testimony, the English court held that the *murabahah* contract entered into by the parties was valid based on the English law of contract. The English court decision had thus validated a purportedly invalid *murabahah* contract.[36]

In another litigated case, *Shamil Bank of Bahrain v Beximco Pharmaceuticals Ltd & Ors*,[37] the English courts refused to apply the Shari'ah and held that the English law was the sole governing law for the *murabahah* contract that was entered into by the disputing parties. The judgment was made although the contracting parties had agreed that their contract shall be governed by the laws of England but subject to the principles of the Shari'ah. The English Court of Appeal upheld the decision of the judge at first instance that the Shari'ah cannot be a binding system of law since it is not the law of a country and is a non-national system. It is evident from this case that although the contract in question involved an Islamic financial transaction, the English courts, however, did not apply the Shari'ah.[38] The court did not recognize the Shari'ah to govern a financial transaction[39] which is contrary to the nature of Islamic financial transactions that shall be compliant with the Shari'ah.

Meanwhile, the litigated case of *The Investment Dar Company KSCC v Blom Developments Bank SAL*[40] demonstrates a perplexed situation. Blom, a Lebanese entity, had placed some money with The Invesment Dar (TID), a Kuwaiti company, pursuant to a *wakalah* (agency) contract. It was agreed that TID would invest the money and subsequently return the money to Blom with an agreed rate of return. When TID failed to honour the contract, Blom brought the matter to the English court. During litigation, TID's counsel argued that TID's transaction with Blom was not Shari'ah-compliant and, thus, void because it was ultra vires the constitutions of TID, which expressly prohibit TID from entering into contracts that do not comply with the Shari'ah. That argument was put forward by TID's counsel despite the fact that the transaction had been previously approved as Shari'ah-compliant by the Shari'ah Committee of TID itself. The English High Court accepted the argument by TID's counsel and held that there was an arguable case that the transaction in question was ultra vires TID's constitutions. That decision would have released TID from its obligations under the contract. However, the disputing parties subsequently negotiated an out of court settlement.

While the above-mentioned cases demonstrate the conundrum of litigating cross-border Islamic financial transactions in the English courts, the predicament is similar in the litigation of domestic Islamic financial transactions in the Malaysian civil courts. In the early days between 1979 and 2002, the Malaysian civil courts[41] simply considered whether the Islamic financial transactions fulfilled the rigours of the common law and ignored the Shari'ah-compliant aspect of the transactions.[42] From 2003 onwards, however, the Malaysian civil courts changed their approach. The courts started to look into the Shari'ah-compliant aspect of Islamic financial transactions and even questioned the permissibility of the transactions under the Shari'ah.[43] The most notable cases are *Malayan Banking Bhd v Marilyn Ho Siok*,[44] *Affin Bank Bhd v Zulkifli Abdullah*[45] and *Arab-Malaysian Finance Bhd v Taman Ihsan Jaya Sdn Bhd & Ors and Other cases*.[46] Nonetheless, what the cases illustrate is that judges who do not have formal training in the Shari'ah gave judgments on the permissibility of the financial transactions from the Shari'ah perspective[47] and this resulted in flawed judicial interpretations of the Shari'ah which consequently led to several anomalies.[48] Meanwhile, in the oft-quoted case of *Bank Kerjasama Rakyat Malaysia Bhd v Emcee Corp Sdn Bhd.*,[49] the court decided that the laws applicable to Islamic banking facilities are the same as those applicable to conventional banking. Therefore, the common law or civil law remedies such as a claim for late payment charges may be awarded in an Islamic finance dispute despite such a claim being considered the prohibited *riba* under the Shari'ah.[50] This approach had the effect of converting an Islamic financial transaction into a conventional one when such an order is made by the courts.[51]

In an effort to remedy the situation, several statutory provisions[52] were enacted by the Malaysian Parliament where it was made mandatory for the courts to take into consideration any published rulings of the Shari'ah Advisory Council (SAC)[53] or to refer to the SAC for the latter's rulings when any question concerning a Shari'ah matter arises in any proceedings relating to Islamic financial transactions. Where reference is made to the SAC, the latter's ruling shall be binding on the court. The intention of these provisions is to render the SAC as the ultimate body that can rule on the Shari'ah aspect of a civil court case concerning Islamic financial transactions.

In several other Muslim jurisdictions where Islamic finance is litigated in the Shari'ah courts, a number of issues continue to exist. Rider points out that the discretionary powers of the Shari'ah courts and lack of judicial precedent in the process of determination may result in different Shari'ah courts within the same jurisdiction taking different approaches in the handling of a similar financial legal issue.[54] This, in turn, creates legal uncertainty that may prejudice the rights that is thought to be attached to a financial instrument, jeopardise the reliability of arrangements entered into good faith and give rise to other types of legal risks.[55] The dilemma is further exacerbated by the fact that the certification by a Shari'ah scholar or a Shari'ah Board comprised of several scholars, that a particular product or service is Shari'ah-compliant is not binding on the Shari'ah courts and these courts will resolve any financial disputes based on their own interpretation of the position under the Shari'ah.[56]

From the foregoing discussions, it is evident that litigation is not a suitable dispute resolution forum for Islamic finance where the judges are not experts in the Shari'ah and Islamic financial transactions. The courts treated the Islamic financial transactions no differently from conventional ones and applied the laws and principles of conventional finance to Islamic finance. In some cases, the courts do not recognise the Shari'ah as an independent system of law that governs financial transactions. As a result, Islamic financial transactions may lose their characteristics as Shari'ah-compliant financial transactions when the court decisions were made.

Arbitration

Key features and foundations of arbitration

Arbitration is an adjudicative dispute resolution process and often based on a contractual arbitration clause to refer any dispute between contracting parties to arbitration.[57] It is a consensual method of dispute resolution. Arbitration 'can be seen as a private version of litigation'[58] and the similarity to litigation is that the adjudicator will hear from both parties and decide on the issue. The parties are bound by the decision of the adjudicator known as 'the arbitral award'. Although arbitration is voluntarily initiated, the process and decision usually become binding upon the parties.[59] Arbitration is more flexible than litigation with regard to the procedures involved.[60] The flexibility ranges from 'choosing in advance or at the time a dispute arises their preferences in arbitrator selection, the language in which proceedings are conducted, and the governing procedures'.[61] In the case of *Filli Shipping Co. Ltd v Premium Nafta Products Ltd*[62] Lord Hoffman held that parties who agreed to submit to arbitration impliedly agreed to be bound by the chosen tribunal in a neutral location with neutral arbitrators, conducted in privacy and in a speedily and effective manner.[63]

In summary the key features and foundations of arbitration are as follows: it is a private form of adjudication outside the court system; the appointment of a neutral and independent third party as an arbitrator or panel of arbitrators is either agreed upon or appointed in accordance to an agreed process of a commercial agreement or by virtue of a statutory obligation; it is impartial, private and confidential and ideally conducted in an effective and speedy manner; the process will determine the obligations and substantive rights of the parties; and the decision is an arbitral award which is final and binding on the parties and not subject to appeal on merits unless irregularities in the decision making process existed.[64]

Domestic and international arbitration

Arbitration as part of alternative dispute resolution (ADR) mechanisms is applicable domestically and internationally. The difference between domestic and international arbitration is that the former takes place when the arbitration proceedings, the subject matter and the merits of the dispute are all governed by the local law, or when the cause of action for the dispute arises wholly under the local jurisdiction or where the parties are otherwise subject to the local jurisdiction. On the other hand, the latter has international elements and deals with cross border transactions that work beyond jurisdiction. The issues relating to international arbitration are basically about the choice of jurisdiction, the law and the applicable procedures. Internationally, the United Nations General Assembly in its resolutions[65] adopted for the establishment of a model national law for arbitration,[66] known as the United Nations Commission on International Trade Law (UNCITRAL) Model Law on International Commercial Arbitration (Model Law).[67]

Accordingly, the Model Law[68] is 'designed to assist States in reforming and modernizing their laws on arbitral procedure so as to take into account the particular features and needs of international commercial arbitration'.[69] The Model Law includes the arbitral process from the arbitration agreement, the composition and jurisdiction of the arbitral tribunal, the extent of court intervention, and the recognition and enforcement of the arbitral award. It was drafted for the purpose of uniformity and the specific needs of the international commercial arbitration process.[70] The Model Law has been adopted by 74 member states of the United Nations as of March 2017.[71] For the recognition and enforcement of foreign arbitral awards, the 1958 New York Convention on the Recognition and Enforcement of Foreign Arbitral Awards (the New York Convention)[72] provides common legislative standards where the 'principal aim is so that foreign arbitral awards will not be discriminated against' and to 'ensure such awards are recognized and generally capable of enforcement' in the States' domestic jurisdiction 'in the same way as domestic awards'.[73] This Convention is applicable in countries that are signatories to the Convention. In other words, cross-border arbitration decisions are enforceable in signatory nations where arbitral awards made under the governing law of a signatory State are recognized and enforced by other signatory countries.

This feature is the main advantage of international arbitration in that the New York Convention facilitates the enforceability of arbitral awards across national boundaries. The European Union Judgments Regulation 1215/2012, which provides a framework for the recognition of court judgments, is limited to European Union countries only. There are also efforts currently under way to establish finance-specific arbitration bodies to ensure that the financial sector clients receive the expertise they require for the effective resolution of disputes. Such bodies include the Panel of Recognised International Market Experts in Finance (PRIME Finance),[74] which is an international arbitration institution in the Hague established in 2012 for the settlement of complex international financial disputes.[75]

Arbitration in Islamic law

Arbitration is termed *tahkim* in Arabic.[76] It involves two or more parties in a dispute who agree to submit their case to a third party called a *hakam* or *muhakkam*.[77] The *hakam* is a neutral decision-maker who is authorized to dispose of rights, settle disputes by suggesting solutions and issue binding decisions.[78] Thus, the *hakam*'s authority is derived from the parties through their voluntary consent.[79] This is the main element that differentiates arbitration from litigation, namely it is the parties, not the State, that authorise the *hakam*.[80]

In pre-Islamic Arabia, the first arbitration case was before Prophet Muhammad became a Prophet where he was chosen as a *hakam* of a dispute due to his honesty and trustworthiness. The dispute was about the positioning of the holy blackstone when there was disagreement between the tribes in Mecca. They disagreed on who should have the honour to posit the holy blackstone in its place. Prophet Muhammad resolved the dispute by taking his robe, asked each syeikh (leader) from each tribe to hold the side of the robe and together they positioned the holy blackstone to a place they agreed. This method resolved the dispute between the tribes and they were satisfied with the way the Prophet resolved it.[81] The practice of arbitration as a form of dispute resolution in the pre-Islamic Arabia was strengthened with the advent of Islam which further streamlined the arbitration procedure to ensure fair dealing and justice.[82]

In the Qur'an, there are numerous verses that directly indicate the use of arbitration as a dispute resolution process.[83] Meanwhile, in *Majallah Al-Ahkam Al'Adliyyah* which is a compilation of Islamic civil law based on the view of Hanafi jurists, there are provisions detailing the appointment of an arbitrator and the effect of arbitration awards. According to the *Majallah*, more than one arbitrator may be appointed to arbitrate on one matter. The disputing parties may also appoint their own arbitrator and this is considered as lawful.[84] However, all the arbitrators need to agree on the issue in dispute. The arbitrators may also appoint an umpire with the permission of the parties.[85] Where the activities of an arbitrator is limited by time, a decision must be made within that period of time. A judgment after that period is considered unlawful or not *nafiz*.[86] Should the disputing parties decide to dismiss the arbitrator that they have appointed, they may do so even before a decision is made.[87]

The decision of an arbitrator is lawful or *nafiz* and binding on all parties concerning the matters under dispute. The arbitration decision shall not go beyond the persons or other matters not relevant to the subject matter.[88] Since the decision of an arbitrator is binding, the disputing parties shall accept it as long as it does not contradict with the Shari'ah.[89] The *Majallah*, however, does not specify the criteria for the appointment of an arbitrator. Cusairi, however, suggests that

> the qualifications of an arbitrator as discussed among jurists of the four schools of law are similar to that of a qadhi. Notwithstanding that, the question is whether an arbitrator has to obtain full qualifications or absolute authority/absolute legal capacity (*al-ahliyah al-mutlaqah*) of a *qadhi*. This

means that even though the four Sunni Schools of Law unanimously agree that a *hakam* must be qualified as a *qadhi*, they differed in defining specifications, limitations and the extent to which the qualifications or the characters of a *qadhi*-competent must be met.[90]

Arbitration in Islamic finance

A well-known Islamic finance dispute that went for arbitration is *Sanghi Polyesters Ltd (India) v The International Investor KSCS (Kuwait)*.[91] In this case, arbitration in London was the chosen dispute resolution forum by the parties who entered into an Islamic *istisna'* contract, namely contract for manufacture.[92] It was stated in the contract that they shall be governed by the 'Laws of England except to the extent it may conflict with Islamic Shari'ah, which shall prevail'. The arbitrator, who is an expert in the Shari'ah, upheld the parties' will to be governed by the English law except where it conflicts with the Shari'ah[93] by awarding the principal and profit claims that are allowed under both the English law and the Shari'ah. The arbitrator, however, refused to award additional damages since it conflicted with the Shari'ah. In this case the arbitrator not only upheld the parties' will but also recognized Shari'ah as an independent system of law capable of governing a financial transaction.[94] This case demonstrates that for Islamic finance, arbitration is a more suitable dispute resolution mechanism than litigation.

Further, the International Chamber of Commerce (ICC) in its 2016 Commission Report on Financial Institutions and International Arbitration suggested that a global legal framework for Islamic finance, through the convergence and codification of Islamic contract law, should be developed with the option to provide for dispute settlement through arbitration when the parties wish the mandatory principles of Shari'ah to prevail.[95] To achieve this end, the training of professionals and experts in the area of Islamic finance is a necessity.[96]

The same 2016 Report by ICC recognised that there are currently two arbitral institutions that are specifically suited to resolve Islamic finance disputes. They are the International Islamic Center for Reconciliation and Mediation (IICRA) and the Kuala Lumpur Regional Centre for Arbitration (KLRCA) with the latter now known as the Asian International Arbitration Centre (AIAC).[97] IICRA[98] was established by the Islamic Development Bank (IDB), the General Council for Islamic Banks and Financial Institutions (CIBAFI), and the United Arab Emirates that serves as the host country for IICRA. IICRA was founded in 2005 but began operations in 2007. It acts as an independent non-profit institution that arbitrates financial and commercial disputes between financial or commercial institutions that implement Shari'ah principles and their clients or other parties. The KLRCA was established in 2012 and has issued i-Arbitration Rules for disputes arising out of commercial agreements based on Shari'ah principles.[99]

However, there are several issues that require attention before arbitration is promoted as the dispute resolution mechanism for Islamic finance. The first issue is the limited number of qualified arbitrators who are knowledgeable in Shari'ah and the intricacies of Islamic financial transactions. Another issue is the cross-border enforcement of arbitral awards.[100] In circumstances where an arbitral award issued in a country needs to be enforced in another, it may be difficult to do so unless there is a reciprocal enforcement treaty in place between the countries or that the countries are signatories to the New York Convention.[101] Even where the countries are signatories to the Convention, a cross-border enforcement of the arbitral award could still be avoided on the basis of 'public policy defence'. National courts may prevent the enforcement of cross-border arbitration awards that they consider to run counter to public policy, for example, on the basis that the arbitral award undermines 'explicit national laws or jurisdictions'.[102] Nonetheless, despite this issue it is still much easier to enforce cross-border arbitral awards than to do so with foreign judgments of the courts. The arrangements for the latter remain fragmented and piecemeal.

Mandatory arbitration clauses in Islamic finance agreements?

One way to ensure that Islamic finance disputes are resolved according to the Shari'ah is by inserting a mandatory arbitration clause in the contract entered into by the parties. Such a clause may stipulate that the disputing parties shall opt for arbitration where the principles of Shari'ah shall apply in resolving the dispute. Among other provisions that may be included in the arbitration clause are the specific procedure to be followed relating to the disclosure of evidence; allowing of remedial powers such as interim relief; rights of appeal; confidentiality; and qualifications of the arbitrator. It is imperative that an arbitration clause should not be a 'midnight clause' thrown in at the last minute without due consideration.[103] It is to be noted that arbitration may only be resorted to when there is an arbitration clause in the contract. However, where there is no such clause, the contracting parties may still go for arbitration by mutually agreeing to do so.

Nonetheless, it was reported in the Price Waterhouse Coopers' 2013 International Arbitration Survey that only 23 per cent of its financial service sector respondents[104] preferred to resolve international disputes through arbitration.[105] Undoubtedly, there is scepticism towards alternative forms of dispute resolution within some entities in the Islamic financial services industry.[106] Efforts, however, have been initiated by the International Swaps and Derivatives Association (ISDA) in 2010 and 2012 to include arbitration clauses in its Islamic Finance *Tahawwut* Master Agreement (TMA)[107] and its *Mubadalatul Arbaah* (Profit Rate Swap) Agreement. The TMA is designed for use with Shari'ah-compliant genuine hedging transactions that utilize *murabahah* (mark-up sale) contracts based on *wa'ad* (promise).[108] ISDA also introduced ISDA Arbitration Guide in 2013 that provides several model arbitration clauses that may be incorporated in an ISDA Master Agreement for derivative trades. Although the efforts by ISDA are laudable, the model arbitration clauses are not mandatory. They would only become mandatory if they are incorporated into the Agreement by mutual consent of the parties involved.

Accordingly, some commentators have suggested compulsory arbitration through the regulatory body by legislating compulsory arbitration applicable to all Islamic finance facilities' disputes.[109] In Malaysia, it has been a legal policy that all Government contracts shall incorporate a mandatory arbitration clause which requires all disputes to go through the arbitration process which is a bar to litigation, unless arbitration fails. However, there is an important issue pertaining to the mandatory arbitration clause as it may amount to denying a party access to the court.[110] Another issue of concern is the legality of mandatory arbitration clause as it 'often raises doubts of constitutionality, as it entails a limitation of the ability of claimants to access to State courts'.[111]

Arbitral award: grounds for review and enforcement

There are at least three types of arbitral awards namely, foreign awards obtained from a foreign country, domestic awards and international awards.[112] The grounds for non-recognition of a foreign award in the New York Convention are very limited. These include awards that are contrary to public policy; where the parties to the agreement were under some incapacity; where the agreement is not valid under the law to which the parties have subjected it; or where there is an absence of a proper notice of the appointment of the arbitrator or of the arbitration proceedings.[113] Article 36 of the Model Law also provides the grounds for refusing recognition or enforcement of an arbitral award[114] which is similar to Article V of the New York Convention relating to the grounds for non-recognition of an arbitral award.[115]

Mediation

Definition and types of mediation

Mediation is another method of alternative dispute resolution available to parties in dispute.[116] It is, by nature, a voluntary process. It is conducted informally by mutual consent of the parties who have disputed claims and unresolved issues pertaining to a matter. Accordingly, mediation is 'an informal process based on agreement, and it is therefore not necessarily jurisdiction specific'.[117] Mediation is a 'non-binding intervention between parties to promote resolution of a grievance, reconciliation, settlement, or compromise'.[118] The United Kingdom Civil Mediation Council described mediation as 'an effective way of resolving disputes without the need to go to court. It involves an independent third party – a mediator – who helps both sides come to an agreement'.[119] Mediation is also defined as 'a voluntary process in which a mediator facilitates communication and negotiation between parties to assist the parties in reaching an agreement regarding a dispute'.[120] Thus, mediation is essentially a negotiation facilitated by a neutral third party, selected by the mutual consensus of the parties.[121] One of the features of mediation which is different from arbitration is that mediation does not involve decision making by the neutral third party. Further, in mediation disputes are settled by way of a private agreement and before the start of the mediation process, parties would normally agree that all evidence are on a 'without prejudice' basis. Hence, if the mediation process fails, the parties cannot use whatever evidence that have been produced during the mediation process. The advantages of mediation include cost effectiveness, informal process, speedier settlement, assistance by a neutral third party, confidential and private process, and amicable settlement which brings an appropriate solution to a dispute.[122]

There are various types or styles of mediation used in different jurisdictions and subject areas. The most common are facilitative mediation, evaluative mediation and transformative mediation. Facilitative mediation is a conventional mediation and 'the primary or true form of mediation'.[123] In facilitative mediation, the mediator assists the disputing parties to reach their goal for an amicable settlement. However, the mediator has the role of testing the strengths and weaknesses of each side's case to ensure that the flow of the mediation is towards the right direction. Facilitative mediation helps the parties to negotiate more effectively, to formulate offers that will be attractive to the other disputing party and to have guidance on timing. Evaluative mediation, which is also known as directive mediation, is similar to conciliation.[124] Evaluative mediation focuses on the strengths and weaknesses of the case.[125] It is 'a mediation in which the mediator will evaluate the dispute and express an opinion on the likely outcome … which the parties should settle'.[126] Therefore, the evaluative mediator will encourage amicable settlement by evaluating the issue and the strengths and weaknesses of both parties.[127] Transformative mediation seeks to improvise communication and relationship between the disputing parties so that they can resolve the dispute on their own.[128] Thus, the nature of the discussion will be controlled by the disputing parties while the mediator takes a reflective role.[129] Apart from these types of mediation, there is also the court's initiative on mediation known as the court-annexed mediation which has been implemented in some parts of the world including Malaysia.[130]

Mediation in Islamic law

In Islam, mediation is called *tawsit*, *wasatah*,[131] *wasitah*,[132] or *wasta*.[133] Apart from mediation, the terminologies are also translated as intermediation[134] and intervention.[135] The definition of mediation from an Islamic perspective is similar to the Western perspective. Mediation in Islam is essentially an intervention to resolve a dispute between two parties or more towards an amicable settlement.[136] It has some similarities to formal litigation or judgment. The main difference, however, lies in the 'source of authority' that is 'between the private versus the public authority of the state courts'.[137] In mediation, each disputing party appoints a representative to negotiate a settlement between them without the presence of and direct input from the parties. The negotiated settlement becomes binding on the parties to the dispute.[138]

Mediation is mentioned in numerous verses in the Qur'an. One of them is translated thus:

> And if two parties (or groups) among the believers fall into a quarrel, then make peace between them both ... with justice and be equitable. Verily, Allah loves those who are fair (and just). The believers are but a single brotherhood, so make reconciliation between two (contending) brothers, and fear Allah, that you may receive mercy.[139]

While mediation is mentioned in the Qur'an, this primary source of Islamic law, however, does not outline the process of mediation in detail. Thus, contemporary practice in mediation is acceptable as long as it does not contradict with the principles of Shari'ah. One of the principles relates to the preservation of other persons' secret or '*ayb*'. Therefore, an important aspect in Islamic mediation is preserving confidentiality.[140] A mediator who has been entrusted with a secret in order to resolve a dispute shall not divulge that secret. In fact, the keeping of secrets is one of the elements of *amanah* or trust which is highly emphasized in Islam.[141] In relation to this, the Prophet Muhammad said: 'One who does not fulfill trust obligations has no Faith (*emaan*) with him; and one who does not stand by his word of promise has no religion with him'.[142] Further, a mediator shall be neutral, impartial, without prejudice, and unbiased.[143] He shall try to get clarification from all the disputing parties to ensure that a just settlement could be achieved. The seeking of clarification from all the parties is the role of a mediator through the act of intervention and is in line with the Qur'anic approach on *tabayyun* (gathering of all evidence).[144] Meanwhile according to Cusairi, 'in general, there is agreement among the jurists that mediators-arbitrators must have qualities such as justice/impartiality (*'adalah*) and be knowledgeable on the law and the principle of disobedience (*nushuz*)'.[145] Cusairi adds to the qualifications of a mediator by saying that 'the arbitrator-mediator must be a Muslim; have attained the age of majority and be of sound mind; be of just character; be of male gender; be a mujtahid (a learned scholar); and be free from physical defects'.[146]

Mediation in Islamic finance

Since mediation is private in nature, Islamic financial disputes that go for mediation are not officially reported. An institution that provide mediation services for Islamic finance is the International Islamic Mediation and Arbitration Centre (IMAC).[147] IMAC is based in Hong Kong and was established in 2008 with an in-house Shari'ah Advisory Council that provides expertise in various Shari'ah-related matters. Mediation by IMAC may be conducted 'in any location which will provide an atmosphere for meaningful dialog and positive participation by all concerned parties'.[148] The mediation does not involve a set procedural process and, instead, operates on what the parties 'want and are willing to give in order to reach resolution'.[149] If a resolution is not obtained, the parties would usually opt for arbitration, which is often agreed to prior to the beginning of the mediation. In such a situation, the whole process would be known as Med-Arb.[150]

For Islamic finance, although mediation has its advantages, the very private nature of mediation could be a double-edged sword. While mediation maintains privacy and confidentiality, at the same time, however, the absence of public documents or access to mediation proceedings does not contribute to the development of legal certainty in the nascent Islamic financial services industry. In the words of Lord Thomas, the Chief Justice of England and Wales, there are 'issues which arise from the resolution of disputes firmly behind closed doors'.[151] Although Lord Thomas was specifically referring to arbitration, His Lordship's remark equally applies to mediation that shares a similar private characteristic to arbitration. According to Lord Thomas, the lack of openness decelerates 'public understanding of the law, and public debate over its application'; does not 'expose issues that call for Parliamentary scrutiny and legislative revision'; deprives individuals' ability 'to access the law, to understand how it has been interpreted and applied'; and 'reduces the degree of certainty in the law', thus, reducing 'individuals' ability to fully understand their rights and obligations, and to properly plan their affairs accordingly'.[152]

Financial ombudsman

Financial ombudsman is akin to a mediation forum. The concept of ombudsman is said to have been introduced in the Western world by the Swedish King Charles XII, who upon returning from self-exile in Turkey in 1713, created the office of Supreme Ombudsman that later became the Chancellor of Justice.[153] Charles XII is said to have been influenced by the example of the second Muslim caliph, namely 'Umar al-Khattab (AD 634–644) and by the concept of *Qadhi al-Qudhat* which was developed in the Muslim world.[154] In Islam, the concept of ombudsman or known as *hisbah*, first emerged more than 1,400 years ago. There are several verses in the Qur'an that mention *hisbah*, one of them is translated thus: 'Let there arise out of you a band of people enjoining what is right forbidding what is wrong and believing in Allah'.[155]

The Qur'anic injunction of 'enjoining what is right forbidding what is wrong' was put into practice by the Prophet Muhammad when he appointed Umar bin Khattab as a *muhtasib* (ombudsman) for Madinah and Sa'ad ibn Al A'as Umayyah as a *muhtasib* for Makkah. The jurisdiction of the *muhtasib* encompassed matters that were generally outside the scope of the law courts,[156] such as keeping an eye on public morals, eliminating fraudulent practices of the traders and generally ensuring the good health of the civil society. The institution of *hisbah* and office of *muhtasib* continued to exist and played an important role during the Muslim reign of Abbasid Caliph Abu Ja'afar al Manur (AD 733), the Fatamids, the Ayyubids and the Ottomans although the office was known by different names in different regions. For example, in the eastern provinces of Baghdad it was known as *muhtasib*, in North Africa *sahib al-suq*, in Turkey *muhtasib aghasi* and in India *kotwal*.[157] In the contemporary world, the ombudsman has become part of the alternative dispute resolution fora in many countries providing a quick, inexpensive, independent and effective redress mechanism.

Acknowledging the necessity for a speedy and yet effective dispute resolution mechanism for the financial services industry, many countries have taken the initiative to establish financial ombudsmen in their respective jurisdiction. Among them are the Financial Industry Disputes Resolution Centre (FIDReC) in Singapore, Financial Ombudsman Service in the United Kingdom, Financial Ombudsman Service in Australia, and Ombudsman for Financial Services (OFS) in Malaysia. The Malaysian OFS is established with the view to assist financial consumers in resolving their complaints or disputes with financial institutions, known as the Financial Service Providers (FSPs) that are under the purview of the Central Bank of Malaysia.[158] The OFS is a non-profit organization and provides its services to financial consumers on a free of charge basis. The decisions of the OFS are binding on the FSPs provided that the decisions are accepted by the complainant/financial consumers.[159] In cases where the complainants do not accept the decisions, they may subsequently institute legal proceedings against the FSPs.[160] It is apparent that the binding effect of the OFS' decisions slightly departs from the original nature of mediation. The Malaysian OFS was formerly known as the Financial Mediation Bureau, which was incorporated in 2004 and commenced operations in 2005. However, it was in 2015 that the Islamic Financial Services (Financial Ombudsman Scheme) Regulations (IFSR) was introduced which provides the mechanism for the settlement of Islamic financial disputes.[161]

Conclusion

Litigation of Islamic financial disputes in several countries demonstrate that litigation is not a suitable dispute resolution fora for Islamic finance. However, Islamic finance dispute resolution cannot dispense with the courts since the latter are needed for several purposes such as foreclosure of properties, enforcement of securities, winding up and bankruptcy. On the other hand, arbitration has demonstrated to be a better dispute resolution forum for Islamic finance than litigation. Nonetheless, there are several issues that require attention prior to promoting arbitration as the suitable dispute resolution forum for Islamic finance. Among the issues are the insufficient number of qualified arbitrators who are knowledgeable in Shari'ah and cross-border enforcement of arbitral awards. Mediation is another option as an Islamic finance dispute resolution forum but the private nature of mediation may not contribute to the overall development of the relatively nascent Islamic financial services industry. Clearly, there is not one solution that provides a suitable dispute resolution forum for the Islamic financial services industry. Nonetheless, the search could draw inspiration from the rich Islamic conflict intervention principles, values and models particularly where Islamic dispute resolution applies a variety of techniques that correspond and adapt to each stage or condition of disputes.

Acknowledgements

This chapter is part of the research output funded by Malaysia's Ministry of Education research grant FRGS/1/2014/SSI10/UKM/02/2.

Notes

1 Henry J Brown and Arthur Marriot, *ADR Principles and Practice* (3rd edn, Sweet & Maxwell 2011) 18.
2 Public Works and Government Services Canada, 'Alternative Dispute Resolution (ADR) and Litigation: Key Features and Considerations' http://studylib.net/doc/18733895/alternative-dispute-resolution-adr-and-litigation-key- accessed 20 February 2018.
3 M Ali Sadiqi, 'Islamic Dispute Resolution in the Shade of the American Court House' (October 2010) www.amjaonline.org/en/academic-research/cat_view/6-islamic-arbitration-guidelines-and-procedures-2010 accessed 20 February 2018. The decision is appealable unless it is a decision of the highest court in the court hierarchy.
4 Public Works and Government Services Canada (n 2).
5 Sadiqi (n 3).
6 Public Works and Government Services Canada (n 2).
7 George E Irani, 'Islamic Mediation Techniques for Middle East Conflicts' (1999) 3 Middle East Review of International Affairs 1.
8 Susan Blake, Julie Browne and Stuart Sime, *A Practical Approach to Alternative Dispute Resolution* (Oxford University Press 2011) 47.
9 Syed Khalid Rashid, 'Alternative Dispute Resolution in the Context of Islamic Law' (2004) 7 *The Vindobona Journal of International Commercial Law and Arbitration* 95.
10 Mohamed M Keshavjee, 'Alternative Dispute Resolution – Its Resonance in Muslim Thought and Future Directions' (Ismaili Centre Lecture Series, London, 2 April 2002) https://iis.ac.uk/alternative-dispute-resolution-its-resonance-muslim-thought-and-future-directions accessed 20 February 2018.
11 John Davidson and Christine Wood, 'A Conflict Resolution Model' (2004) 43 *Theory into Practice Conflict Resolution and Peer Mediation* 6.
12 Public Works and Government Services Canada (n 2).
13 Davidson and Wood (n 11).
14 Umar Aimhanosi Oseni, 'Dispute Resolution in Islamic Banking and Finance: Current Trends and Future Perspectives' (International Conference on Islamic Financial Services: Emerging Opportunities for Law/Economic Reforms of the Developing Nations, Nigeria, October 2009). See generally, Walter Olson, *The Litigation Explosion: What Happened When America Unleashed the Law Suit* (Truman Tally Books 1991); Rashid (n 9).
15 See Lord Woolf's report on Access to Justice which introduced reforms in the civil justice system in the United Kingdom by recommending the court-annexed ADR as part of the case management role of a judge. The recommendations were introduced in the amended Civil Procedure Rules (CPR) in May 2000 with case management as its main objective. The five main areas of delay in litigation as mentioned in the report were delay in progressing the case from issue to trial, delay in reaching settlement, delay in obtaining a hearing date, delay due to time taken by the hearing, and low priority given to civil cases. Harry Woolf, *Access to Justice: Final Report to the Lord Chancellor on the Civil Justice System in England and Wales* (Her Majesty's Stationery Office 1996).

16 However, there are certain advantages for litigation over arbitration. For example, litigation provides injunction which is a quicker way to preserve status quo or to conserve assets pending final decision. Appointment of arbitrators is also a tedious process of selection to be agreed upon by the parties, as well as the security for cost that must be paid. See Brown and Marriot (n 1) 125.
17 Wahbah Al-Zuhayli, *Al-Fiqh Al-Islam WaAdilatuh* (Juz' 6 Dar al-Fikr 1996) 739.
18 Ibid.
19 Ibid. See the meaning of fard kifayah at Oxford Islamic Studies Online, 'Fard Kifayah' www.oxfordislamicstudies.com/article/opr/t125/e625 accessed 3 November 2017.
20 The Qur'an, *Surah An-Nisa'* (4) verse 58.
21 The Qur'an and *Sunnah* are the primary sources of the Shari'ah or Islamic law. Qur'an is the Holy Book for Muslims. *Sunnah* refers to the utterances, conducts and tacit approvals of the Prophet Muhammad and reported as *Hadith*.
22 Abdul Monir Yaacob (ed.), *Sistem Kehakiman Islam* (IKIM 2001) 15.
23 Mahomed Ullah Al-Haj, *A Dissertation on the Administration of Justice of Muslim Law* (The Book House 1980) 49.
24 *Ijtihad* is an exercise of individual opinion arrived at through a well-defined methodology of legal reasoning and legal interpretation called *usul al-fiqh*. Two forms of *ijtihad* are *ijma'* (consensus of jurists) and *qiyas* (analogy).
25 Sadiqi (n 3).
26 Al-Zuhayli (n 17) 744.
27 Art 1848 Majallah Al-Ahkam Al'Adliyyah, which reads:

> As the decision of judges in respect of all the inhabitants in their District must be enforced, so also the decision of arbitrators in respect of the persons who appointed them, and the matter for which they are appointed are binding
>
> in Charles Robert Tyser, DG Demetriades and Ismail Haqqi Effendi, The Mejelle: Being an English Translation of Majallah El-Ahkam-I-Adliya and a Complete Code on Islamic Civil Law (The Other Press 2001) 326

28 Art 1837 Majallah Al-Ahkam Al'Adliyyah, which reads: 'It is not permitted to reconsider and hear claims, when there is a decision (hukm) and written judgment (I'lam) in conformity with the principles of Sher' law, i.e. when the conditions and grounds of the judgment exist' in Tyser, Demetriades and Effendi (n 27) 325.
29 Martin Shapiro, 'Islam and Appeal' (1980) 68 California Law Review 350.
30 Malaysia Syariah Judiciary Department, 'Court Procedure According to the Level of Appellate Court' (In Malay) www.esyariah.gov.my/portal/page/portal/Portal%20E-Syariah%20BM/Portal%20E-Syariah%20Prosedur%20Mahkamah/Portal%20E-Syariah%20Prosedur%20Mahk.%20Tinggi/Portal%20E-Syariah%20Prosedur%20Mahk.%20Rayuan accessed 23 February 2018.
31 Jonathan Lawrence, Peter Morton and Hussain Khan, 'Dispute Resolution in Islamic Finance', (Global Islamic Finance Report, April 2012) http://klgates.com/files/Publication/0b2f56b0-d738-4217-85ee-6670f2101659/Presentation/PublicationAttachment/3e2c3cd0-43fd-4ef4-ac96-700e33340e6a/Dispute_Resolution_in_Islamic_Finance.pdf accessed 20 February 2018.
32 Ibid.
33 See further Siti Faridah Abdul Jabbar, 'Islamic Finance and Dispute Resolution' (2014) 35 *Company Lawyer* 65.
34 [2002] WL 346969 (QB Comm. Ct 13 February 2002).
35 For an elaboration on *murabahah*, see Siti Faridah Abdul Jabbar, 'Islamic Finance: Fundamental Principles and Key Financial Institutions' (2009) 30 *Company Lawyer* 23.
36 Oseni (n 14).
37 [2004] 2 Lloyd's Rep. 1, [2004] EWCA Civ 19.

38 Oseni (n 14).
39 Camille Paldi, 'Dubai as the Dispute Resolution Center for the Islamic Finance Industry', (30 December 2010) www.jdsupra.com/legalnews/dubai-as-the-dispute-resolution-center-f-54362/ accessed 20 February 2018.
40 [2009] EWHC 3545 (Ch).
41 As opposed to the Malaysian Shari'ah courts that do not have jurisdiction in matters relating to finance. The Shari'ah courts have jurisdiction in matters relating to Islamic personal law only.
42 A few of the cases are *Tinta Press v Bank Islam Malaysia Bhd* [1986] 1 MLJ 474; *Bank Islam Malaysia Bhd v Adnan bin Omar* [1994] 3 CLJ 735; *Dato Hj Nik Mahmud bin Daud v Bank Islam Malaysia Bhd* [1996] 4 MLJ 295 (High Court), [1998] 3 MLJ 396 (Supreme Court).
43 Zulkifli Hasan and Mehmet Asutay, 'An Analysis of the Courts' Decisions on Islamic Finance Disputes' 2011 3 *ISRA International Journal of Islamic Finance* 41.
44 [2006] 7 MLJ 249.
45 [2006] 3 MLJ 67.
46 [2008] 6 MLJ xiv.
47 Oseni (n 14).
48 Aisha Nadar, 'Islamic Finance and Dispute Resolution: Part 1' (2009) 23 Arab Law Quarterly 1.
49 [2003] 2 MLJ 408 CA.
50 See for example *Malayan Banking Bhd v Marilyn Ho Siok Lin* [2006] 7MLJ 249, at 267 where the Malaysian court imposed late payment charges on the defendant albeit the terminology used by the court was profit: 'profit per day thereafter … until the date of satisfaction of the sum owing under the charge'.
51 Paldi (n 39); Engku Rabiah Adawiah Engku Ali, 'Constraints and Opportunities in Harmonisation of Civil Law and Shariah in the Islamic Financial Services Industry' [2008] 4 MLJ i.
52 Central Bank of Malaysia Act 2009, ss 56 and 57; Capital Markets and Services Act 2007, ss 316A(1), 316F and 316G.
53 There are two SACs in Malaysia. One is under the purview of the Central Bank of Malaysia while the other is under the Securities Commission of Malaysia. The former issues rulings on Islamic banking and takaful while the latter on Islamic capital market. See further Siti Faridah Abdul Jabbar, 'The Islamic Financial Services Industry: Shari'ah Board's Governance Framework' (2013) 34 *Company Lawyer* 297.
54 Barry Rider, 'Islamic Financial Law: Back to Basics' in IFSB, *The Changing Landscape of Islamic Finance: Imminent Challenges and Future Directions* (IFSB 2010) 115–116.
55 Ibid.
56 Ibid.
57 Blake, Browne and Sime (n 8) 371.
58 Ibid. 372.
59 Sadiqi (n 3).
60 Lawrence, Morton and Khan (n 31).
61 Ibid.
62 [2007] UKHL 40.
63 *Filli Shipping Co. Ltd v Premium Nafta Products Ltd* [2007] UKHL 40 para 6. Lord Hoffman held that:

> In approaching the question of construction, it is therefore necessary to inquire into the purpose of the arbitration clause. As to this, I think there can be no doubt. The parties have entered into a relationship, an agreement or what is alleged to be an agreement or what appears on its face to be an agreement, which

may give rise to disputes. They want those disputes decided by a tribunal which they have chosen, commonly on the grounds of such matters as its neutrality, expertise and privacy, the availability of legal services at the seat of the arbitration and the unobtrusive efficiency of its supervisory law. Particularly in the case of international contracts, they want a quick and efficient adjudication and do not want to take the risks of delay and, in too many cases, partiality, in proceedings before a national jurisdiction.

64 For further important features of arbitration, see Lawrence, Morton and Khan (n 31). This article was first published in the Global Islamic Finance Report 2012 which mentioned that other important features of arbitration are that the procedural framework for the arbitration is stipulated in the arbitral rules, the seat of arbitration is typically, but not always, where the arbitral hearing is held (the seat is an important choice as the law of the seat will govern the arbitral procedure) and neutrality in jurisdiction and law if arbitration is conducted in a third country.

65 United Nations, 'General Assembly Resolution 40/72 (11 December 1985)' www.un.org/en/ga/search/view_doc.asp?symbol=A/RES/40/72 accessed 15 November 2017 and United Nations, 'General Assembly Resolution 61/33 (4 December 2006)' www.un.org/en/ga/search/view_doc.asp?symbol=A/RES/61/33&Lang=E accessed 15 November 2017.

66 United Nations, 'Official Records of the General Assembly, Fortieth Session, Supplement No. 17 (A/40/17), annex I' www.uncitral.org/pdf/english/texts/arbitration/NY-conv/New-York-Convention-E.pdf accessed 15 November 2017 and United Nations, 'Official Records of the General Assembly, Sixty-first Session, Supplement No. 17 (A/61/17)' http://unctad.org/en/Docs/a61d17_en.pdf accessed 15 November 2017. See United Nations, 'UNCITRAL Model Law on International Commercial Arbitration 1985 with amendments as adopted in 2006'. www.uncitral.org/pdf/english/texts/arbitration/ml-arb/07-86998_Ebook.pdf accessed 15 November 2017.

67 The United Nations Commission on International Trade Law (UNCITRAL) is a subsidiary body of the United Nations General Assembly. UNCITRAL is 'a legal body with universal membership specializing in commercial law reform worldwide for over 50 years, UNCITRAL's business is the modernization and harmonization of rules on international business'. For more information on UNCITRAL, see United Nations, 'A Guide to UNCITRAL, Basic facts about the United Nations Commission on International Trade Law' www.uncitral.org/pdf/english/texts/general/12-57491-Guide-to-UNCITRAL-e.pdf accessed 15 November 2017.

68 There is also UNCITRAL Technical Notes on Online Dispute Resolution. See United Nations, 'UNCITRAL Technical Notes on Online Dispute Resolution (2016)' www.uncitral.org/uncitral/en/uncitral_texts/odr/2016Technical_notes.html accessed 18 November 2017.

69 United Nations, 'UNCITRAL Model Law on International Commercial Arbitration (1985), with amendments as adopted in 2006' www.uncitral.org/uncitral/en/uncitral_texts/arbitration/1985Model_arbitration.html accessed 29 December 2017.

70 United Nations, 'General Assembly Resolution 40/72 (11 December 1985)' and United Nations, 'Resolution 61/33 (4 December 2006)' (n 65). For case law on UNCITRAL Texts (CLOUT), see United Nations, 'Case Law on UNCITRAL Texts (CLOUT)' www.uncitral.org/clout/index.jspx?lng=en#legislativeText accessed 15 November 2017 and for UNCITRAL 2012 Digest of Case Law on the Model Law on International Commercial Arbitration, see United Nations, 'Digests' www.uncitral.org/uncitral/en/case_law/digests.html accessed 15 November 2017.

71 See International Arbitration Law Network and Resources, '74 Jurisdictions Have Adopted the UNCITRAL Model Law to Date' http://internationalarbitrationlaw.com/74-jurisdictions-have-adopted-the-uncitral-model-law-to-date/ accessed 29 December 2017.

72 United Nations, 'Treaty Series 330/4739 (7 June 1959)' https://treaties.un.org/pages/showDetails.aspx?objid=080000028002a36b accessed 15 November 2017.

73 The objectives of the Convention on the Recognition and Enforcement of Foreign Arbitral Awards (the Convention) are to provide common legislative standards for the recognition of arbitration agreements and court recognition and enforcement of foreign and non-domestic arbitral awards. In clear words, the provisions are applicable to awards made in any State other than the State in which recognition and enforcement is sought. It also applies to awards 'not considered as domestic awards'. See United Nations, 'Convention on the Recognition and Enforcement of Foreign Arbitral Awards (New York, 1958) (the "New York Convention")' www.uncitral.org/uncitral/en/uncitral_texts/arbitration/NYConvention.html accessed 20 November 2017.

74 For a history of PRIME Finance, see PRIME Finance, 'History' https://primefinancedisputes.org/page/history accessed 3 March 2018.

75 PRIME Finance, 'Media Coverage' https://primefinancedisputes.org/page/media-coverage accessed 3 March 2018.

76 Harith Suleiman Faruqi, *Faruqi's Law Dictionary: English–Arabic* (Librairie Du Liban 1991) 51.

77 Samir Saleh, *Commercial Arbitration in the Arab Middle East* (Graham & Trotman Limited 1984) 20.

78 Zeyad Al-Qurashi, 'Arbitration under the Islamic Sharia' (2004) 1 TDM www.transnational-dispute-management.com/article.asp?key=4 accessed 3 March 2018.

79 Ibid.

80 Ibid.

81 Aseel Al-Ramahi, 'Sulh: A Crucial Part of Islamic Arbitration' (2008) LSE Legal Studies Working Paper 12/2008 https://papers.ssrn.com/sol3/papers.cfm?abstract_id=1153659 accessed 20 February 2018.

82 Oseni (n 14).

83 To name a few, *Surah an-Nisā'* (4), verse 35, which is translated thus:

> If you fear a breach between them twain (the man and his wife), appoint (two) arbitrators, one from his family and the other from her's; if they both wish for peace, Allah will cause their reconciliation. Indeed, Allah is Ever All-Knower, Well-Acquainted with all things.

Surah an-Nisā' (4), verse 65, which is translated thus: 'But no, by your Lord, they can have no Faith, until they make you judge in all disputes between them, and find in themselves no resistance against your decisions, and accept (them) with full submission'.

84 Art 1843 of the Majalla Al-Ahkam Al-'Adliyyah in Tyser, Demetriades and Effendi (n 27).

85 Ibid. Art 1845.

86 Ibid. Arts 1846, 113.

87 Ibid. Art 1847.

88 Ibid. Art 1842.

89 Ibid. Art 1848.

90 Rafidah Mohamad Cusairi, 'The Application of Islamic Shari`ah to the Muslim Minority Living in the UK: A Comparative Study on Family Mediation Between English Law and Faith-Based Med-Arb At Shari`ah Councils' (PhD thesis, Glasgow Caledonian University 2013) 170.

91 [2001] CLC 748.

92 For an elaboration on *istisna'*, see Jabbar (n 35).

93 Nadar (n 48).

94 See further Jabbar (n 33).

95 International Chamber of Commerce (ICC), 'Commission Report on Financial Institutions and International Arbitration (Report) 2016' https://cdn.iccwbo.org/content/uploads/sites/3/2016/11/ICC-Financial-Institutions-and-International-Arbitration-ICC-Arbitration-ADR-Commission-Report.pdf accessed 18 November 2017. The report was released on 9 November 2016. The report focuses on the view and expectations of financial institutions in the field of international arbitration.

96 Ibid.

97 It is worth noted that an arbitration clause is mandatory in all contracts executed by the Government of Malaysia which was at first being a policy to promote the KLRCA and to reduce litigation costs if matters are proceeded in court.

98 International Islamic Center for Reconciliation and Mediation, 'Establishment' www.iicra.com accessed 4 March 2018.

99 Asian International Arbitration Centre, 'i-Arbitration' www.aiac.world/arbitration/i--arbitration accessed 26 August 2018.

100 Mark Hoyle, 'Specific Issues in Islamic Dispute Resolution' (2009) 75 Arbitration 219.

101 Oliver Agha, 'Islamic Finance Dispute Resolution' [2009] *Islamic Finance News* 31.

102 Ibid.

103 Lawrence, Morton and Khan (n 31).

104 The respondents were in-house counsel who identified their primary industry as being financial services including 'rating agencies, investment research providers and financial consultancy'. See n 2 of the report at Price Waterhouse Coopers, 'Corporate Choices in International Arbitration: Industry Perspectives' www.pwc.com/gx/en/arbitration-dispute-resolution/assets/pwc-international-arbitration-study.pdf accessed 21 February 2018.

105 The International Chamber of Commerce Arbitration and ADR Commission's report into the use of arbitration in the financial sector, published in November 2016, reflected similar findings to the Price Waterhouse Coopers' 2013 International Arbitration Survey. It noted that 70 per cent of interviewees were not aware whether their financial institutions had participated in any international arbitrations in the last five years. Only 24 per cent had participated in a small number, resulting in international arbitration representing less than 5 per cent of all financial institutions' disputes. See Duncan Speller and Francis Hornyold-Strickland, 'International Arbitration in the Finance Sector: Room to Grow' www.cdr-news.com/categories/arbitration-and-adr/featured/7122-international-arbitration-in-the-finance-sector-room-to-grow accessed 21 February 2018.

106 Presentation by Hakimah Yaakob at the Asia Pacific Regional Arbitration Group Conference 2011 who stated that, following a survey that she conducted of 10 Islamic banks and 12 *takaful* operators (Islamic insurance providers) in Malaysia, she found that there was a 'credit policy' in many of these institutions to not include alternative dispute resolution clauses in their contracts, but to opt for litigation instead. This was said by the financial institutions to have been done, in many cases, in order to avoid credit risks for legal uncertainty. See Hakimah Yaakob, 'Arbitration – Consistent with the Spirit of Islamic Banking? The Benefits and Challenges of Arbitrating in Islamic Banking and Finance Disputes' (Asia Pacific Regional Arbitration Group Conference, Kuala Lumpur, 9–10 July 2011).

107 See also Workshop on IIFM Standards by Habib Motani (September 2017) on the ISDA/IIFM Tahawwut Master Agreement as guidelines regarding the sorts of transaction that may be entered into under the ISDA/IIFM Tahawwut Master Agreement at www.iifm.net/sites/default/files/Session%201%20-%20Hedging%20Legal%20Aspects%20by%20Habib%20Motani.pdf accessed 15 November 2017 and International Swaps and Derivatives Association, 'ISDA/IIFM Tahawwut Master Agreement Clarification Summary' at www.iifm.net/sites/default/files/TMA%20clarification%20summary_0.pdf accessed 15 November 2017.

108 International Swaps and Derivatives Association (n 107).

109 Hamid Sultan Abu Backer, *International Arbitration: With Commentary to Malaysian Arbitration Act 2005* (Janab (M) Sdn Bhd 2016) ch 5, 465–466. Justice Hamid Sultan of the Malaysian Court of Appeal suggested amendments of the relevant legislation for a provision that all financial institutions providing Islamic financial facilities to incorporate an arbitration clause in their agreements and that the Court shall order the parties in a contested matter involving Islamic finance to enter into an arbitration agreement. It was further contended that 'compulsory arbitration is not alien to Islamic Jurisprudence' which has been practiced in the Syariah Courts in many States in Malaysia. Accordingly, the mandatory arbitration that was suggested is an example of a codified initiative by the US in its Alternative Dispute Resolution Act 1998. See Umar Aimhanosi Oseni, 'A Review of Malaysia as a Choice Jurisdiction for Dispute Resolution in the Global Islamic Finance Industry' in Backer, *International Arbitration: With Commentary to Malaysian Arbitration Act 2005*, ch 5, 470. Australia has also legislated for mandatory arbitration as a prerequisite requirement before litigation. See Australia National Alternative Dispute Resolution Advisory Council (NADRAC), 'Legislating for Alternative Dispute Resolution, A Guide for Government Policymakers and Legal Drafters' (2006) www.ag.gov.au/LegalSystem/AlternateDisputeResolution/Documents/NADRAC%20Publications/Legislating%20for%20Alternative%20Dispute%20Resolution.PDF accessed 16 February 2018.

110 See US Consumer Financial Protection Bureau, 'CFPB Issues Rule to Ban Companies From Using Arbitration Clauses to Deny Groups of People Their Day in Court' www.consumerfinance.gov/about-us/newsroom/cfpb-issues-rule-ban-companies-using-arbitration-clauses-deny-groups-people-their-day-court/ accessed 16 February 2018. See also Tom Cotton and Keith Rothfus, 'Repeal The CFPB's Anti-Consumer Ban On Mandatory Arbitration Clauses' www.forbes.com/sites/realspin/2017/07/25/repeal-the-cfpbs-anti-consumer-ban-on-mandatory-arbitration-clauses/#7ac953347fb0 accessed 16 February 2018. For further reading, see Amanda R James, 'Comment: Because Arbitration Can Be Beneficial, It Should Never Have To Be Mandatory: Making A Case Against Compelled Arbitration Based Upon Pre-Dispute Agreements To Arbitrate In Consumer And Employee Adhesion Contracts' 2016 *Loyola Law Review* 531.

111 See Pietro Ortolani and Barbara Warwas, 'Arbitration In Southern Europe: Insights From A Large-Scale Empirical Study' 2015 (26) American Review of International Arbitration 187 at n 132.

112 Arbitration Act 2005 of Malaysia recognizes at least three types of arbitral awards namely: (i) foreign arbitral awards arising from international arbitration outside Malaysia; (ii) international arbitration awards arising from Malaysia; (iii) domestic awards from Malaysia. The relevant sections are ss 38, 39, 30.

113 See the New York Convention.

114 See the text of the Model Law (n 66).

115 Explanatory Note by the UNCITRAL secretariat, p. 35 para 47, UNCITRAL Model Law on International Commercial Arbitration 1985 (n 66).

116 According to Hamid and Mohammad, mediation has been practiced by many eastern communities, such as the Chinese, Arabs, Indians and Malays, for many centuries as the customary means of dispute resolution. See Mohamed Ishak Abdul Hamid and Nik Azahani Nik Mohammad, 'Cross-Culture Jurisprudential Influence on Mediation in Malaysia' [2016] 4 MLJ xli.

117 Blake, Browne and Sime (n 8) 11, para 1.27.

118 Merriam Webster Online Dictionary, 'Definition of Mediation' www.merriam-webster.com/dictionary/mediation accessed 14 November 2017.

119 UK Civil Mediation Council, 'What is Mediation?' www.civilmediation.org/about-mediation/29/what-is-mediation accessed 14 November 2017.

120 Mediation Act of Malaysia 2012 [Act 749], s 3.

121 Blake, Browne and Sime (n 8) 177, para 11.07. See also Michael Palmer and Simon A Roberts, *Dispute Processes: ADR and the Primary Forms of Decision Making* (Butterworths 1998).
122 For further reading on the advantages of mediation, see Blake, Browne and Sime (n 8) 181–182, para 11.14; and for disadvantages of mediation, 185, para 11.22. See also Brown and Marriot (n 1), 75–107 for a further insight about ADR and the Courts.
123 Blake, Browne and Sime (n 8) 197.
124 Ibid. 199.
125 For further reading, see Blake, Browne and Sime (n 8).
126 Ibid. 198.
127 For a comparison of facilitative and evaluative mediation, see ibid.
128 Blake, Browne and Sime (n 8) 200, para 11.94.
129 Ibid.
130 For Malaysia, the Kuala Lumpur Court Mediation Centre (KLCMC) was established on 1 April 2011 as an initiative by the courts to encourage mediation. See further Asean Law Association, 'Kuala Lumpur Court Mediation Centre: Court-Annexed Mediation' www.aseanlawassociation.org/11GAdocs/workshop5-malaysia.pdf accessed 26 August 2018.
131 Faruqi (n 76) 451.
132 The term '*Al-Wasathah*' also connotes the same meaning. The term '*wasitah*' is mostly used by the Lebanese, who usually change the letter 'alif' to 'ya'. See Asma Hakimah Ab Halim, Interview with Dr Mahdi Zahraa, Reader in Law, Glasgow School for Business and Society, Glasgow Caledonian University (Glasgow, 11 May 2015).
133 Al-Ramahi (n 81) 4.
134 Shin Nomoto, 'An Early Isma'ili-Shi'i Thought on the Messianic Figure (the Qa'in) according to al-Razi (d. *c.*322/933–4)' (2009) 44 Orient 19.
135 Sadiqi (n 3).
136 Faruqi (n 76) 451.
137 Sadiqi (n 3).
138 Ibid.
139 The Qur'an, *Surah Al-Hujurat* (49), verses 9–10.
140 JAMS Mediation Services, 'Mediators Ethics Guidelines' www.jamsadr.com/mediators-ethics/ accessed 31 October 2017.
141 The Qur'an, *Surah An-Nisa'* (4), verse 58.
142 Reported by al-Baihaqi in Shu'ab al-Iman. See Quran-Al-Hakeem, 'Excellent Advice From Allah' http://quranalhakeem.com/excellent-advice-from-allah/ accessed 20 February 2018.
143 JAMS Mediation Services (n 140).
144 The Qur'an, *Surah Al-Hujurat* (49), verse 6.
145 Cusairi (n 90) 171.
146 Ibid. 172.
147 International Islamic Mediation and Arbitration Centre, 'About Us: Establishment' www.arabcci.org/IMAC accessed 4 March 2018.
148 International Islamic Mediation and Arbitration Centre, 'FAQs: Arbitration' www.arabcci.org/IMAC_faqs.htm accessed 4 March 2018.
149 Ibid.
150 Ibid.
151 The Right Hon. The Lord Thomas of Cwmgiedd, Lord Chief Justice of England and Wales, 'Developing Commercial Law Through the Courts: Rebalancing the Relationship Between the Courts and Arbitration', The Bailii Lecture, 9 March 2016 www.judiciary.gov.uk/wp-content/uploads/2016/03/lcj-speech-bailli-lecture-20160309.pdf accessed 22 February 2018.

152 Ibid.
153 Ahmed Akgunduz, *Introduction to Islamic Law* (IUR Press 2010) 30–31, citing Marcel A Boisard, 'On the Probable Influence of Islam on Western Public and International Law' (1980) 11 International Journal of Middle East Studies 429. See also Victor Pickl, 'Islamic Roots of Ombudsman System' (1997) 6 *The Ombudsman Journal* 101.
154 Akgunduz (n 153).
155 The Qur'an, *Surah Al Imran* (3), verse 104.
156 Ibn Taimiyyah, *Al-Hisbah fi al-Islam wa Wazifat al Hukkam al-Islamiyyah* (*Hisbah in Islam and Duties of Islamic Officials*) (Madinah University n. d.) 10.
157 Syed Khalid Rashid, 'Peculiarities and Religious Underlining of ADR in Islamic Law' (Conference on Mediation in the Asia Pacific: Constraints and Challenges, Kuala Lumpur, 16–18 June 2008).
158 Ombudsman for Financial Services, 'Background' www.ofs.org.my/en/background accessed 4 March 2018.
159 Islamic Financial Services (Financial Ombudsman Scheme) Regulations 2015, reg.18(1).
160 Central Bank of Malaysia, 'Financial Ombudsman Scheme Concept Paper (29 August 2014)', www.bnm.gov.my/guidelines/10_business_conduct/5_financial_ombudsman_scheme.pdf accessed 4 March 2018.
161 See further Siti Faridah Abdul Jabbar, 'Dispute Resolution in Islamic Finance: Malaysia's Financial Ombudsman Scheme' (2016) 37 *Company Lawyer* 130.

4 Islamic dispute resolution in the United Kingdom

Maria Bhatti

Introduction

Islamic dispute resolution is a crucial part of the Islamic legal system, which has very recently gained some publicity in the Western world[1] after pressure from minority groups to accommodate different legal structures under the secular and pluralistic Western legal system. Dispute resolution in Islam consists of both arbitration (*tahkim)* and mediation (*sulh*), and similar to the Western structures the former is normally binding in nature and the latter is non-binding and conciliatory. However, while the focus in Islam is on the collective and dispute resolution mechanisms which are 'intuitive and informal', the West prefers a 'cognitive and formal' method of dispute resolution.[2] Furthermore, the dispute resolution processes in Islam are part of a larger Islamic legal framework, known as Shari'ah, which is a highly complex and varied legal system. It is divided into different schools of jurisprudence, varying interpretations and adapts to changing circumstances and contexts depending on whether Shari'ah is literally construed or liberally interpreted. The interesting question following the theological and historical analysis of Shari'ah and its dispute resolution mechanisms is whether *sulh* and *tahkim* can co-exist with Western dispute resolution processes under one legal structure or whether the two systems are mutually exclusive. This chapter will analyse the role of Islamic dispute resolution in the West with a specific case study on the United Kingdom. In this chapter, I will discuss the framework in which Islamic dispute resolution has been construed in the West, as this analysis is important to ensure that Islamic finance disputes are effectively resolved through Shari'ah courts in the United Kingdom.

Theoretical similarities and differences between *Sulh* and contemporary mediation in the West

Islamic jurisprudence administers the way disputes are mediated in Islam. In a Shari'ah court, the judge is known as the *qadi* (literally, meaning to settle or resolve) who determines whether a dispute should be settled through *sulh* (negotiation, mediation), *tahkim* (arbitration) or administered in court.[3] *Sulh*, known as amicable settlement, conciliation or peacemaking was used in pre-Islamic Arabia where chieftains, soothsayers, healers and other influential noble men acted as arbiters and mediators in tribal disputes.[4] Since tribal society was governed by unwritten laws, there was no formal court system and law was typically enforced through arbitration or conciliation.[5] This process is similar to modern day mediation, where negotiators and mediators reconciled disputes and tried to negotiate a peace settlement.[6] Often the sons of tribes were taught family mediation skills from an early age. The father was often used as a *wasta* or mediator to resolve problems in the family. *Wasta* literally means 'the middle' and is similar to the Arabic verb *yatawassat*, which means 'to steer parties towards a middle point or compromise'.[7] In comparison, *tahkim* or arbitration was used to administer justice and the arbitrator was known as the *hakam* or *muhakkam*.[8] They took a more coercive role and decided the outcome based on the arguments presented and customary law.[9] The *hakam* had to be someone of exceptional personal qualities. In the pre-Islamic period, the priest of a pagan cult (*kahin*) or tribal chieftains were typically chosen to occupy the role.[10]

After the advent of Islam in the sixth century, Prophet Muhammad gained power and the authority shifted from people and customs to representatives of Islamic government.[11] Even during the Prophet's time, the difference between *sulh* and *tahkim* was evident because *sulh* was equivalent to modern-day mediation where parties compromised or negotiated upon a peaceful settlement with the help of a third party. On the other hand, *tahkim* was similar to modern day arbitration where the third party made a binding decision and the arbitrator was someone who was well-versed in Islamic law.[12] There are, however, differences of opinion on the enforcement of the decisions made by arbitrators, and depending on the Islamic schools of jurisprudence followed, arbitral decisions have different enforcement power.[13] The potential overlap between mediation and arbitration in Islamic law arises because of the following verse of the Quran: 'If you [believers] fear that a couple may break up, appoint one arbiter from his family and one from hers. Then if the couple want to put things right, God will bring about a reconciliation between them …'.[14] This verse arises in the context of family law and defines the procedure for mediating conflict between a husband and wife. It is interesting to note that the verse uses the word 'arbiter' or *hakam* in Arabic, which raises the query of whether the process defined is a binding arbitration or a non-binding mediation. The structure of dispute resolution has been interpreted differently by Islamic jurists, however, there is a strong argument that the process defined here is in fact mediation. This is because the verse notes that 'if they wish for peace, Allah will cause their reconciliation', which means that the final decision is given to the husband and the wife and the process used is mediation/conciliation.[15] Mediation is therefore, seen as the better avenue for dispute resolution to avoid the more serious consequences of divorce, which the Prophet notes is an abhorrent thing that is permissible but should always be the last resort.[16] The major difference between *tahkim* and *sulh* is twofold: first, *sulh* does not require the involvement of a third party in order to reach a conclusion whereas an impartial third party is a pre-condition for *tahkim*. Second, *sulh* is not binding and *tahkim* is binding according to most Islamic jurists. However, both forms of dispute resolution must be based on principles of 'fair play, justice, equity and good conscience' as firmly set out in the Quran.[17] One of the most famous acts of dispute resolution in Islamic history was when the Prophet Muhammad became the new leader of the city of Medina, a city in which the Jewish and Christian tribes had settled for a long time. Being aware of the religious, social and political divisions in the city, the Prophet decided to resolve the potential conflict and draft a charter known as the 'Medina Charter' to which non-Muslims, Medina natives, immigrants, Christians and Jews were signatories.[18] The Charter called for justice and equality among all signatories and that the rights of each person would be protected by the entire community. Even if there was a conflict between the monotheists and polytheists, it was important for everyone to stand together and not enter separate alliances.[19] More importantly, there was a dispute resolution clause in the contract stating that the Prophet would act as a mediator to ensure the agreement was enforced equitably.[20] His role was to 'assemble the conflicting groups, discuss the wants and needs of each, and devise a plan that was accepted by all parties involved, thereby ending the strife that had long existed among them'.[21]

An interesting question is whether *sulh* (negotiation, mediation) and Western dispute resolution processes can co-exist under one legal structure or whether they are mutually exclusive dispute resolution systems.[22] On the one hand, the differences between the two are apparent. The focus in Islam is on the collective and its dispute resolution mechanisms are 'intuitive and informal', whereas the West prefers a 'cognitive and formal' method of dispute resolution.[23] Under the Islamic system, the focus is not simply business relationships but the preservation of family and societal connections through *sulh* rather than adjudication.[24] More importantly, the third-party intervener under the two systems differ.[25] Under the Islamic system, pre-conditions to becoming a mediator include a high status, kinship connections, religious merits and knowledge of customs and the community.[26] However, the West highly regards impartiality, proper training, education and experience.[27]

From another perspective, the underlying concept of mediation in both cultural contexts is justice, reconciliation, providing a common ground for negotiation and recognizing that interdependent goals give way to shared ideas, compromise and productivity.[28] An example of such shared ideas is the Medina Charter, which was 'based on the recognition of diverse affiliations … principles of justice, equality, and equal dignity for all the signatories were mentioned in it'.[29] This indicates that despite the culturally specific mediation processes, there are many shared assumptions governing dispute resolution. According to Said and Funk, 'peace and conflict resolution are both universal and particular; similar as well as divergent approaches derive form and vitality from the cultural resources of a people'.[30] They further note that it is only natural that 'different religious traditions view conflict resolution through their own unique lenses, and prioritize some values and ideals over others'.[31]

The interaction of Western and Islamic dispute resolution mechanisms is most apparent in the contemporary example of Western democratic, pluralistic and multicultural governments consisting of a legal system accessed by people from different cultures, religions and backgrounds. For example, Jewish laws have been successfully incorporated into most Western legal structures, including the UK, America, Canada and Australia. According to the Jewish law of Halakha, all disputes should be resolved through the Beth Din (House of Judgment) and the Beth Din now operates as the primary forum for dispute resolution in nearly all Western countries. However, its decisions are consistent with the Western legal structures within which it operates, for example the Beth Din of America affirms that it conducts its cases in a manner consistent with the requirements of secular arbitration law.[32] One of the reasons why the Beth Din structure is more established and has historically received less controversy is because there has been a long Jewish presence in most Western countries. On the other hand, Muslims are new immigrants in the West and recent global events, especially those related to women and terrorism have created Muslims as the 'dangerous other' in the conscience of many people in the West. This chapter does not discuss the differences between Jewish and Islamic dispute resolution processes. Instead, the focus of the case-study presented is on the United Kingdom and how *sulh* operates within the context of the British legal system, especially in light of the establishment of the Muslim Arbitration Tribunal in 2007, which is still in operation today.

Islamic dispute resolution in the United Kingdom

In a report, Living Apart Together: British Muslims and the Paradox of Multiculturalism was published in Britain in May 2007 by the research group Policy Exchange. This report notes the following:

> 59% of Muslims would prefer to live under British law, compared to 28% who would prefer to live under sharia law. 37% of 16–24 year olds prefer sharia compared to 17% of 55+ year olds and it noted that 37% of British Muslims preferred to be governed by some form of *sharia* law.[33]

Some academics have strongly criticized the methodological framework of this report and its accuracy in reflecting the actual view of Muslims in Britain.[34] However, it does reflect the move of Britain towards understanding and accommodating cultural and religious diversity. Many view this as a response to addressing the issue of segregated communities and home grown terrorism through an accommodative legal and political framework.[35] For example, Shah argues that law must be re-evaluated in a pluralistic and culturally diverse society in order to make it relevant to minority ethnic communities in the UK.[36] Similarly, it is noted by Griffiths that the relationship between law and cultures 'raises important questions about power – where it is located, how it is constituted, what forms it takes – in ways that promote a finely tuned and sophisticated analysis of continuity, transformation and change in society'.[37]

While the British legal system caters for ethnic customs and cultures and also contains anti-discrimination legislation, the *Race Relations Act 1976*, it is only recently that the question of establishing Shari'ah courts has emerged. Some attribute the emergence of Shari'ah to the closer ties formed within the Muslim community and the emergence of Shari'ah Councils through the social-political role that mosques play.[38] Others attribute this to legal pluralism in Britain, which is defined as 'a situation where two or more legal systems co-exist in the same social field'.[39] The framework in which Shari'ah courts are based are defined as 'semi-autonomous fields', which is a field that:

> can generate rules and customs and symbols internally, but that … is also vulnerable to rules and decisions and other forces emanating from the larger world by which it is surrounded. The semi-autonomous field has rule-making capacities, and the means to induce or coerce compliance; but it is simultaneously set in a larger social matrix which can, and does, affect and invade it, sometimes at the invitation of persons inside it, sometimes at its own instance.[40]

This is the framework in which Islamic Alternative Dispute Resolution ('ADR') is introduced in Britain, not as the introduction of pure Shari'ah law but one which is consistent with the law of Britain. This construct is defined by many as a combination of Islamic law and English law to form 'Angrezi [English] Shari'ah'.[41] The reconstruction of the Muslim legal system occurs within the overarching British legal system in order to accommodate the needs of the Muslim communities. Shari'ah courts conduct mediations and arbitrations within the British legal system and also act to preserve Islamic legal principles within a secular legal system.[42]

Nature of ADR in Britain/Enforcement

Shari'ah councils in the UK are structured as unofficial dispute resolution mechanisms existing in Muslim communities that adopt the processes of *sulh* to resolve disputes in accordance with Shari'ah law. They fit the model of a 'semi-autonomous social field' because they can coexist within the British legal structure without placing any strain on it. They are autonomous bodies yet they recognize the power of British law.[43] The informal structure of Shari'ah Councils has been established in Britain for more than 30 years; they mostly deal with Islamic family and personal law and in some instances, they try to resolve disputes between parties through *sulh* in order to encourage reconciliation. They do not act under the *British Arbitration Act 1996* and their decisions are not binding. Instead reliance is placed on the goodwill of parties who can choose to implement and follow the decisions.[44] Furthermore, it is a private process which is usually presided over by a single Islamic scholar, who is typically not legally qualified. The informal structure of Shari'ah councils was the reason why the Muslim Arbitration Tribunal (MAT) was established in 2007. Its goal is to provide Muslims access to a more formal dispute resolution process operating within the legal framework of England and Wales, and allow for the enforcement of decisions. However, the process is similar to both *sulh* and *tahkim* because although the final decision is binding, it is possible for the parties to appeal the decision in the civil courts if they are dissatisfied. Furthermore, it makes sure that its decisions are consistent with both English law and Shari'ah law. This is noted in Clause 8(2) of the Procedural Rules where the use of the word 'and' is indicative of the fact that Shari'ah law which is inconsistent with the laws of England cannot be applied.[45]

Furthermore, the MAT has jurisdiction over most areas of civil and personal religious law, including Islamic finance disputes[46] except for divorce proceedings (it can only offer a religious divorce), child custody and criminal matters. In all other matters, disputants are referred to the civil court. The decision makers are selected in accordance with Clause 10(2) of the Procedural Rules, which notes that the Tribunal should consist of a minimum of two members including a solicitor or barrister of England and Wales and a scholar of Shari'ah law.[47] The decisions reached by the MAT can be enforced through the normal civil courts since the body operates under the *Arbitration Act 1996*. According to Clause 23 of the Procedural Rules, 'No appeal shall be made against any decisions of the Tribunal. This rule shall not prevent any party applying for Judicial Review with permission of the High Court'.[48] The MAT notes that its status in English law is simply 'evidence before the civil court'.[49]

Public reaction

The traditional process of *sulh* takes place through Shari'ah Councils and now binding arbitration or *tahkim* is also possible in Britain through the establishment of the Muslim Arbitration Tribunal. These two methods of ADR are in reality a merger of Western and Islamic concepts of dispute resolution because they operate as an alternative to the Western ADR process with the only difference being that they apply Shari'ah laws. Another qualification that exists is that Shari'ah must operate within the operation of English law in both *sulh* and *tahkim* processes. This qualification was the reason most of the public was pacified by the idea of Shari'ah law operating in England. However, not everyone was satisfied with the procedural rules set out on the MAT website clarifying that the tribunal operates in accordance with English law. For example, an article published in the Daily Mail UK notes that the introduction of the MAT

> sparked uproar … with warnings that the fundamental principles of equal treatment for all – the bedrock of British justice – was being gravely undermined. Critics fear Britain's Islamic hard-liners will now try to make sharia law the dominant legal system in Muslim neighborhoods, and warn that women often receive less favorable treatment at the hands of traditional Islamic courts.[50]

The article in the Daily Mail news is published online and fails to identify the exact nature of the unfavourable treatment women may be subject to; instead it is accompanied with a picture of a woman in a burka whose face is completely covered.

Controversy was also sparked in the UK after the Archbishop of Canterbury, Dr Rowan Williams gave a lecture at the Temple Foundation Royal Courts of Justice on 'Islam and the English Law' in February 2008. He noted in this lecture that a Shari'ah Court should be available for Muslims in a similar way the British Orthodox Jewish Courts, the Beth Din, operates in light of the Talmud. He said that Shari'ah could be used as a basis for mediation or other forms of ADR. This was in light of the fact that the British common law system had been organically developed to consider jurisprudence from all over the world. He noted that extreme punishments and oppressive treatment of women as adopted in certain Islamic states would not be adopted and that issues such as abortions would be treated as secular matters. He also made it clear that the existence of Shari'ah would not threaten the edifice of the British legal system nor did it mean the existence of a parallel legal system.[51] Despite this clear statement, the reaction from the Conservative's shadow community cohesion minister, Sayeeda Warsi was that 'Williams seems to be suggesting that there should be two systems of law, running alongside each other, almost parallel, and for people to be offered the choice of opting into one or the other … that is unacceptable'.[52]

However, the Archbishop makes it clear in his speech that this is not the case and that 'nobody in their right mind would want to see in this country the kind of inhumanity that's sometimes been associated with the practice of the law in some Islamic states; the extreme punishments, the attitudes to women as well'.[53] A British Muslim woman and legal scholar, Samia Bano, has been critical of the context in which this debate is taking place. Her major concern relates to the way in which the debate is being framed in the context of the 'dangerous' Muslim other and a 'disloyal Archbishop who was not only out of step with the concerns expressed by the majority British society (Christians) but was seeking to undermine Western liberal legality with 'demands for the recognition of plural systems of law'.[54] It has been noted by the scholar Reza Banaka that the Archbishop has been criticized by the Government, his own Church, representatives of other religious and even the Muslim Council of Victoria and Liberal Judaism.[55]

Many British sceptics have been critical of the agenda behind the Archbishop's statements and whether it was merely an attack on secular governments to enhance a greater role of Christianity in public life in the same way he was advocating for Islamic law.[56] In order to clarify the Archbishop's comments, Lord Phillips – the most senior judge in England and Wales jumped to his defence and noted that Shari'ah suffered from 'widespread misunderstanding' and that:

> there is no reason why sharia principles, or any other religious code, should not be the basis for mediation or other forms of alternative dispute resolution

> … it must be recognized, however, that any sanctions for a failure to comply with the agreed terms of mediation would be drawn from the laws of England and Wales.[57]

He also made the comment that physical punishments such as flogging, stoning and the cutting off of hands would be unacceptable. In his opinion, therefore, the Archbishop had been misunderstood and Shari'ah would only play a role in certain marital and commercial disputes and this had already been occurring in the country for the past 30 years through Shari'ah Councils.[58]

As a result of these discussions, on 7 June 2011, Baroness Cox of the House of Lords introduced the *Arbitration and Mediation Services* (*Equality Bill*)[59] to amend the *Equality Act 2010* and the *Arbitration Act 1996*. One of the main aims of the Equality Bill is to address the issue of discrimination in private arbitration proceedings.[60] The *Equality Bill* seeks to amend the *Equality Act 2010* by inserting in s 29 (after sub-s 10): 'A person must not, in providing a service in relation to arbitration, do anything that constitutes discrimination, harassment or victimization on grounds of sex'.[61] Furthermore, the *Equality Bill* will amend the *Arbitration Act 1996* to include a provision under s 6A, entitled 'Discriminatory Terms of Arbitration', which will prohibit arbitration agreements and processes from stipulating 'any other term that constitutes discrimination on the grounds of sex'.[62]

Although the *Equality Bill* was introduced as a result of efforts to combat gender discrimination in the area of family law arbitration, it may also impact arbitration of Islamic finance matters where parties stipulate that the arbitrator must be Muslim and male. Criteria based on gender will not only be in direct breach of the *Equality Bill* if and when it is passed, but thereafter, the amendments proposed in the *Equality Bill* could also be used to argue that the public policy of the United Kingdom views gender restrictions as discriminatory.[63]

Regardless, the *Equality Bill* has been the subject of criticism. The Islamic Shari'ah Council's secretary, Dr Hasan, argues that Cox does not understand the complexities surrounding the Shari'ah arbitration process, and is simply basing her opinions on common misconceptions surrounding Shari'ah.[64] For example, the MAT consults an expert panel consisting of women to ensure that there is no discrimination based on gender throughout the arbitration process.[65] In his second reading speech, Lord Bishop of Manchester notes that

> as currently drafted, the Bill appears to present anomalies which could create problems for those who are well aware of their rights, are independently advised and want to approach their faith tribunals for adjudication in a matter which they believe to be covered by the rules of their faith.[66]

Bano is critical and puts forward extensive arguments about whether Shari'ah courts will mean the introduction of burqa laden women and outdated punishments and serve to simply reaffirm stereotypes and construct a dangerous Muslim other in the minds of the community – even if one was arguing against the concept itself.[67] She observes that the Archbishop quotes distinguished Islamic scholars such as Professor Tariq Ramadan and Mona Siddiqui to assume that 'accommodation of sharia could support the Muslim reformists in introducing a new interpretation and new practices of sharia that are in line with the democratic underpinnings of English law'.[68] This assumption ignores the wider social and political context and falls into the 'traps of cultural essentialism and homogeneity that reproduce the binaries that it seeks to dismantle and displace'.[69] The discourse in which the debate about Shari'ah law is taking place is based upon the assumption that as a Muslim, you either belong to the community and demand that English law accommodate Shari'ah or that you are disconnected from your community and are simply happy with living under secular law.[70]

In Bano's opinion, it is important to recognize the complex ways in which Muslims engage with Shari'ah in the UK and she calls for a more inclusive approach by having a dialogue with Muslims who are the primary users of these bodies.[71] The complex way with which Muslims engage with Shari'ah is briefly highlighted above when explaining basic Islamic law. Islamic law is not one comprehensive body, its interpretation depends on different religious leaders and communities. Two main groups of Muslims exist, Sunnai and Shi'a Muslims. Moreover, there are different sectarian divisions such as Ismaili Muslims who are part of the Shi'a group but practice distinct laws. Additionally, there are four different schools of thought in Islam and Shari'ah councils do not represent a single view of Islamic thought but are made up of various bodies representing these different schools of thought in Islam.[72]

The issue of Shari'ah being subject to a variety of interpretations was also raised in the case of *Shamil Bank v Beximco*[73] ("*Shamil Bank*"), an Islamic finance agreement contained the following governing law clause: 'subject to the principles of the Glorious *Shari'ah*, this Agreement shall be governed by and construed in accordance with the laws of England'. It was argued by Beximco that Shamil Bank had charged them interest under the guise of an Islamic contract known as *murabahah* and therefore, the contract was unenforceable.[74] The English Appellate Court ("the appellate court") decided that Shari'ah did not replace English law in this case but reflected the nature of the business.

It was argued by Potter J that:

> [t]he general references to *Sharia* ... affords no reference to, or identification of, those aspects of *Sharia* law which are intended to be incorporated into the contract, let alone the terms in which they are framed … [t]hus the reference to the "principles of … *Sharia*" stand unqualified as a reference to the body of Shari'ah generally. As such, they are inevitably repugnant to the choice of English law as the law of the contract and render the clause self-contradictory and therefore meaningless.[75]

Colon argues that this reasoning was 'hasty' because the appellate court did not consider prior negotiations of the parties or the common practices of the Islamic financial industry. The result of the appellate court's reasoning "was that the words "[s]ubject to the principles of the Glorious Sharia'a are rendered superfluous, but Shamil bank is still left to represent itself to its British customers as an 'Islamic bank" '.[76] According to Colon, the reference to Shari'ah is to ensure that Islamic financial transactions remain Shari'ah compliant despite the litigation process. The reason why parties decide to deal with Islamic banks that include Shari'ah law clauses in their agreements is to ensure that they are participating in Shari'ah compliant deals.[77] Otherwise, they would choose to gain finance from mainstream financial institutions.[78]

Possible solutions

One possible solution to the above-mentioned problem of having non-standard Shari'ah rules governing the arbitration of Islamic finance disputes in the United Kingdom could be to adopt standardized arbitral rules which are both Shari'a compliant and recognized internationally. To date, the most developed arbitration rules have been introduced by the Asian International Arbitration Centre (AIAC) called, the *i-Arbitration Rules* (the prefix 'I' indicates compliance with Shari'ah), which were first presented in 2012 at the Global Financial Forum.[79] The *i-Arbitration Rules* are based on the *United Nations Commission on International Trade Law (UNCITRAL) Rules 2010*. They are recognized internationally and aspire to cater for Shari'ah-based disputes in international commercial arbitration. Since they are private rules, they have global appeal and can be used worldwide as they provide a procedure through which arbitral tribunals can refer matters to Shari'ah advisory councils.[80] The *i-Arbitration Rules 2018* recently came into effect on 8 March 2018 and have been recently revised and have been reformed to include new sections on the joinder of parties and consolidation of arbitral proceedings.[81] As arbitration is a private dispute resolution process, adopting the *i-Arbitration Rules* which cater for Islamic finance matters will address the issue of multiple interpretations of Shari'ah as the parties can elect to direct any disputes matters to a Shari'ah council of their choice in the United Kingdom. Furthermore, they are based on the *UNCTIRAL Rules 2010* which are internationally renowned, and therefore should be accepted in the United Kingdom without causing further controversy.

Conclusion

Traditionally, Islamic dispute resolution has been extensively used under Shari'ah law and Islamic jurists have identified these processes as *sulh* (mediation) and *tahkim* (arbitration). Numerous examples of the Prophet Muhammad, verses from the Quran and examples from the *hadith* are indicative of this fact. The complex and fragmented nature of the Shari'ah means that there is no one concise form of Shari'ah law that identifies the exact process of *sulh* and *tahkim*. It is for this reason that interpretations have evolved and changed over time depending on the place, situation and context. A contemporary example can be observed in the introduction of Islamic dispute resolution processes through the advent of Shari'ah Councils and Shari'ah courts in the UK. While Shari'ah Councils have been around for more than 30 years, the Muslim Arbitration Tribunal (MAT) was established more recently – however, this has triggered public controversy. For example, many women's rights groups including non-Muslim and Muslim alike have criticized Shari'ah councils and the MAT for establishing intra-group inequalities and adhering to interpretations of Shari'ah which may conflict with Western values.

However, Shari'ah has historically shown great emphasis on mediation and reconciliation through the example of the Prophet Muhammad and the second caliph, Umar ibn Al-Khattab. Furthermore, Umar ibn Al-Khattab also provides an example of how accommodative and flexible Shari'ah law can be especially if it is interpreted according to its higher objectives which includes justice, fairness and the preservation of life, honour and dignity. In light of this, Umar ibn al-Khattab eradicated corporal punishment in the early seventh century in order to preserve the dignity and honour of his community in the context of extreme hunger and poverty. Similarly, extensive empirical research needs to be conducted into the experiences of Muslims with the Islamic dispute resolution process and loopholes that contradict the laws and values of the United Kingdom need to be addressed in order for the two systems to exist harmoniously. This will enable effective resolution of Islamic finance disputes through Shari'ah courts. One practical solution to resolve Islamic finance disputes in the United Kingdom is to adopt the *i-Arbitration Rules* as standardized rules which provide an internationally recognized arbitral procedure as well as complying with Shari'ah by giving parties the autonomy to select a Shari'ah Advisory Council of their choice.

Notes

1 The term 'Western world' is used by Brower and Sharpe generally to refer to European nations, the United States of America, Australia and New Zealand. It is important to note that such terminology is subject to debate. See Samuel P Huntington, *The Clash of Civilizations and the Remaking of World Order* (Simon & Schuster 1996). *Contra* Edward Said, 'The Clash of Ignorance' (2001) 273(12) *The Nation* 11.
2 Aseel al-Ramahi, '*Sulh*: A Crucial Part of Islamic Arbitration' (2008) *Islamic Law and Law of the Muslim World: Research Paper Series* 1, 18.
3 Syed Khalid Rashid, 'Peculiarities & Religious Underlining of ADR in Islamic Law' (2008) *Mediation in the Asia Pacific: Constraints and Challenges* 1.
4 Aida Othman, 'And Amicable Settlement is Best: *Sulh* and Dispute Resolution in Islamic Law' (2007) *Arab Law Quarterly* 64, 65.
5 Aseel al-Ramahi, '*Sulh*: A Crucial Part of Islamic Arbitration' (2008) *Islamic Law and Law of the Muslim World: Research Paper Series* 1, 3.
6 Faisal Kutty, 'Shari'a in International Commercial Arbitration' (2006) *The Loyola of Los Angeles International and Comparative Law Review* 565, 589.
7 Aseel al-Ramahi, '*Sulh*: A Crucial Part of Islamic Arbitration' (2008) *Islamic Law and Law of the Muslim World: Research Paper Series* 1, 3.
8 'Procedure' *The Oxford International Encyclopedia of Legal History*. Oxford University Press, 2009 www.oxfordreference.com/ accessed 1 November 2017.
9 Aida Othman, 'And Amicable Settlement is Best: *Sulh* and Dispute Resolution in Islamic Law' (2007) *Arab Law Quarterly* 64, 66.

10 Aseel al-Ramahi, '*Sulh*: A Crucial Part of Islamic Arbitration' (2008) *Islamic Law and Law of the Muslim World: Research Paper Series* 1, 5.
11 Ibid. 7.
12 Aida Othman, 'And Amicable Settlement is Best: *Sulh* and Dispute Resolution in Islamic Law' (2007) *Arab Law Quarterly* 64, 68.
13 Faisal Kutty, 'Shari'a Factor in International Commercial Arbitration' (2006) *The Loyola of Los Angeles International and Comparative Law Review* 565, 590.
14 Translated by MAS Abdel Haleem, *The Qur'an* (OUP 2004) (Chapter 4, Verse 35).
15 Ratno Lukito, 'Religious ADR: Mediation in Islamic Family Law Tradition' (2006) *Al-Jami'ah* 326, 336.
16 Ibid. 332.
17 Syed Khalid Rashid, 'Peculiarities and Religious Underlining of ADR in Islamic Law' (2008) *Mediation in the Asia Pacific: Constraints and Challenges* 1, 2.
18 Tariq Ramadan, *The Messenger: The Meanings of the Life of Muhammad* (Allen Lane 2007) 88–89.
19 Ibid.
20 Ibid.
21 Yerkin Yildirim, 'The Medina Charter: A Historical Case of Conflict Resolution' (2009) *Islamic and Christian-Muslim Relations* 439, 441.
22 Yerkin Yildirim, 'The Medina Charter: A Historical Case of Conflict Resolution' (2009) *Islamic and Christian-Muslim Relations* 439, 444.
23 Aseel al-Ramahi, '*Sulh*: A Crucial Part of Islamic Arbitration' (2008) *Islamic Law and Law of the Muslim World: Research Paper Series* 1, 18.
24 Ibid.
25 Ibid. 19.
26 Ibid.
27 Ibid.
28 Yerkin Yildirim, 'The Medina Charter: A Historical Case of Conflict Resolution' (2009) *Islamic and Christian-Muslim Relations* 439, 444.
29 Tariq Ramadan, *The Messenger: The Meanings of the Life of Muhammad (*Allen Lane 2007) 88–89.
30 Abdul Aziz Said and Nathan C. Funk, *Peace and Conflict Resolution in Islam: Precept and Practice* (University Press of America 2001), 58.
31 Ibid. 59.
32 Kellie Johnston, Gus Camelino and Roger Rizzo, 'A Return to Traditional Dispute Resolution' *Canadian Forum on Civil Justice* (2000).
33 Munira Mirza, Living Apart Together: British Muslims and the Paradox of Multiculturalism (2007) 5 www.policyexchange.org.uk/wp-content/uploads/2016/09/living-apart-together-jan-07.pdf accessed 1 November 2017.
34 Samia Bano, 'Islamic Family Arbitration, Justice and Human Rights in Britain' *Law, Social Justice & Global Development* (2007) 1, 3.
35 Ibid.
36 Prakash Shah, *Legal Pluralism in Conflict: Coping with Cultural Diversity in Law* (Psychology Press 2005) 2.
37 A Griffiths, 'Ideological Combat and Social Observations: Recent Debate About Legal Pluralism' *Journal of Legal Pluralism and Unofficial Law* (1998) 28.
38 Samia Bano, 'Islamic Family Arbitration, Justice and Human Rights in Britain' *Law, Social Justice & Global Development* (2007) 1, 11.
39 Ibid. 7.
40 Ibid. 8.
41 Ibid. 9.
42 Ibid. 10.
43 Ibid. 12.
44 Muslim Arbitral Tribunal, (2015) www.matribunal.com accessed 1 November 2017.

45 Ibid.
46 Muslim Arbitral Tribunal, (2015) www.matribunal.com/commercial-and-debt-disputes.php, accessed 1 January 2018.
47 Ibid.
48 Ibid.
49 Telegraph, 'What can sharia courts do in Britain' www.telegraph.co.uk/news/newstopics/lawreports/joshuarozenberg/2957692/What-can-sharia-courts-do-in-Britain.html accessed 1 November 2017.
50 Daily Mail, 'Islamic sharia courts in Britain are now legally Binding' www.dailymail.co.uk/news/article-1055764/Islamic-sharia-courts-Britain-legally-binding.html accessed 1 November 2017.
51 Prospect Magazine, 'Sense on Sharia' www.prospectmagazine.co.uk/2008/02/senseonsharia/ accessed 15 November 2017.
52 Ibid.
53 BBC, 'Sharia law in UK is unavoidable' http://news.bbc.co.uk/2/hi/uk_news/7232661.stm accessed 14 November 2017.
54 Samia Bano, 'In Pursuit of Religious and Legal Diversity' *Ecclesiastical Law Journal* (2008) 283, 284.
55 Ibid.
56 Ibid.
57 BBC, 'Sharia law could have UK Role' http://news.bbc.co.uk/2/hi/uk_news/7488790.stm accessed 14 November 2017.
58 BBC, 'Sharia law could have UK Role' http://news.bbc.co.uk/2/hi/uk_news/7488790.stm accessed 14 November 2017.
59 'Bill stages — *Arbitration and Mediation Services (Equality) Bill*' [HL] 2014–15. http://services.parliament.uk/bills/2014-15/arbitrationandmediationservicesequality/stages.html accessed 20 November 2017.
60 The *Equality Bill* also seeks to amend the *Family Law Act* 1996, *Criminal Justice and Public Order Act* 1994 and the *Courts and Legal Services Act* 1990 – this chapter does not deal with these amendments.
61 *Arbitration and Mediation Services (Equality) Bill* (11 June 2014) www.publications.parliament.uk/pa/bills/lbill/2014-2015/0021/15021.pdf accessed 17 December 2017.
62 Ibid.
63 Craig Tevendale, '*Jivraj* – It's Back and This Time it's at the European Commission' (28 September 2012) *Kluwer Arbitration Blog* http://kluwerarbitrationblog.com/2012/09/28/jivraj-its-back-and-this-time-its-at-the-european-commission/ accessed 20 December 2017. See *Jivraj v Hashwani* [2009] EWHC 1364; *Jivraj v Hashwani* (2010) EWCA (Civ) 712.
64 Rebecca E Maret, 'Mind the Gap: The Equality Bill and Sharia Arbitration in the United Kingdom' (2013) 36(1) *Boston College International and Comparative Law Review* 255, 276.
65 *Muslim Arbitral Tribunal, History* (2015) www.matribunal.com accessed 1 November 2017.
66 United Kingdom, *Parliamentary Debates*, House of Lords, 19 October 2012, Column 1683, (*Baroness Cox*) www.publications.parliament.uk/pa/ld201213/ldhansrd/text/121019-0001.htm#12101923000438 accessed 15 November 2017.
67 Samia Bano, 'In Pursuit of Religious and Legal Diversity' *Ecclesiastical Law Journal* (2008) 283, 287.
68 Ibid.
69 Ibid.
70 Ibid. 288.
71 Ibid.
72 Ibid. 291.
73 Shamil Bank, [2004] EWCA (Civ)19, [54],1 W.L.R. at 1800.

74 Shamil Bank, [2004] EWCA (Civ)19, [54],1 W.L.R.
75 [2004] EWCA Civ19, [52].
76 Julio Colón, 'Choice of Law and Islamic Finance' (2011) 46 Texas Intl LJ 411, 427.
77 Ibid.
78 Ibid.
79 Kuala Lumpur Regional Centre for Arbitration, 'KLRCA Arbitration Rules (Revised 2013)' (2013) http://klrca.org/rules/arbitration/.
80 Global Arbitration Review, 'KLRCA to unveil Islamic Arbitration Rules', *Global Arbitration Review* (online), 17 September 2009 http://globalarbitrationreview.com/article/1031606/klrca-to-unveil-islamic-arbitration-rules.
81 Practical Law, 'KLRCA Publishes New Rules', *Practical Law: A Thomson Reuters Legal Solution* (online), 30 October 2013, http://us.practicallaw.com/2-547-2965?q=&qp=&qo=&qe=. This chapter does not delve into a discussion on these new updates. For more information, see Jones Day, 'Kuala Lumpur Regional Center for Arbitration Rebrands as Asian International Arbitration Centre', Jones Day, February 2018 www.jonesday.com/Kuala-Lumpur-Regional-Centre-for-Arbitration-Rebrands-as-Asian-International-Arbitration-Centre-02-14-2018/?RSS=true.

5 Settlement of Islamic finance disputes in the United States of America

Julio C Colón

Introduction

Islamic finance in the United States (the US) is a nascent industry. Currently there are few Islamic finance institutions in the country, which include both capital financing and investment vehicles such as mutual funds.

The US is highly regulated. Some of the regulations which the banking industry is subject to in its retail sector are the National Bank Act, The Federal Deposit Insurance Act, and the Truth in Lending Act, among others. Those are in addition to regulations promulgated by the Office of Comptroller of the Currency (OCC), the Federal Deposit Insurance Corporation (FDIC), the Securities Exchange Commission (SEC), and other agencies which affect the banking and finance industry. Furthermore, each of the over 50 state and territorial jurisdictions have distinct laws which can affect the finance industry in ways different to that of the federal system.

This chapter discusses dispute resolution in Islamic finance in the US by analysing case law, as well as some statutes that may be relevant in future cases. There is some overlap between this chapter and Chapter 2: Choice of Law, particularly in the sections entitled 'Shari'ah in Common Law Courts' and 'Islamic Law Influenced Jurisdictions'. As such, this chapter will not address questions regarding the choice of law and will focus on (1) the legal framework for Islamic finance in the US; (2) the juristic approaches employed by courts to manage disputes (irrespective of choice of law); and (3) arbitration in Islamic finance in the US.

The US legal framework for Islamic finance

Islamic finance in the US is composed of both retail and wholesale finance.[1] Early on, in an attempt to be Shari'ah-compliant at least one US bank experimented with profit-sharing deposit accounts.[2] Islamic finance in the US, however, started in earnest by providing an alternative to traditional mortgages, which in retrospect is not surprising given the coincidence that home ownership is generally encouraged by the government at all levels.[3]

In retail investment, several companies have emerged which cater to investors seeking Shari'ah-compliant options in the form of mutual funds and other advisor-directed investments.[4] Wholesale finance remains on a more limited basis within the country. Large US banks such as AIG, however, maintain Islamic banking windows in their foreign offices as well as subsidiaries, and they underwrite *sukuk* for investors interested in the US bond market.[5] On the private investor side, various partnerships have been created for the purposes of engaging in Shari'ah-compliant investments or marketing Islamic finance ventures.[6]

To accomplish this, the participants rely on the same myriad of statutes, regulations, and administrative rulings that apply generally to US finance. Thus it is necessary to provide a general description of the legal framework as it relates to three areas: (1) consumer banking and investment laws (2) state and Federal regulatory agencies; and (3) state and Federal courts.

Banking and investment laws

In the US, in all respects the same laws that govern conventional banking still apply to Islamic finance.[7] The National Bank Act proscribes purchase or holding of legal title by national banking associations for a period exceeding five years.[8] The purpose of this provision was to prevent banks from speculating in real estate,[9] which for Islamic finance presents a problem, at least on the surface. Contracts based on *musharikah*, *ijarah*, and *murabahah* require the financial institution to take legal title of the property to be acquired; as it happens those three financial arrangements are utilized for home acquisition.

The Federal Deposit Insurance Act defines 'deposit' – in part– as 'the unpaid balance of money or its equivalent received or held by a bank or savings association in the usual course of business and for which it has given or is obligated to give credit [...]'.[10] The purpose of this act is to protect the deposits of banking consumers. Because the Federal Deposit Insurance Act defines 'deposit' in such a way as to limit the ability of the financial institution to put consumers' deposits at risk, it would seem to also inhibit financial institutions' ability to create Shari'ah-compliant, profit-sharing deposit accounts along the line of conventional consumer deposits and savings accounts.[11]

A complex regime of securities laws governs various aspects of the financial sector activity implicating Islamic finance, such as the Securities Act of 1933 ('The Securities Act'), the Trust Indenture Act of 1939 ('The Trust Indenture Act'), and a range of regulations promulgated by enforcement agencies. The Securities Act governs the registration and disclosure of information concerning securities sold in the US.[12] The Trust Indenture Act governs the sale of bonds and similar products.[13] While the full extent of the application of these laws cannot yet be examined, based on current practices it is clear that lawyers working within the field will structure deals in such a way that they comply with these laws. For example, one popular model upon which to structure a real estate purchase is a *musharikah mutanaqisah*, or diminishing partnership. In order to achieve this in the US companies may structure the *musharikah* through some form of limited liability entity organized under state law. One could imagine structuring a *sukuk* as a publicly traded Master Limited Partnership, which would necessitate filing a registration statement and completion of all other disclosure requirements required by securities laws.[14]

Federal and state agencies

Statutes often empower federal and state agencies with regulatory and enforcement authority. This means that the interpretation of statutes by agencies – governmental offices composed of non-elected individuals – may carry as much weight as a statute that was passed through the rigors of the legislative process. The following agencies are endowed with such authority.

Office of the Comptroller of the Currency

The Office of the Comptroller of the Currency (OCC) is an office within the Department of the Treasury which is charged with the responsibility to regulate banks. It charters banks, ensures compliance with consumer banking laws, and monitors their investments and holdings.[15] As one of the measures of the National Bank Act, national banks were chartered under the administration of the OCC, which as a result created a system of financial institutions utilizing the newly adopting federal fiat currency.[16]

With respect to Islamic finance, the OCC's responsibility to regulate banks' investments directly affects the ability of nationally chartered banks to offer financial products, particularly those related to real estate acquisition. While there are a variety of loan products that are known to comply with the banking laws, the OCC has responded favourably to at least two requests for opinions regarding Shari'ah-compliant offerings.

First, the OCC issued a widely circulated interpretive letter in response to a request for an opinion from the United Bank of Kuwait (UBK) as to whether the National Bank Act permitted it to offer a 'Net Lease' product as part of its mortgage lending business.[17] A 'Net Lease' product is essentially a rent-to-own agreement. UBK proposed an *ijarah-wa-iqtina'* arrangement whereby: (1) the lessee makes a downpayment on a home; (2) lessee and UBK execute a 'Net Lease Agreement and a Purchase Agreement'; (3) lessee accepts the property; (4) UBK supplies the remainder of the funds to complete the purchase from seller; (5) UBK retains legal title to the property and records its property interest as it would for a mortgage.[18] Various tangential aspects of UBK's business, however, distinguished this transaction from a rent-to-own agreement between the seller and prospective buyer, such as the facts that the prospective lessee/buyer was responsible for identifying a property to purchase and the lessee would be responsible for maintaining the property.[19] According to UBK's explanation, 'Monthly lease payments will be sufficient to cover principal and interest, and pay insurance and property taxes [..., and] Lessee will amortize the entire principal by the end of the lease term'.[20] The agreement envisioned that in the case of default, 'UBK will have remedies against the Lessee for nonpayment similar to those available to a lender on a "traditional" nonrecourse mortgage'.[21] UBK's obstacle in immediately implementing this plan was the prohibition found in the National Bank Act of nationally chartered banks holding legal title by national banking associations for a period exceeding five years as discussed earlier. Typically when financing a home, legal title is recorded in the name of the purchaser while the bank records a lien on the property. In addressing this discrepancy, *OCC Interpretive Letter No 806* noted, 'UBK's residential real estate financing proposal is functionally equivalent to [...] mortgage lending [... and] banks [already] structure leases so that they are functionally equivalent to lending secured by personal property'.[22] Making analogies to several court decisions preceding the request for interpretation, the OCC then concluded that UBK's proposed Net Lease would not violate 12 USC §29 as its 'legal title is largely cosmetic' because it does not 'actually hold real estate', in the sense that despite having title, UBK will not 'operate the property, pay taxes, insurance, and other charges, maintain upkeep of the premises, make repairs when necessary, assume liability for injuries or other accidents on the property, or otherwise exercise dominion and control over the property'.[23,24] The OCC concluded its opinion by finding that UBK's proposed Net Lease was permissible.[25]

In a second important opinion, an unnamed financial institution (FI) with a federal branch located in the US requested an opinion from the OCC as to whether *murabahah* financing could be offered as part of a banking business under 12 USC §24 (the same statute in question in the preceding paragraph).[26] Under its *murabahah* model, the FI intended to 'acquire the property on behalf of the customer and then resell the property to the customer at a mark up on an installment basis'.[27] Though under this arrangement title would immediately pass to the purchaser upon execution of the closing transaction,[28] the question remained whether the acquisition of real estate title fit within one of the four named exceptions in 12 USC §29, namely: (1) 'Such as shall be necessary for its accommodation in the transaction of its business'; (2) 'Such as shall be mortgaged to it in good faith by way of debts previously contracted'; (3) 'Such as shall be conveyed to it in satisfaction of debts previously contracted in the course of its dealings'; and (4) 'Such as it shall purchase at sales under judgments, decrees, or mortgages [...] or shall purchase to secure debts due to it'. Again highlighting that its opinion will emphasize function over form, the interpretive letter concluded, '[T]he economic substance of the Murabaha financing transactions is functionally equivalent to [...] a real estate mortgage transaction [...]'.[29] In giving its opinion, the OCC placed significant weight on the aspects of the *murabahah* program which showed that its interest in the property was merely in furtherance of providing financing for the consumer. For example:

> [T]he Murabaha financing transaction does not conflict with any of the purposes underlying the restrictions of section 29 [...]. The Branch will not actually hold real estate. It will not operate the property, pay taxes, insurance, or other charges, maintain upkeep of the premises, make repairs when necessary, assume liability for injuries or other accidents on the property, or

> otherwise exercise dominion or control over the property. Although the Branch will have legal title for a moment in time, it will not take actual possession of the property at any point during the term of the financing.[30]

The letter also made comparisons between *murabahah* and 'riskless principal securities transactions', which had already been approved as part of the business practices of a national bank in *OCC Interpretive Letter No 371*.[31] According to the letter, in riskless principal securities transactions, the bank functions as a securities broker; similarly in the *murabahah* arrangement in question, FI would not purchase the asset except at the customer's direction, at which point the customer would immediately repurchase the property per the terms of the agreement.[32] Ultimately, the OCC found no objection to FI's proposed *murabahah* transactions.[33]

Federal Deposit Insurance Corporation

The FDIC is the agency responsible for insuring bank deposits and maintaining other consumer protections related to the banking industry, such as monitoring the soundness of the financial institution as measured by its level of capitalization.[34] As suggested by its name, the primary purpose of the FDIC is to administer deposit insurance. In doing so, the FDIC has interacted with Islamic finance industry on at least one occasion.

One perceived obstacle to consumer deposit accounts within Shari'ah-compliant profit-sharing accounts is the way that the Federal Deposit Insurance Act defines 'deposit', which is 'The unpaid balance of money or its equivalent received or held by a bank or savings association in the usual course of business and for which it has given or is obligated to give credit [...]'.[35] Because the bank is required to give full credit to amount of money previously received, a member cannot maintain federal deposit insurance benefits on a 'deposit' which is structured as a profit-and-loss sharing account, as may be found in Islamic banks outside of the US.

The FDIC did make a ruling as such in regard to a request from the Islamic banking intelligence and consulting company Shape Financial. The ruling itself was made pursuant to a private request and as such was unpublished in legal reporters and has not been made public otherwise.[36] However, based on various interviews and media releases, there are enough facts to relate the following and draw some conclusions.

In 2002 Shape Financial sought a ruling from the FDIC as to whether its Shari'ah-compliant Profit Sharing Deposit (PSD) qualified for deposit insurance.[37] The product was based on a true model of risk and reward, whereby the returns were based on the bank's profit and losses.[38] Because the value of the 'deposit' could decline, the FDIC's opinion was that this was not a product that would be covered by deposit insurance.[39] Subsequently, Shape Financial altered the product as to fluctuate regarding profits only – not loss – at which point the FDIC issued a favourable ruling qualifying PSD as an account that would be covered.[40,41] Notes from an informal interview with counsel for the FDIC provide some insight into this decision:

> The FDIC has approved this product for protection, because it is again a 'functional equivalent' to deposits already allowed under their regulation. John Stevens, FDIC chief counsel for the Chicago regional office, explained that banks are allowed to set their rate of return on deposits wherever the bank chooses; if it sets that rate of return based on profits from a certain portfolio, that is the prerogative of the bank.[42]

Two propositions can be gleaned from this brief statement: (1) for any 'insured depository institution',[43] no exception will be made as to the statutory definition of 'deposit' in respect of the requirement that it be represented as an obligation for which the bank must give credit; and (2) the phrase 'interest credited' within the 'deposit' need not be represent interest per se.[44] As the US still lacks a nationally chartered Islamic bank, this opinion along with the previously cited letters from the OCC are useful in crafting policies and arguments that take in account the bases of antecedent FDIC rulings as they do serve as a form of informal precedent.

Other agencies

The Securities and Exchange Commission (SEC) enforces securities laws and regulates the securities industry.[45] There are several examples of SEC interaction with Islamic finance. Shari'ah-compliant mutual funds must comply with SEC regulations which control liquidity, diversity, transparency, and other requirements. Regulations adopted by the SEC affect the issuance and administration of *sukuk* and the administration in their various forms, such as *musharikah* and *ijarah*. This author has not encountered case law involving shareholder, bondholder, or securities enforcement litigation directly involving Islamic finance activity; however, SEC compliance can be secured administratively before disputes arise such as in the cases described above in the passage concerning the OCC. For example, the SEC can issue a 'No-Action Letter', which based on facts described in a request for 'no-action' is essentially a recommendation from an SEC staff member that no enforcement action commence for the activity described in the request.[46,47]

State agencies play a similar, often identical role as federal agencies; however, they operate within a smaller jurisdiction within the nation. Several instances from New York state agencies demonstrate that state jurisdictions are inclined to utilize the same principles as their federal counterparts. For example, in 1999 the New York Department of Financial Services (NYDFS) reviewed the legality of the 'Net Lease Agreement' described in *OCC Interpretive Letter No 806* discussed earlier as applied to regulations pertaining to New York state-chartered banks.[48] Relying on the assumption that the financial institution would provide the same structure as the *ijarah-wa-iqtina'* described in HBK's proposal, the NYDFS wrote the following:

> The Banking Department has no objection to a lender entering into a proposal such as the one described above. We agree with the Office of the Comptroller of the Currency that this is 'functionally equivalent to or a logical outgrowth' of secured real estate lending or mortgage lending, activities that are part of the traditional business of banking.[49]

Similarly, in 2001 in reference to a similar request for interpretation regarding *murabahah* home financing as described above in *OCC Interpretive Letter No 867*, the NYDFS wrote, '[T]he risks associated with Murabaha real estate financings are essentially the same as those associated with underwriting "traditional" mortgage loans'.[50] Then concluding that *murabahah* home financing was not objectionable under New York law, NYDFS once again agreed 'with the OCC that such financings are "functionally equivalent" to conventional financing transactions'.[51]

Other state agencies in New York have made similar allowances in order to allow 'functionally equivalent' transactions to conventional mortgages to operate unimpeded under New York law. For example, the 2007 advisory opinion of the New York Office of Tax Policy Analysis in response to a request from Ahli United Bank, which exempted the second conveyance of title to the lessee/buyer from state real estate transfer tax in cases of the *ijarah-wa-iqtina'* transaction described in *OCC Interpretive Letter No 806*.[52] Similar rulings have been made in other states as well, such as Illinois.[53]

State and federal courts

Court-based remedies for Islamic finance are available by means of three areas of law regardless of the presence of Shari'ah-related issues; namely – contract law, civil claims (tort), and actions based on regulation or with regulatory authorities such as those described in the previous subsections.[54]

In terms of process, all are very much alike. A petition is filed in a court with jurisdiction to hear the case, and opposing parties are given legal notice. Each party is permitted to engage in a period of legally sanctioned fact-finding called 'discovery', and pretrial motions may be filed and argued before the court. If no settlement is reached and a final judgment is not ordered based on prior motions, then the case will be set for trial which will most often be before a jury. In the case of an action based on regulation initiated by the relevant agency or a state or federal prosecutor, the discovery and pretrial motions available to each party may differ from that which is available in a purely civil proceeding.

For this chapter, we focus on lawsuits initiated by private parties. The following discussion is a brief description of the underlying theory in the field of law which may be used to gain relief in a case dealing with an Islamic finance arrangement, followed by an illustrative example from a real or hypothetical case.

Contract law

The body of law that encompasses obligations and protections of parties with respect to agreements, sales, purchases, services, and the remedies at law for default are considered under the umbrella of contract law. The theory of default can apply to a number of Islamic finance agreements, even those where the alleged default was based on the Islamic finance institution's lack of Shari'ah-compliance.[55] Consider, for example the following hypothetical:

> An Islamic Bank receives a national charter to operate in the U.S. Among the products that it advertises is its profit-sharing Cash Deposit account. Islamic Bank advertises that its operations, including its Cash Deposit account, are supervised by a Shari'ah board and operates under the premises of the 1998 *fatwa* devised by the Shari'ah supervisory board for the Dow Jones Islamic World Market Index. A client invests $100,000 in a Cash Deposit account, signing agreements containing the above-mentioned principles. After one year, the client withdraws their investment. During the process, it is divulged that Islamic Bank's Shari'ah supervisory board had actually operated according to the principles adopted by the Kuala Lumpur Stock Exchange Islamic Index and devised by the Shariah Advisory Council of the Securities Commission of Malaysia. The client contends that certain real estate properties would have been included in Islamic Bank's portfolio but for its reliance on the Shariah Advisory Council of the Securities Commission of Malaysia criteria rather than that of the Dow Jones Islamic World Market Index. The client sues for breach of contract.

The above hypothetical is a similar situation to that of *Jacob & Youngs, Inc. v Kent*, 230 NY 239 (1921), a case taught in probably every first-year contracts course in the US.[56] Although that case involved plumbing rather than investments, and sentimental loss rather than missed opportunity, the underlying issues would still need to be addressed in the hypothetical; such as, was the breach major or minor and how to calculate damages in such a case. Fundamentally however, the area of contract law is one that potentially allows a consumer to recover in the case of non-fulfilment of contract terms by the Islamic finance institution.

Tort

Initiating a civil suit based on a common law claim, such as fraud or misrepresentation, is another practical strategy of resolving disputes in Islamic finance.[57] For example, in *Jama v Guidance Residential, LLC*, Civil No 12-77(DSD/JSM) (D Minnesota 16 August 2012), the plaintiff sued the US Islamic home finance provider Guidance Residential for alleged 'misrepresentations [that] caused him "to [q]ualify for the loan at the [i]nterest [r]ate that [Guidance] offered"', alleging violation of the Minnesota Consumer Fraud Act, which states:

> The act, use, or employment [...] of any fraud, false pretense, false promise, misrepresentation, misleading statement or deceptive practice, with the intent that others rely thereon in connection with the sale of any merchandise, whether or not any person has in fact been misled, deceived, or damaged thereby.[58]

While the suit for fraud was dismissed for failure to state a claim,[59] this case demonstrates the possibility of using tort law as an avenue for recovery against a company that falsely markets itself, potentially even with respect to its Shari'ah-compliance.

Securities litigation

Lawsuits based on laws such as those described in earlier, are often based on securities regulation. In those cases, the prospectus which describes the investment to prospective investors in a public or private placement may contain misrepresentations which an investor claims was responsible for a loss.[60] Of course, the SEC is the entity primarily charged with enforcing securities regulation. For Islamic finance, up to this time I have not encountered any Securities Exchange Act litigation stemming from actions involving untrue statements and making use of the national securities exchanges, whether initiated by the SEC or through private actions. Though, some Islamic finance institutions have been involved in SEC enforcement actions.[61] Given that a private right of action is authorized by the Securities Exchange Act, one can hypothesize situations in the future in which a company that chooses to market itself as an Islamic finance institution could be sued by private citizens for activity that is not Shari'ah-compliant. For example, consider the language of 17 CFR 240.10b-5:

> It shall be unlawful for any person, [... by use of] facility of any national securities exchange,
>
> (a) To employ any device, scheme, or artifice to defraud,
> (b) To make any untrue statement of a material fact or to omit to state a material fact necessary in order to make the statements made, in the light of the circumstances under which they were made, not misleading, or
> (c) To engage in any act, practice, or course of business which operates or would operate as a fraud or deceit upon any person, in connection with the purchase or sale of any security.

In view of this particular regulation, imagine a hypothetical set of facts involving a lawsuit initiated on the basis of a publicly traded company which is marketed in its prospectus as Shari'ah-compliant (e.g. an Islamic bank or Shari'ah-compliant mutual fund), and as observing standards as set by the Dow Jones Fatwa of 1998. In the case that such a company ignored Shari'ah board guidance in opposition to the claims of its prospectus, a shareholder would have a cause of action based on 17 CFR 240.10b-5 for such misrepresentations. That stated, the more important consideration is to note that the existing legal regime offers avenues for consumers of Islamic finance products to resolve their disputes with companies that market such products within state and federal courts, and this same regime incentivizes companies to follow through on their claims.

The US court approach

Thus, the following represents a summary of courts' first encounters with Islamic finance in the US. While the explanations described in the previous section describe some legal theories and procedures for recovering in a civil dispute or administrative procedure involving Islamic finance, the following discusses the likely analysis of such claims by the courts and other adjudicatory bodies, particularly their techniques of statutory interpretation and their approach in analysing the arguments of parties in Islamic finance disputes.

Tendencies concerning religious issues

The US is a secular jurisdiction. Whereas the official religion of say Yemen or Pakistan is Islam, the official position of the US regarding religion is that they are the same before the government, and the government will not engage in interpreting religious principles. Given that the foundational philosophy of Islamic finance is the resort to prophetic knowledge, how does the court employ its reasoning in resolving disputes in Islamic finance.

Honoring parties' choice of law

In the US, parties are generally able to choose the governing law of their contracts. US courts will ordinarily honour the applicable law chosen by the parties.[62] Once the applicable law is determined, the trial court judge is tasked with determining how a judge sitting in that jurisdiction would adjudicate the dispute. For example, a judge presiding over a contract dispute in Texas who determines the applicable law to be that of New York will then analyse issues such as fraud and damages according to New York law rather than the law of his own jurisdiction. Thus, in *National Group for Communications & Computers v Lucent Technologies Intl*, 331 F Supp 2d 290 (DNJ 2004), before making conclusions concerning the dispute itself the court notes that 1) the contract is governed by Saudi Arabian law; and 2) the court therefore needed to determine 'how Saudi Arabian law would construe the Plaintiff's claim for the loss of its Projects Department'.[63]

In making determinations concerning foreign law, the court has a wide array of tools at its disposal. To illustrate, the Federal Rules of Civil Procedure R. 44.1 provides, '[T]he court may consider any relevant material or source, including testimony' and its sources need not even be admissible under the Federal Rules of Evidence.[64] As a court determining Shari'ah issues for trial purposes is focused on legal concepts applicable to a particular case, it is able to gather legal standards from the ILIJ in conceptual forms. Thus, in *National Group v Lucent Technologies* the court was able to use clearly non-secular sources to make its decision without questioning whether it was straying into making a religious ruling because disputes were identified, then sources were gathered, and legal (though religious) concepts were abstracted into principles that could be used, absent faith, in the ultimate truth of the primary sources.

Using that process, the *National Group v Lucent Technologies* court (1) identified the Hanbali school as generally controlling; (2) the 'Qur'an, the Sunnah, and fiqh' as primary sources; (3) the concept of *gharar* as applicable after defining the said term; and (4) utilized available commentaries on the above in order to determine that expectation damages as requested by the plaintiff fell under the legal prohibition of *gharar*.[65] The court was able to accomplish this because the legal tradition being utilized, which also sustains modern Islamic finance, contained principles that are discoverable and abstract; the court did not make determinations that *gharar* was prohibited from the primary sources, but rather used the primary sources only in understanding the nature of the prohibition in order to draw analogies to the case at bar.

In summary, the court will continue to respect parties' choice of law, and the religious nature of Islamic finance does not necessarily contradict the fundamental policy of remaining neutral in sectarian matters.

Judicial estoppel

Inconsistent positions concerning the applicability of Shari'ah principles are seldom permitted when the first position has already been accepted by the court. While the doctrine of judicial estoppel is not uniformly accepted or applied between courts within the US, the practice exists to varying degrees even in the absence of mention of the doctrinal elements.[66] The general policy is easily understood when thought of in practical terms; the court will defend the integrity of the judicial process from abuse arising from 'cynical gamesmanship, achieving success on one position, then arguing the opposite to suit an exigency of the moment'.[67]

With regard to Islamic finance, two patterns of inconsistent positions can occur. The first is a matter of Shari'ah principles as applied to the substantive component of the case, such as an objection being made regarding the validity of the contract, but only made after an adverse decision was handed down; this is essentially what occurred in *Shamil Bank v Beximco*.[68]

The second pattern is an objection regarding Shari'ah principles as applied to the procedure, but only made after consenting to the procedural element and receiving an adverse judgment. This is in substance what occurred in *Saudi Basic Industries Corp v Mobil Yanbu Petrochemical Co*, in which the plaintiff brought a suit in Delaware court, only to later bring into question the qualifications of the trial court judge to practice *ijtihad* according to Saudi Arabian law. Rejecting the plaintiff's post-trial manoeuvre, the trial judge responded, 'It is remarkable that SABIC, having [purposefully] selected this forum instead of a Saudi Court [...], comes forward after a verdict against it to claim that no American judge is qualified to interpret and apply Saudi law'.[69]

To sum up, principles of estoppel operate as a restraint on a party's collateral attacks on factual or procedural decisions on the basis of subsequently-contrived arguments utilizing Shari'ah principles.

Interference in religion

In the *National Group for Communications* and the *Saudi Basic Industries Corp* cases, the respective courts applied the law chosen by the parties in spite of the necessity of delving into religious texts. In fact, it appears that neither party, nor the court questioned the ability of the court to do so based on First Amendment ground.[70] However, the constitutional restriction is there; so, it follows to question the length to which the court will go to accommodate not only the parties' choice of law, but the very terms of the contract itself even when being evaluated under US law.

In *El-Farra v Sayyed*, the Supreme Court of Arkansas was called upon to decide whether or not the trial court had subject matter jurisdiction to hear the complaints of Monir Y El-Farra against the Islamic Center of Little Rock and members of its executive committee.[71] In that case, El-Farra, the plaintiff, had previously been contracted to serve as the imam of the Islamic Center of Little Rock ('the center', 'defendant').[72] As part of his contract, the center's executive committee could terminate El-Farra's contract by unanimous vote on the basis of 'Islamic Jurisdiction (Shari'a)'.[73] Several months after warning El-Farra concerning the content of his Friday sermons, the executive committee served El-Farra a letter, placing him on probation with regard to his employment and citing conduct that 'contradicts the Islamic law'; he was terminated a short while later.[74] El-Farra filed a lawsuit against the center, alleging *inter alia*, defamation and breach of contract.[75] In response, lawyers for the center filed a motion for summary judgment, arguing that 'the First Amendment to the United States Constitution [...prohibited] the circuit court from exercising jurisdiction in this case'.[76] The trial court agreed with the defendant's reasoning and granted the motion, effectively dismissing the case.[77]

The plaintiff appealed, and his lawyers argued that his breach of contract claim did not involve 'matters related to Islamic doctrine, but only interpersonal matters concerning his relationship with the Executive Committee', and because he was not seeking reinstatement, but merely damages, 'his claim is purely secular, [and] does not involve the court in selection of a minister'.[78] However, the appellate court disagreed, citing several appellate court rulings; including the US Supreme Court ruling in *Serbian Eastern Orthodox Diocese v Milivojevich*,[79] which applying the First Amendment that 'held that civil courts are not a constitutionally permissible forum for a review of ecclesiastical disputes'.[80] In further support of its decision to uphold the summary judgment for lack of subject matter jurisdiction on plaintiff's breach of contract claims, the court noted that 'the First Amendment protects the act of decision rather than the motivation behind it'[81] and 'whether the termination [...] was based on secular reasons or Islamic doctrine, this court will not involve itself in ICLR's right to choose ministers without government interference'.[82] The court then proceeded to affirm the dismissal El-Farra's defamation claim based on similar reasoning.[83]

While the many jurisdictions in the US possess distinctive jurisprudence applicable to similar issues, *El-Farra* is representative of Islamic finance disputes for two main reasons. The first is that the courts are loath to interfere in matters involving a religious institution and that pertain to a religious thought even when such issues may arguably be distilled to secular topics. In other words, the First Amendment's protections can extend to the mundane operations of the religious institution. The second consideration is that while Islamic financial institutions in the US are not religious institutions, Islamic finance or Shari'ah-compliant business may be carried out in such a manner that it becomes situated in the same space covered by the aforementioned considerations. For example, consider the situation of a religious charity whose goal is to increase access to higher education to future Islamic scholars by providing Shari'ah-compliant student loans, or imagine the case of two businessmen in a *musharikah* arrangement who contract in writing to conduct all business according to 'Islamically acceptable' standards as adjudged by the local imam.

Contractual interpretation

Conventional loan providers in the US will prefer an interpretation of Islamic finance agreements that interpret terms as analogous to loans and interest because it is what the industry is generally based on.[84] This raises the question: have state and federal regulators given their blessing to certain Islamic finance arrangements merely because they could substitute various terms for those used in conventional loans? Perhaps, but in the absence of bench-made law saying as much, I believe that the regulatory interpretations deserve more analysis beyond the hidden *riba* arguments.

Analogizing to common transactions

As discussed in the previous section, in permitting the use of *murabahah* and *ijarah* products, the OCC decided that these products were at their core similar to credit transactions and bore the same risks.[85] Indeed, the regulatory authority in this case based its decision on the purposes behind the law, noting that the public policy of limiting a bank's risk simply was not present in *murabahah* and *ijarah* real estate transactions given the brief moments that the financial institution would incur ownership.[86]

Similarly, the New York State Banking Department's decisions regarding *murabahah* and *ijarah* products were cited in the OCC interpretive letters.[87] What is the policy behind this interpretation? Is the point that because it is similar to a mortgage, it is permitted? Not exactly. In understanding the decisions of New York regulators and others, one must take into account two other facts concerning home ownership within the country.

First, homeownership in the US is nurtured by use of preferential tax-treatment. Borrowers can deduct interest paid on mortgages from their taxable income.[88] That is just one potential deduction. On an investment level, an investor that places his profits into purchasing real estate can defer paying certain capital gains tax on the original investment.[89] Second, New York and other states have also eliminated the second title transfer tax that can occur in *ijarah* transactions in real estate.[90]

Given these facts, it would seem that there are three important issues for regulators: (1) the transaction encourages a type of business which is desired (e.g. home purchases); (2) the risks to the consumer are similar to already permitted transactions; and (3) the existing laws permit it. In regard to risk and regulatory agencies, it appears that the agency weighs risks to the consumer against approval of the product. For example, as discussed previously, SHAPE, a private Islamic finance intelligence company, was denied insurance from the FDIC for a Shari'ah-compliant deposit product based on the banks profit and loss; however, a revised product based solely on the bank's profits was approved.[91]

While these decisions have proven favourable to the growth of Islamic finance at an agency level, none of the examples that I note in this passage is a court decision. To my knowledge, the US has yet to have its version of *Shamil Bank* (United Kingdom), whose outcome was in part dictated by contractual language regarding Shari'ah-compliance which the court may have found ambiguous as to its character. The decision in that case was ultimately based on the court making an analogy to conventional transactions.[92] On the other hand, making analogies is part and parcel of the common law system, i.e. controlling cases are not necessarily directly 'on point', and the process of comparing and contrasting facts in order to determine whether or not a law or doctrine applies is a process of legal analysis of Islamic finance in US courts.

For example, in *United Islamic Society v Masjed Abubakr Al-Seddiq, Inc*, No A16–0140 (Mich Ct App 29 August 2016), United Islamic Society (UIS) sued requesting declaratory relief clarifying UIS to be the beneficiary of a trust in place of Masjed Abubakr Al-Seddiq (MAAS).[93] The trust was made in the form of a *waqf*, which the petition defined as 'an Arabic word meaning endowment typically of a building or plot of land for religious or charitable purposes'.[94] MAAS objected to the court having jurisdiction due to the Establishment Clause of the First Amendment of the US Constitution because the court would have to 'analyze the religious term "waqf" to determine when a trust was created, whether UIS is fulfilling Islamic objectives for the community, and whether NAIT is fulfilling its duties as trustee'; in doing so, the court would essentially be analysing a religious doctrine.[95] However, both at trial and appellate levels, the court was more convinced by the possibility of resolving property rights based on established law if the purported *waqf* fits neatly within the confines of existing legal doctrines; that is, by analogy. At trial level, the court addressed the Establishment Clause objection in part by making the following observations:

(1) Even if the court must determine the meaning of *waqf*, it could still 'resolve the issues raised in the [p]etition by neutral principles of law and without regard to religious doctrines'; and (2) 'The purported trust [*waqf*] created by MAAS might be an illegal passive trust', which was to say that the court would apply the elements of existing law to the character of the *waqf* in comparison.[96] At the appellate level, the court also seemed content to apply state trust laws to the dispute, noting that, 'UIS makes no mention of any religious doctrine [..., and] requests a determination that it is the intended beneficiary of the trust based on the lease, warranty deeds, meeting minutes, and MAAS resolution'.[97] Ultimately, the appellate court decided in favour of appellees on the question of jurisdiction, giving in part the reason that 'determining when a trust was created and which party was intended to be the trust beneficiary likely involves neutral principles of law rather than religious doctrine'.[98]

Upholding distinctions based on contractual terms

For cases in which contractual interpretation is the core issue of litigation, US courts are not likely to engage in the same analogous reasoning as regulatory agencies, but rather will hold sophisticated parties to the terms of their agreement. This is the case even in those instances in which the court has a clearly analogous conventional agreement which could have served the parties had Shari'ah-compliance been a non-factor.

The arguments in *In Re East Cameron Partners, LP* presents a good background from which to analyse this principle.[99,100] In *In re East Cameron Partners, LP*, East Cameron Partners L.P. (ECP) entered into a complex *sukuk* arrangement in order to facilitate their oil and gas business.[101] The *sukuk* was structured by creating a limited liability company named East Cameron Gas Company (ECG) which acted as the trustee of the *sukuk* trust. ECG proceeded to issue *sukuk* certificates in a private placement under Regulation D and an international offering under Regulation S,[102] which in a regulatory sense means that the *sukuk* certificates essentially represented an ownership stake in ECG. The proceeds were then used to purchase an Overriding Royalty Interest (ORRI) in gas properties from ECP.[103] Various other entities were created or involved as intermediaries in order to facilitate payments and holding of property. ECP was to make quarterly payments to which would transfer to ECG, which in turn would make distributions to the *sukuk* certificate holders.[104] After ECP delivered a specified amount of hydrocarbons in cash or in kind, the ownership of the ORRI would revert back to ECP.[105] However, production lagged, and ECP was unable to make quarterly payments.[106] On 16 October 2008, ECP filed a voluntary petition for bankruptcy.[107]

Alongside its petition, ECP filed a complaint requesting, among other things, declaratory relief and to obtain an order in its favour clarifying the following:

> [T]hat this court provide declaratory relief declaring that: (i) the sukuk transaction described herein [...] constitute[s] a simulation and antichresis

> under Louisiana law; (ii) the Purchase Conveyance [...] did not transfer ownership of the ORRI to LOH [an agent of ECG]; (iii) the ORRI remains an asset of ECP [...] which is subject to a pledge [...] as security for the loan of funds to ECP.[108]

As is clearly stated above, ECP requested that the bankruptcy court declare (1) the *sukuk* transaction was a loan; (2) that the conveyance of the ORRI, i.e. the underlying asset securitizing the *sukuk* and making the private/international offering of ECG a worthwhile investment, did not transfer ownership of the ORRI to ECG; and (3) the ORRI, was merely security for ECG's loan to ECP.[109] In essence, ECP requested the court to interpret the distinctions of the *sukuk* transaction that made it Shari'ah-compliant as ineffective, as nothing more than a conventional secured loan. In order to support its argument, ECP notes that Louisiana law is controlling, and under such law the *sukuk* was a simulation of a loan and antichresis, a type of loan involving pledging and taking possession of immovable property.[110] ECP pointed to convincing case law which permits parties to secure a debt by means of a false, simulated sale. In doing so, ECP relied heavily on *In re Senior-G & A Operating Co, Inc*, 957 F2d 1290 (5th Cir 1992). In that case, the debtor had conveyed royalty interests to the creditor in return for $12,750,000.[111] During the bankruptcy case, the creditor contended that it was indeed the owner of the royalty interest, but the court disagreed, and reasoned that the conveyance was actually a pledge for a secured loan because the payment of the royalty itself was secured – as opposed to a pure royalty interest which is merely passive and does not prompt the mineral owner to develop the land – thus the creditor had the right to foreclose on the well itself.[112] The agreement also provided that the royalty interest would revert back to the debtor once a certain amount of value had been returned to the creditor.[113] Furthermore, the parties agreed to treat the transaction as a loan for tax purposes.[114] The court found that the actions of the parties demonstrated that the conveyance was intended merely to secure a loan, a simulation in other words.[115] ECP argued that the agreement in the *sukuk* transaction contained many parallels to *In re Senior-G & A*, noting that (1) parties agreed to treat the transaction as a loan for tax purposes; (2) the agreement gave the ORRI holder the right to foreclose on the property for failure of ECP to meet its production obligations (similar to a mortgage); and (3) the ORRI would revert back to ECP once a certain value had been paid to ECG.[116] Thus according to ECP, that analogy was enough for the court to discover that the intentions of the parties was never to actually convey the ORRI, but rather to secure a loan by means of an antichresis.[117]

In a motion to dismiss ECP's complaint and accompanying memorandum of law, the Sukuk Certificateholders responded to the request for declaratory judgment by arguing: 1) that the ORRI conveyance was indeed a true sale under controlling Louisiana law; 2) that ECP's statements of law should be disregarded in favour of Louisiana's version of the Uniform Commercial Code; 3) that the complaint should be dismissed because it asked the court to rewrite the contract; and 4) the complaint should be dismissed because though asking the court to recharacterize the sukuk as a loan, it left out every major detail of what that loan should be.[118] To support its argument that the ORRI was a true sale, Sukuk Certificateholders argued that the plain language of the agreement supports this interpretation in various sections, for example section 1.01 of the Purchased Overriding Conveyance:

> GRANTS, BARGAINS, SELLS, CONVEYS, ASSIGNS, SETS OVER AND DELIVERS unto [LOH [an agent of ECG]], an overriding royalty interest in each of the Subject Interests and in and to the Hydrocarbons in and under and that may be produced and saved from the Subject Interests equal to the respective Overriding Royalty Percentage applicable to each Subject Interest (after deduction of the pro rata part of the Lease Use Hydrocarbons attributable to the Subject Interests) of all Hydrocarbons produced and saved that Month, together with all and singular the rights and appurtenances thereto in anywise belonging (the 'Purchased Overriding Royalty').[119]

Regarding the counterarguments of ECG that this conveyance was merely simulated, Sukuk Certificateholders noted that the Louisiana Commercial Code governed the agreement rather than Louisiana Civil Code's provisions on antichresis, which among other things provided that 'the parties' characterization of a transaction as a sale of accounts [...] shall be conclusive that the transaction is a true sale and is not a secured transaction'.[120] Addressing ECP's arguments that *In re Senior A & G* is controlling, Sukuk Certificateholders pointed out that the agreement in that case was made prior to the relevant changes in the Louisiana Commercial Code, but furthermore that the parties in that case used other language indicative of a mortgage; first by entitling the agreement as 'Production Payment Loan Agreement' and second by stipulating that the 'production payment granted thereby shall constitute a lien upon the subject minerals conveyed'.[121] On the other hand, the conveyance in the *sukuk* provided that it was an 'absolute conveyance' and was entitled 'Purchase and Sale Agreement', among other distinctions.[122] *Sukuk* holders went on to argue that because the Declaratory Judgment Act can only be used to declare rights rather than to revise agreements, no declaratory relief should be given because doing so would ignore the parties' unambiguous 'objectives', and no proof had been provided as to how the Court should rewrite the Mortgage in the event that the Court recharacterizes the Sukuk Securitization.[123] Sukuk Certificateholders closed with a similar argument, this time stating that given the above considerations, ECP failed to state a claim in its request for declaratory relief due to that very lack of detail concerning the supposed loan.[124]

In its decision, the court granted Sukuk Certificateholders' motion to dismiss without elaborating on its reasoning for doing so.[125] However, in its order the court does note that it did so on the basis of Federal Rule of Civil Procedure 12(b)(6), for failure to state a claim upon which relief could be granted.[126] Therefore, we can deduce that the court probably accepted one of the arguments that

Sukuk Certificateholders made under that rule. First, the court may have been swayed by the assertion that the characterization of the conveyance as a loan would fail under Louisiana law. Second, the court may have accepted the line of reasoning that ECP was attempting to use the Declaratory Judgment Act to revise an agreement in spite of the parties' objective intent. Or last, the court may have been convinced that by requesting the court to recharacterize the *sukuk* as a loan, that ECP failed to state a claim by not including all relevant details of that ostensible loan agreement. All three arguments were made under Federal Rule of Civil Procedure 12(b)(6). The Federal Rule of Civil Procedure 12(e) request from Sukuk Certificateholders for an order that ECP give a more definite statement of its claims became moot, obviously as the claim itself was dismissed. But interestingly, the court did exercise jurisdiction by deciding on these motions; thus, it did not accept Sukuk Certificateholders' third argument that the court should decline to exercise jurisdiction over the complaint under Federal Rule of Civil Procedure 12(b)(1),[127] as the various revisions would constitute an improper use of the Declaratory Judgment Act; i.e. the lack of real notice given to *sukuk* certificateholders as to the specifics of this supposed revision reduces the matter to non-justiciable controversy.[128]

Whatever its reasoning, it is evident that the court was reluctant to deviate from the objective terms of the of the *sukuk* agreement. This is a fair result, because of the sophistication and equal bargaining power of the parties, in spite of any parallels to a mortgage arrangement. The logic of the debtors in *In re East Cameron Partners, LP* shows that deals mirroring those arranged to be Shari'ah-compliant already exist in US jurisdictions and the objective intent of the parties in entering Islamic finance agreements must be taken into account.

US arbitration

Arbitration in the US is generally permitted, and a clear policy exists in favour of enforcement of arbitration agreements and awards at both state and federal levels. At a federal level, arbitration is largely governed by the Federal Arbitration Act (FAA). Agreements to arbitrate arising out of transactions under the jurisdiction of the federal government, that is to say maritime activity and interstate and international commerce, are 'valid, irrevocable, and enforceable, save upon such grounds as exist at law or in equity for the revocation of any contract'.[129] With respect to the enforcement of commercial arbitration awards, particularly foreign judgments, the US is a member of the Convention on the Recognition and Enforcement of Foreign Arbitral Awards ('New York Convention'), which is enforced by means of the FAA.[130] The FAA incorporates the New York Convention in 9 USC §§201–208, which provides in part, 'The Convention on the Recognition and Enforcement of Foreign Arbitral Awards of 10 June 1958, shall be enforced in United States courts in accordance with this chapter'.[131] Similar provisions exist at the local level for disputes enforceable in state courts.[132]

While the New York Convention provides exceptions for enforcement of arbitral awards, most notably in cases for which enforcement would be against the law or public policy of that country.[133] Regarding use of the public policy exception in the US, the clause has been applied narrowly in favour of the pro-enforcement inclination of the convention; the general supposition is that 'enforcement of arbitral awards can be denied only when enforcement would "violate the forum state's most basic notions of morality and justice"'.[134] There has been little cause for concern that a US court's pro-enforcement bias would switch in the context of Islamic finance transactions; though this presumes the absence of new legislation prohibiting the consideration of international law and Shari'ah in certain courts in the aforementioned example. In fact, at least one court has enforced an agreement to arbitrate before a religious tribunal in the sensitive family law setting.

In *Jabri v Qaddura*, a Texas appellate court held that the trial court erred in finding the Arbitration Agreement to be invalid and in denying Appellants' motions to compel arbitration under the Texas General Arbitration Act.[135] In doing so, the court considered the arbitration agreement signed by the parties, and cited portions within its decision, to wit:

> [A]fter consultation with their respective attorneys, agree to submit all claims and disputes among them to arbitration by the TEXAS ISLAMIC COURT;
>
> 1. The Parties agree to arbitrate all existing issues among them in the above mentioned Cause Numbers [... including] the Divorce Case, the child custody of the [*sic*] Noor Qaddura and Farah Qaddura, the determination of each party's responsibilities and duties according to the Islamic rules of law by Texas Islamic Court.[136]

It is significant that though the agreement to arbitrate clearly comprehended the custody of children, the appellate court was still convinced by the language favouring enforcement, 'The Arbitration Agreement does not contain any language purporting to except the applicability of the Agreement to certain issues,' and in enforcing the agreement the court pointed out on its own that there was no agreement concerning the future residence of the children.[137]

In conclusion, arbitration agreements and subsequent awards are favoured by a pro-enforcement policy in the US. Also, the distinctions of Islamic finance, including sensitivities arising from choice of law do not impede enforcement by virtue of objections based on public policy.

Conclusion

Islamic finance in the US is still in its early phase. However, the sector is growing due to the increase in consumers that prefer a Shari'ah-compliant banking option, as well as the expansion of capital investment in the US from Shari'ah-influenced jurisdictions, such as those of the Arabian peninsula. Legal cases resulting from this sector of business permit us to make the following broad observations. First, on a regulatory basis, Shari'ah-compliant transactions are reasonably permitted when they provide at least the same level of consumer protection as existing US regulations. At that point, decision makers can draw similarities between different terms in Shari'ah-compliant and traditional US financial agreements. Second, US courts may be willing to analyse Shar'iah-compliant agreements according to religiously-derived principles when the contract calls for it, but they are unlikely to do so in regard to calling into question their own jurisdiction. That is to say, Shari'ah matters will have to be addressed in the substantive phase of the case, and even then such issues must lend themselves to the application of widely-understood principles. Last, sophisticated parties to a contract are likely to be held to the specific terms of their agreements. Whether for or against Islamic finance influenced provisions, parties to a contract will rarely find success in court by arguing a contrary intent, whether such arguments are based on US or Shari'ah traditions.

Notes

1 Andrew M. Metcalf, 'United States' [2016] The Islamic Finance and Markets Review (1st edn) ('The retail market involves products such as home purchases and small business financing. [...] The wholesale market concentrates on providing equity and financing facilities for major investments').

2 See Abdulkader Thomas, 'Methods of Islamic Home Finance in the United States' (2001) Shape Knowledge Services http://consultshape.com/wp-content/uploads/methods2017.pdf accessed 10 October 2017. ('University Islamic Financial Corp. (UIFC) [... grew] to include an FDIC [Federal Deposit Insurance Corporation] insured profit sharing deposit [...]').

3 Indeed, at least one example exists of a municipal government providing instalment sales financing without interest (similar to a *murabahah* contract). See Thomas (n 2) ('In 2000, the Council on American Islamic Relations (CAIR) [...] highlighted the plight of Somali refugees in that city [...] CAIR worked with [...] the State and County to structure an installment sales project [...]').

4 See Riyadh Mohammed, 'Hot trend in 2017: Rise of Islamic banks on Main St. USA' (*CNBC*, 2 December 2016) www.cnbc.com/2016/12/02/under-the-radar-islamic-banks-rise-in-th.html accessed 9 October 2017 ('But one of the earliest pioneers is Saturna Capital, an investment advisor and fund-management company founded in 1989. It now manages more than $3.5 billion in assets that are invested in mutual funds consistent with Islamic finance principles'); Interestingly, 'the United States is the fourth-largest domicile of Islamic investment funds, due almost entirely to the Amana Mutual Funds Trust based in Bellingham, Wash., whose income and growth funds hold almost $3.5 billion in assets'. Renee Haltom, 'Islamic Banking, American Regulation' [2014] 2nd quarter Econ Focus 15–19, 18 www.richmondfed.org/~/media/richmondfedorg/publications/research/econ_focus/2014/q2/pdf/feature1.pdf accessed 10 October 2017.

5 For example, *Murray v U.S. Department of Treasury*, 681 F3d 744 (6th Cir 2012) was a United States taxpayer litigation case arising from an Establishment Clause challenge to the federal government dispersing relief funds to multinational bank AIG because six of its subsidiaries sold 'Sharia-compliant financing ("SCF") products [...]'. The managers of these subsidiaries ensured 'the Sharia-compliance of its SCF products by obtaining consultation from "Sharia Supervisory Committees"'. Also see, Shirley Chiu, 'Islamic Finance in the United States: A Small but Growing Industry' [2005] no 214 Chicago Fed Letter ('HSBC has several other offices in its global Islamic services division overseas').

6 See Michael JT McMillen, 'Islamic Capital Markets for United States Parties: Overview and Select Shariʿah Governance Elements' in *Inside the Minds: Financial Services Enforcement and Compliance* (Aspatore 2013)

> Very few Islamic finance structures have been developed [... relating] primarily to only a handful of industries and business activities (real estate investing, a small portion of private equity, a limited array of equity investment funds, three or so securitizations, and some project and infrastructure finance needs [...];

and also Shayerah Ilias, 'Islamic Finance: Overview and Policy Concerns' [2008] Congressional Research Service (Order Code RS22931) CRS-1-CRS-2 ('Additionally, U.S.-based companies have taken advantage of alternative funding sources through Islamic-financing abroad. According to Standard & Poor's, Loehmann's Holdings, Inc. and East Cameron Gas Company have issued rated shariah-compliant bonds' (citing Standard & Poor's, 'The Islamic Financial Industry Comes of Age', Commentary Report, 25 October 2006).

7 John H Vogel, 'United States' [2016] Getting the Deal Through: Islamic Finance & Markets 51, 51.

8 12 USC § 29. Also see John H Vogel, 'Current Status of Islamic Finance in the United States' [2012] no 27 Cayman Financial Review Magazine B43 http://caymanianfinancialreview.cay.newsmemory.com/?date=20120404&goTo=B43 accessed 9 October 2017

> In addition, the National Bank Act prohibits commercial banks from the purchase, holding of legal title, or possession of real estate to secure any debts to it for a period exceeding five years. This ban would effectively restrict Islamic home finance products, such as the availability of a murabaha.

9 See 'Letter from Charles F Byrd to James M Kane, District Counsel' [1984] 3 Comptroller of the Currency QJ No 2 at 51 (June 1984) ('In my opinion, precluding national banks from trading their OREO for new real estate is consistent with the purpose of 12 USC 29: ensuring that national banks do not speculate in real estate'); also see *National Bank v Matthews*, 98 US 621, 625–26 (1878) ('The object of the restrictions was obviously [...] to deter them [banks] from embarking in hazardous real estate speculations, and to prevent the accumulation of large masses of such property in their hands [...]').

10 12 USC §1813(l)(1).

11 See Vogel (n 8) ('The United States does not permit a deposit at a bank to be at risk [...] [T]he Islamic banking model [...] profit-loss sharing scheme [...] puts the initial deposit at risk. Thus, the US statutory definition of 'deposit' poses a potential obstacle to Islamic financing'); also see Greg Cavanagh, 'Regulatory Aspects of Islamic Banking in the United States' (Lecture) [2011] (4th U. California Berkeley Islamic Finance Forum, Berkeley School of Law) ('Deposit accounts that do not bear interest are not problematic from either a bank regulatory or shariah perspective[.] But what if a customer wants a return on his or her deposit?').

12 See generally ibid., 'Securities Law History' *Wex* (Legal Information Institute at the Cornell Law School) www.law.cornell.edu/wex/securities_law_history accessed 2 January 2018.

13 See 15 USC §77bbb ('Necessity for regulation').

14 Pursuing regulatory compliance while achieving *Shari'ah*-compliance milestones has been contemplating theoretically within the framework of US securities law in other aspects of Islamic finance as well. See Vogel (n 8):

> It remains to be seen whether a financial institution operating in the US may seek US regulatory approval for a deposit product that would pass on the financial institution's losses to the depositor under a UK-style 'waiver approach' or some other arrangement that has the same substantive effect. One suggestion has been

made to treat a profit and loss sharing depository account as an 'investment security' regulated by the SEC, rather than a banking product regulated by federal and state banking regulators.

15 Lee Hudson Teslik, 'The U.S. Financial Regulatory System' (*Council on Foreign Relations*, 4 October 2008) at 4 www.cfr.org/backgrounder/us-financial-regulatory-system accessed 9 October 2017.
16 Ibid. 3–4.
17 *OCC Interpretive Letter No 806*, reprinted in [1997–1998 Transfer Binder] Fed Banking L Rep (CCH) 81,253 (17 October 1997) www.occ.gov/static/interpretations-and-precedents/dec97/int806.pdf accessed 5 December 2017.
18 Ibid. 2.
19 Ibid.
20 Ibid.
21 Ibid.
22 Ibid. 4.
23 12 USC §29 (Banks may

purchase, hold, and convey real estate [... but] no such association shall hold the possession of any real estate under mortgage, or the title and possession of any real estate purchased to secure any debts due to it, for a longer period than five years [...].

24 OCC Interpretive Letter No 806 (n 17) 11.
25 Ibid. 16.
26 *OCC Interpretive Letter No 867*, www.occ.gov (November 1999) www.occ.gov/static/interpretations-and-precedents/nov99/int867.pdf accessed 5 December 2017.
27 Ibid. 1.
28 Ibid. 5.
29 Ibid. 2.
30 Ibid. 8.
31 Ibid. n 7 (citing to *OCC Interpretive Letter No 371*, reprinted in [1985–1987 Transfer Binder] Fed Banking L Rep (CCH) 85, 541 (13 June 1986)).
32 Ibid.
33 Ibid. 8.
34 Teslik (n 15) 7.
35 12 USC §1813(l).
36 The ruling was issued to Shape Financial as part of a license application for a product licensed to a community bank. Although of scholarly interest, due to professional ethics principles, members of Shape Financial were unable to share the actual document, but I thank them here for the historical background of the request for ruling of which they were able to inform me.
37 Haltom (n 4) 18.
38 Ibid.
39 Ibid.
40 Ibid.
41 A second *fatwa* was issued regarding the permissibility of the Profit Sharing Deposit on the basis of the limitations imposed by federal law and the understanding that 'the Company and its licensees are working for the implementation of the optimal form of *mudaraba* deposit'. Nisam Yaqubi, Yusuf T DeLorenzo, Ahmed Shleibak, 'Fatwa: SHAPE Profit Sharing Deposit (Letter)' [July 2005] Shape Financial.
42 Victoria Lynn Zyp, 'Islamic Finance in the United States: Product Development and Regulatory Adoption' at 18 (Masters of Arts thesis, Georgetown University 2009) (citing to Victoria Lynn Zip, Interview with John Stevens, Chief Counsel FDIC-Chicago regional office, Georgetown University (Georgetown 25 February 2009)).

43 12 USC §1813 (c)(2) ('The term "insured depository institution" means any bank or savings association the deposits of which are insured by the Corporation pursuant to this chapter').

44 See 12 CFR §204.2 (a)(1):

> 'Deposit' means: (i) The unpaid balance of money or its equivalent received or held by a depository institution in the usual course of business and for which it has given or is obligated to give credit, either conditionally or unconditionally, to an account, including interest credited, or which is evidenced by an instrument on which the depository institution is primarily liable [...] (emphasis added).

45 Ibid. 5.

46 See generally ibid., 'Fast Answers: No Action Letters' (23 March 2017) U.S. Securities and Exchange Commission www.sec.gov/fast-answers/answersnoactionhtm.html accessed 3 January 2018.

47 See for example, 'Letter from Bursa Malaysia Securities Berhad to Securities and Exchange Commission', US Securities and Exchange Commission, 1 (10 September 2010) www.sec.gov/divisions/corpfin/cf-noaction/2010/bursamalaysia091010-902b-incoming.pdf accessed 3 January 2018 (US lawyer requested on behalf of Malaysian company Bursa Malaysia Securities Berhad/Bursa Malaysia Bonds Sdn Bhd a recommendation of no-action from the SEC regarding its operation as a designated offshore securities market (DOSM), which is essentially a request for approval of such status. Among other activities, the company listed *sukuk* on its trading platform).

48 *Re: Net Lease and Purchase Agreement*, NYSBL 96(1), NYS DFS – Banking Interpretations (12 April 1999) www.dfs.ny.gov/legal/interpret/lo990412.htm accessed 5 December 2017.

49 Ibid.

50 *Re: Murabaha Financing Facility/Islamic Home Finance Product*, NYSBL 96(1), NYS DFS – Banking Interpretations (27 August 2001) www.dfs.ny.gov/legal/interpret/lo010827.htm accessed 5 December 2017.

51 Ibid.

52 *Ahli United Bank (UK) PLC (Petition No M071001A)*, Advisory Opinion TSB-A-08(2)R (NYSDTF Taxpayer Services Div 28 April 2008).

53 See Vogel (n 7) 54. ('In addition, states such as New York and Illinois have enacted legislation intended to encourage Islamic finance transactions, such as the elimination of a double real estate transfer tax in an ijarah sale-leaseback transaction').

54 See ibid. 52:

> In the event that Islamic-structured products have been falsely marketed in the US as shariah-compliant, [...] there are three potential remedies available to an investor. [... A] contractual remedy, [...] may enable the investor to call an event of default (arising from the misrepresentation by the IFI of a material term of the contract) [...]. The second remedy is to institute a civil claim for misrepresentation. [...] The third remedy is only applicable if the relevant product is a securities offering that is made through a public or private offering and where a prospectus or private placement memorandum is issued that is untrue or misleading as to the shariah-compliance of the securities offered.

55 See ibid.

56 *Jacob & Youngs, Inc v Kent*, 230 NY 239 (1921).

57 See Vogel (n 16) 52.

58 *Jama v Guidance Residential, LLC*, Civil No 12-77(DSD/JSM) (D Minnesota 16 August 2012) (citing to Minn Stat §325F.69(1)).

59 Ibid.

60 See Vogel (n 7) 52.

61 For example, *Securities and Exchange Commission v Al-Raya Investment Company and Waleed Khalid Al-Braikan as Representative of the Heirs of Hazem Khalid Al-Braikan, et al.*, Civil Action No 1:09-CV-6533 (NRB) (SDNY) (alleging that the CEO for Al-Raya engineered false press releases to drive up the price of a company listed on the New York Stock Exchange ('NYSE'), and then afterwards closed his positions reaping huge profits).
62 See generally Restatement (Second) of the Conflicts of Laws §187 (Am Law Inst 1971) ('The law of the state chosen by the parties to govern their contractual rights and duties will be applied [...]').
63 *National Group for Communications & Computers v Lucent Technologies Intl*, 331 F Supp 2d 290, 293 (DNJ 2004).
64 Ibid. at 294; Federal Rules of Civil Procedure 44.1 ('In determining foreign law, the court may consider any relevant material or source, including testimony, whether or not submitted by a party or admissible under the Federal Rules of Evidence').
65 *National Group for Communications & Computers v Lucent Technologies Intl*, 331 F Supp 2d at 295–301.
66 See Kira A Davis, 'Judicial Estoppel and Inconsistent Positions of Law Applied to Fact and Pure Law' [2003] 89 Cornell L R 192, 198 ('Notwithstanding their uniform justification of the doctrine, the circuits have not agreed on its precise contours').
67 *Warda v Commr*, 15 F3d 533, 538 (6th Cir 1994) (quoting *Teledyne Indus, Inc v NLRB*, 911 F2d 1214, 1218 (6th Cir 1990)).
68 See *Shamil Bank of Bahrain EC v Beximco Pharm Ltd*, [2004] EWCA (Civ) 19, [1] at para 10, [2004] 1 WLR 1784 (appeal taken from Eng.)

> Until their defences were filed in this action, the appellants had never given any indication to the bank that they were dissatisfied on religious grounds with the arrangements agreed between the parties or that they sought to challenge them on the grounds that they did not comply with the principles of Sharia.

69 Saudi Basic Industries Corp. v Mobil Yanbu Petrochemical Co, 866 A 2d 1, 11, 32 (Del 2005).
70 The First Amendment to the US Constitution provides, 'Congress shall make no law respecting an establishment of religion, or prohibiting the free exercise thereof [...]'. US Constitution amendment I.
71 *El-Farra v Sayyed*, 226 SW3d 792, 793 (2006).
72 Ibid.
73 Ibid.
74 Ibid.
75 Ibid.
76 Ibid.
77 Ibid.
78 Ibid. 795.
79 *Serbian Eastern Orthodox Diocese v Milivojevich*, 426 US 696, 710, 96 SCt 2372, 49 LEd2d 151 (1976).
80 *El-Farra v Sayyed*, 226 SW3d at 794.
81 Ibid. 796 (citing *Cha v Korean Presbyterian Church of Washington*, 262 Va 604, 553 SE2d 511 (Va 2001) (church's decisions about appointment and removal of minister is beyond subject-matter jurisdiction of civil courts).
82 Ibid.
83 Ibid. 796–797.
84 See Metcalf (n 1) ('Parties choose New York law with the expectation that these contracts will be treated essentially like loan agreements under New York law. Conventional US lenders favour this treatment, because they understand the interpretation of loan agreements').

85 See Vogel (n 7) 51 (stating that the OCC approved the *ijarah* structure for residential financing because it was ' "functionally equivalent" to conventional secured real estate lending' and that it approved use of the *murabahah* structure 'because this structure was deemed to be "functionally equivalent" to conventional real estate mortgage transactions').

86 See Haltom (n 4) 18:

> In the OCC's view, because the purchase and sale transactions are executed simultaneously, the bank's ownership is merely for "a moment in time," and therefore the Islamic contracts avoid the type of risk that real estate restrictions were intended to limit. (The joint ownership that defines musharaka contracts, on the other hand, is not currently approved for use by banks and is used in the United States only by nonbank mortgage lenders.) From an accounting standpoint, the transaction appears as a loan (an asset) on the bank's balance sheet.

87 See Metcalf (n 1) ('The New York State Banking Department also approved similar home mortgage financing products during the same period, and specifically referred to and agreed with the reasoning adopted by the OCC in its approvals').

88 See 26 USC § 163(a) ('There shall be allowed as a deduction all interest paid or accrued within the taxable year on indebtedness') and 26 USC § 163(h)(3)(B)(ii) ('The aggregate amount treated as acquisition indebtedness for any period shall not exceed $1,000,000 ($500,000 in the case of a married individual filing a separate return)').

89 See 26 USC §1031(a)

> No gain or loss shall be recognized on the exchange of property held for productive use in a trade or business or for investment if such property is exchanged solely for property of like kind which is to be held either for productive use in a trade or business or for investment.

90 See Vogel (n 7) 51 ('In addition, states such as New York and Illinois have enacted legislation intended to encourage Islamic finance transactions, such as the elimination of a double real estate transfer tax in an ijarah sale-leaseback transaction').

91 Haltom (n 4) 18.

92 See *Shamil Bank*, [2004] EWCA (Civ) 19, [1] at para. 60, [2004] 1 WLR 1784

> In that respect, the submissions [...] demonstrate that their sole interest was to obtain advances of funds to be used as working capital and that they were indifferent to the form of the agreements required by the Bank or the impact of Sharia law upon their validity.

93 *United Islamic Society v Masjed Abubakr Al-Seddiq, Inc*, No A16–0140 (Mich Ct App 29 August 2016) (unpublished).

94 Ibid.

95 Ibid.

96 The trial court wrote as well, 'UIS's allegations could be analyzed according to trust law and the rule of majority representation, both neutral principles of law'. ibid.

97 Ibid.

98 Ibid.

99 The documents pertinent this discussion, i.e. the arguments to recharacterize the *sukuk* as a loan, are not widely available. The documents to which I cite are mostly trial documents and unpublished memorandum orders obtained from www.pacer.gov/, which is the electronic documents database for US federal courts. These documents are available to the general public for a fee; however, I advise researchers interested in this case to begin their investigation in the documents available under the adversarial case *In re East Cameron Partners, LP*, Adv Proc No 08-05041 (Bankruptcy Court WDLa).

100 See Michael J T McMillen, 'An Introduction to Shari'ah Considerations in Bankruptcy and Insolvency Contexts and Islamic Finance's First Bankruptcy (East Cameron)' [2010] http://ssrn.com/abstract=1826246 accessed 20 October 2017.
101 Please note that the following is an abbreviation of both the facts and legal arguments. Various agents and entities are unnamed for the sake of clarity and are instead identified with whose interests they are aligned, i.e. ECG and the Sukuk Certificateholders or ECP. Furthermore, the intricacies of the bankruptcy and various temporary orders sought in this case do not provide as much insight as to the purpose of this passage as do the arguments in the adversarial proceedings concerning the declaratory judgment; thus, such matters are left out, once again for the sake of clarity and brevity.
102 *In re East Cameron Partners, LP*, 'Memorandum in Support of the Sukuk Certificateholders' Mot (I) to Dismiss Pl ['s] Verified Compl for TRO, Prelim Injunction, & Declaratory J, or in the Alternative (II) for More Definite Statement, 22 December 2008' [10], Bankruptcy Case No 08-51207; Adv Proc No 08-05041 (Bankruptcy Court, WDLa) (hereinafter 'Memorandum in Support').
103 Ibid. [12].
104 McMillen (n 100) 22.
105 Memorandum in Support (n 102) [29]; *In re East Cameron Partners, LP*, 'Verified Complaint Of East Cameron Partners, LP for TRO, Preliminary Injunction, & Declaratory J, 16 October 2008', Bankruptcy Case No 08-51207 [92]; Adv Proc No 08-05041 (Bankruptcy Court, WDLa) (hereinafter 'Verified Complaint').
106 McMillen (n 100) 23.
107 Ibid.
108 Verified Complaint (n 105) [107].
109 Ibid.
110 An antichresis under Louisiana law is a loan arrangement which provides for the transfer of possession of pledged property as security for a loan, similar to when one pawns and item but with immovable property. La Civ Code art 3135; Verified Complaint (n 105) [69–72].
111 *In re Senior-G & A Operating Co, Inc*, 957 F2d 1290, 1293 (5th Cir 1992).
112 Ibid. 1296.
113 Ibid. 1294.
114 Ibid. 1293.
115 Ibid. 1301–02.
116 Verified Complaint (n 105) [89]–[92].
117 Ibid. [95].
118 *In re East Cameron Partners, LP*, 'The Sukuk Certificateholders' Mot (I) to Dismiss Pl ['s] Verified Compl for TRO, Prelim Injunction, & Declaratory J, or in the Alternative (II) for More Definite Statement, 22 December 2008' [8–10], Bankruptcy Case No 08-51207; Adv Proc No 08-05041 (Bankruptcy Court WDLa).
119 Memorandum in Support (n 102) [25].
120 Ibid. [52] (citing La UCC §9–109(e).
121 Ibid. [64] (citing *In re Senior-G & A*, 957 F2d at 1296).
122 Ibid. [65].
123 Ibid. [75].
124 Ibid. [79].
125 *In re East Cameron Partners, LP*, 'Order on Def [s'] Rule 12 Motions' at 3, Bankruptcy Case No 08-51207; Adv Proc No 08-05041 (Bankruptcy Court WDLa 2009) (unpublished order 17 April 2009).
126 Ibid.
127 Federal Rule of Civil Procedure 12(b)(1) ('[A] party may assert the following defenses by motion: (1) lack of subject-matter jurisdiction; [...]').

128 Ibid.; also see Memorandum in Support (n 102) [91]–[94] (referring to Sukuk Certificateholders' request that court decline to exercise jurisdiction pursuant to the Declaratory Judgment Act).
129 9 USC §2.
130 9 USC §1 et seq.
131 9 USC §201.
132 For example, the Texas General Arbitration Act provides similar protections. See Tex Civ Pract & Rem Code Ann §171.001 ('A written agreement to arbitrate is valid and enforceable [...]'), and also, Tex Civ Pract & Rem Code Ann §171.087 ('Unless grounds are offered for vacating, modifying, or correcting an award under Section 171.088 or 171.091, the court, on application of a party, shall confirm the award').
133 Convention on the Recognition and Enforcement of Foreign Arbitral Awards art. V 2(b), 10 June, 1958, 21 UST 2517, 330 UNTS 38 [hereinafter New York Convention]:

> 2. Recognition and enforcement of an arbitral award may also be refused if the competent authority in the country where recognition and enforcement is sought finds that: (a) The subject matter of the difference is not capable of settlement by arbitration under the law of that country; or (b) The recognition or enforcement of the award would be contrary to the public policy of that country.

134 Richard A Cole, 'The Public Policy Exception to the New York Convention on the Recognition and Enforcement of Arbitral Awards' [1985–86] vol. 1:2 Ohio St J on Disp Resol 365.
135 *Jabri v Qaddura*, 108 SW3d 404, 413 (Tex App—Fort Worth 2003, no pet).
136 Ibid. 407–408.
137 Ibid. 413 ('Each wants to be appointed sole managing conservator of the two children, with the possessory conservator ordered to pay child support').

6 Settlement of Islamic finance disputes in Malaysia

Adnan Trakic

Introduction

Malaysia is a global leader in Islamic finance. Thomson Reuters's Islamic Finance Development Indicator 2017 recognized Malaysia as the most developed Islamic finance market globally for the fifth consecutive year.[1] Similarly, the Islamic Finance Country Index 2017 also ranked Malaysia first in terms of Islamic finance leadership.[2] Malaysia has a robust Islamic finance industry which is made up of Islamic banking, *takaful* (insurance), Islamic money market, and Islamic capital market. As at the end of 2017, Malaysia's total Islamic banking assets stood at US$204.4 billion, placing it third globally, immediately after Iran and Saudi Arabia.[3] Malaysia also continues to be the world leader in *sukuk* (Islamic bonds). In July 2017, Malaysia's Tadau Energy Sdn Bhd issued the world's first green *sukuk*.[4] One month later, another green *sukuk* was issued by Quantum Solar Park Malaysia Bhd.[5] By the end of 2017, Malaysia's total outstanding *sukuk* amounted to US$202.2 billion. Malaysia is also a key destination for Islamic funds globally in terms of Islamic wealth management with some US$28.3 billion of Islamic assets under management as of 2017.

Malaysia's achievements in Islamic finance occurred gradually over the last 40 years.[6] Innovative thinking and a constant quest to improve the state of Islamic finance industry spearheaded by Bank Negara Malaysia (BNM),[7] the Government of Malaysia, and various Islamic financial institutions (IFIs), resulted in a steady and robust, two digit annual growth of Islamic finance. There has also been a steady growth of products and services offered by IFIs. These products and services needed to comply with two sets of laws; Shari'ah as well as conventional Malaysian finance laws. This necessitated the development of a legal framework which will not only support and recognize the Shari'ah underlying nature of what appears to be ordinary conventional banking and finance products but also to ensure that the unique Shari'ah compliant nature of these products and services will be enforced when disputes arise.

Having adequate laws requiring Shari'ah compliance from IFIs is important. Of equal importance is, however, having an adequate dispute resolution mechanism which will enforce these laws. It is often the case that the significance of dispute resolution mechanisms for Islamic finance disputes is underestimated.

Litigation of an Islamic finance dispute before a secular court or a court which is not willing to recognize the Shari'ah underlying nature of Islamic finance contract may result in a pronouncement which will effectively convert Islamic finance contract into a conventional interest-bearing agreement. This is well illustrated in *Islamic Investment Company of the Gulf (Bahamas) Ltd v Symphony Gems NV. & Ors*[8] and *Shamil Bank of Bahrain EC v Beximco Pharmaceuticals Ltd*[9] where the English court did not enforce the Shari'ah aspect of *murabahah* (mark-up sale) agreement and, instead, treated it as a conventional loan agreement.[10] Similar problems arose with Islamic finance disputes adjudicated before the courts in Malaysia until steps were taken by both the Malaysian Parliament and the courts to remedy the problem. Therefore, it is worthwhile exploring how Islamic finance disputes are resolved in Malaysia.

As Malaysia has both civil and Shari'ah courts,[11] an appropriate starting point for this chapter would be to establish which of the two courts has jurisdiction over Islamic finance disputes. This is done in the next section. The chapter then proceeds to provide a brief overview of the wider legal context in which IFIs operate in Malaysia. In particular, this section examines the role of federal legislation, such as Central Bank of Malaysia Act 2009 and Islamic Financial Services Act 2013 in the regulation and supervision of IFIs. One significant aspect of that supervision is in relation to Shari'ah compliance. These laws provide a unique framework for the resolution of Islamic finance disputes involving questions on Shari'ah compliance. The litigation of Shari'ah questions in the Malaysian courts will, arguably, not only ensure that the Shari'ah underlying nature of Islamic finance agreement is upheld but it will also recognize and enforce other civil (common law) aspects of the agreement. The chapter then explores the alternatives to litigation, such as mediation and arbitration. So far, these alternatives have not been a popular choice for the settlement of Islamic finance disputes. Why is that so? Is there something inherent in mediation and arbitration that makes them less appealing, particularly to IFIs? This chapter seeks to explore the strengths and weaknesses of both litigation and the alternatives, and assess their suitability in the context of Islamic finance industry in Malaysia.

Jurisdiction of the courts

Malaysia has a dual court system which consists of civil and Shari'ah courts. Civil (common law) courts have exclusive jurisdiction to hear matters on which the Federal Parliament is allowed to legislate. These are the matters mentioned under List I (Federal List), Schedule Nine of the Federal Constitution.[12] Finance, including Islamic finance, is one of the matters which falls under the jurisdiction of the Federal Parliament and, by extension, the civil courts. Shari'ah courts, on the other hand, have exclusive jurisdiction over the matters stated under List II (State List), Ninth Schedule of the Federal Constitution.[13] These are the matters on which the respective State Legislative Assemblies may legislate and the Shari'ah courts adjudicate. List II is mostly in relation to personal matters of Muslims, such as marriage, divorce, inheritance and, to a limited extent, some criminal offences not mentioned in the Penal Code.[14] The Shari'ah courts' jurisdiction is only over Muslims (human beings).[15] It does not extend to companies or other incorporated entities.[16]

The question as to whether an IFI can be considered as a Muslim was raised, in a form of preliminary objection, in the case of *Bank Islam Malaysia Berhad v Adnan bin Omar*.[17] The defendant (Adnan) claimed that the High Court (civil court) does not have jurisdiction to hear the case as it involves Muslim parties and an Islamic financing facility. Instead, he argued that the Shari'ah court should hear the case. He relied on article 121 (1A) of the Federal Constitution which prohibits the civil courts usurping the jurisdiction of the Shari'ah courts.[18] The plaintiff (Bank Islam Malaysia Berhad) countered by saying that the plaintiff was an incorporated company, and as such, does not have a religion. In other words, the plaintiff cannot be considered a Muslim or non-Muslim. One of the consequences of incorporation is that an incorporated legal entity is separate in law from its members and personal features of the members, such as religion, race, and gender cannot be imputed onto the corporate entity. The High Court agreed with the plaintiff's submission and held that the jurisdiction of the Shar'ah courts is confined to the matters mentioned under the State List. Islamic finance is a commercial matter, and as such, is included under the Federal List. The court also observed that the plaintiff, being a corporate entity, could not be considered a Muslim. Therefore, the defendant's preliminary objection was rejected.

There has, however, been an argument that the Shari'ah courts' jurisdiction over Islamic finance could be implied from some of the items mentioned expressly under the State List.[19] For example, 'Zakah, Fitrah and Baitulmal or similar Islamic religious revenue' fall under the exclusive jurisdiction of the Shari'ah courts.[20] Could revenue generated by IFIs be considered as 'Islamic religious revenue'? The answer is perhaps in the affirmative. But, before the phrase 'Islamic religious revenue' there is the word 'similar' denoting that it is similar to the revenue generated through *zakat*, *fitrah* and *baitulmal*. The revenue generated by IFIs cannot be considered 'similar' to that of the above three. IFIs are incorporated and profit-driven companies. This is not to say that the institutions of *zakat*, *fitrah* and *baitulmal* are not interested in generating profits and becoming sustainable. But, unlike IFIs and other incorporated companies, their primary objective is not profit maximization and the generation of shareholder value. Their main purpose is the socio-economic welfare of the society, eradication of poverty, and equitable distribution of wealth. They are there to serve the society and not to serve their own interests. Should IFIs have the same objectives? Have they deviated from what they were supposed to be? These questions will not be addressed in this chapter, but are worthy of discussion in other forums.

Another argument raised in favour of the Shari'ah courts having jurisdiction over Islamic finance disputes is that Shari'ah courts already have exclusive jurisdiction over 'matters of Islamic law and doctrine'.[21] Islamic finance is inseparable from Islamic law and doctrine. The word 'Islamic' denotes that it is a finance rooted in Islamic jurisprudence. There is no doubt that Shari'ah questions raised in Islamic finance disputes are matters of Islamic law and doctrine. But, would reference of these disputes to Shari'ah courts really solve the problem? Are the Shari'ah courts more competent in Islamic finance than the civil courts? They may well be but it is worth noting that current Islamic finance contracts are far more complex and sophisticated than those discussed in classical Islamic jurisprudence. Islamic finance products now are developed by not only Shari'ah scholars but also by individuals with expertise in conventional finance and law. The Malaysian court has rightly pointed out that even though the facility provided by IFI is an Islamic finance transaction, the law applicable to that transaction is the same law which applies to conventional finance transaction, such as the National Land Code and the Rules of High Court.[22] Therefore, the fact that Islamic finance is governed by both Islamic and conventional laws raises the question of which of the two, the civil or Shari'ah court, is more competent to decide Islamic finance disputes. The answer is each, in their respective areas. Shari'ah court judges are likely to be more competent and knowledgeable in Islamic law, while the civil courts judges are better equipped with the procedural and conventional aspects of the law.

It was thought that the solution to the above dilemma was found when the Muamalat Division of the High Court of Malaya was established to hear and decide only *muamalat* (Islamic commercial) cases. Muamalat Court, however, is not a separate court. It is an administrative arrangement made only in the High Court at Kuala Lumpur. The judge deciding these cases is likely to have some knowledge on Islamic law but that does not necessarily make him/her competent to make the rulings on the Shari'ah questions raised. The Former Chief Justice of Malaysia, Tun Abdul Hamid Mohamad, was of the view that Muamalat Court does not solve the problem.[23] Muamalat Court, according to him, is nothing but a name given to a division of the existing High Court in Kuala Lumpur.[24] In other words, it is still the same conventional court. Therefore, he suggested the amendment of the relevant laws to enable Shari'ah questions raised before the civil courts to be referred to the Shari'ah Advisory Council of BNM. The current legislative framework for the dispute resolution of Islamic finance cases in Malaysia is precisely what Tun Abdul Hamid envisaged.

Legal framework for Islamic finance

Malaysia's financial system consists of both conventional and Islamic financial elements. Malaysia appears to be the only country which has officially recognized the duality of its financial system by enacting a specific provision in the Central Bank of Malaysia Act 2009 (CBMA) to that effect. Section 27 of the CBMA provides the following: 'The financial system in Malaysia shall consist of the conventional financial system and the Islamic financial system'.[25] The enactment of this section was a significant step forward and meant that Islamic finance is no longer a peripheral development in the Malaysian financial sphere. To ensure that the Islamic financial system continues to develop and prosper in par with its conventional counterpart, the CBMA has entrusted BNM with the task of developing and promoting Malaysia as an international Islamic financial centre.[26]

In line with its statutory duty, BNM has been actively involved in the enactment of laws, standards, and guidelines which have been of critical importance to the industry.[27] One of BNM's most important contributions to Islamic finance was the development of what is known today as Shari'ah governance. It is the Shari'ah governance as an additional layer of overall corporate governance that makes IFIs different from their conventional counterparts. Shari'ah governance provides the necessary assurances to the stakeholders of the IFIs that their products and services comply with Shari'ah principles.

Shari'ah governance, in Malaysia, is two-tiered. At the institutional level, every IFIs is required to have a Shari'ah Committee (SC) whose main task is to ensure that products, services, operations and documentation of the IFIs comply with Shari'ah. This is required by the Shari'ah Governance Framework for Islamic Financial Institutions of BNM (the Guidelines) which came into force in 2011.[28] Even though the Guidelines were issued pursuant to, *inter alia*, the laws which have been repealed, such as the Islamic Banking Act 1983 (IBA) and the Takaful Act 1984, their continuation and enforceability has been ensured by the Islamic Financial Services Act 2013 (IFSA).[29] IFSA is a federal law and it provides for the regulation and supervision of IFIs. It is a significantly improved version of its predecessor, IBA, whose content was kept brief.[30] An IFI, according to section 28 of IFSA, '... shall at all times ensure that its aims and operations, business, affairs and activities are in compliance with Shariah'.[31] Non-compliance with this section would, on conviction, render a person[32] liable 'to imprisonment for a term not exceeding eight years or to a fine not exceeding twenty-five million ringgit or to both'.[33] IFSA also requires IFIs to establish SCs, appointment of which is to be done in accordance with BNM's Guidelines.[34]

In addition to the SCs, BNM was instrumental in the creation of the Shari'ah Advisory Council (SAC) at the national level. The SAC was first established in 1997 by virtue of section 16B of the old Central Bank of Malaysia Act 1958. The main purpose behind the creation of the SAC was to have one single authority at the national level to ensure uniformity in the process of approving products and services and to avoid any possible inconsistencies in rulings among SCs of various banks.[35] Section 16B of the Act 1958 provided that the SAC shall be:

> the authority for the ascertainment of Islamic law for the purposes of Islamic banking business, takaful business, Islamic financial business, Islamic development financial business, or any other business which is based on Syariah principles and is supervised and regulated by the Bank.[36]

Section 16B also provided the SAC with power to make rulings on Shari'ah questions referred to it by a court or arbitrator. The courts, however, were not under obligation to refer the Shari'ah questions to the SAC and, even if they did make the reference, the rulings made by the SAC were not binding on them.[37]

As a result, the courts, in some cases, have not referred Shari'ah questions to the SAC.

The High Court decision in *Arab-Malaysian Finance Bhd v Taman Ihsan Jaya Sdn Bhd & Ors*,[38] in particular, stands out as the judge in this case, who was not trained in Shari'ah, decided, without any reference to the SAC, that *bai bitham ajil* (deferred payment sale), which at the time was one of the most popular Islamic banking contracts, was null and void due to its non-compliance with the religion of Islam. This decision caused discomfort and uncertainty among the industry players. Very soon after that, the Court of Appeal in *Bank Islam Malaysia Berhad v Lim Kok Hoe & Anor (and 8 Other Appeals)*[39] reversed the High Court decision by saying that:

> …judges in civil court should not take upon themselves to declare whether a matter is in accordance to the Religion of Islam or otherwise … it needs consideration by eminent jurists who are properly qualified in the field of Islamic jurisprudence … The court, will have to assume that the Syariah advisory body of the individual bank and now the Syariah Advisory Council under the aegis of Bank Negara Malaysia, would have discharge their statutory duty to ensure that the operation of the Islamic banks are within the ambit of the Religion of Islam.[40]

The above Court of Appeal decision was, according to the representatives from BNM and the Attorney General Chambers, one of the main reasons for the repeal of the Central Bank Act 1958.[41] The Central Bank of Malaysia Act 2009 (CBMA) was passed to replace the 1958 Act and the entire Part VII of the CBMA (sections 51–58) has been dedicated to the SAC and its role in the ascertainment of Islamic law for the purpose of Islamic finance.

The CBMA, like its predecessor, provides for the establishment of the SAC.[42] Section 100 of the CBMA 2009 provides that the SAC and its members appointed under the old Act shall be deemed to be established and appointed under the new Act.[43] Likewise, all BNM's directives, notices or circulars on Islamic finance and all rulings made by the SAC under the old Act shall be deemed to have been made or done under the corresponding provisions under the new Act. This provision ensures that there is a continuity of BNM's and the SAC's efforts in the development of Islamic finance. Members of the SAC are appointed by the Malaysian King on the advice of the Finance Minister and in consultation with BNM.[44] The fact that members of the SAC are appointed by the King, who is the head of state, symbolizes the importance of the SAC. The appointed members must be either Shari'ah experts or have knowledge and experience in Shari'ah and in banking, finance, law or other related disciplines. The SAC consists of 10 members who meet 12 times a year and their decisions are based on a two-thirds majority.[45] BNM has formed a secretariat to assist the SAC in carrying its functions.[46]

The SAC has two main functions.[47] First, is to act as an advisor to BNM and IFIs on any matters pertaining to Islamic finance. While it is mandatory for

BNM to consult the SAC on any Shari'ah compliance matters and implement its rulings made upon such reference, IFIs are under no obligation to refer to the SAC's rulings or seek its advice.[48] IFIs have, as indicated earlier, their own SCs from which they can resolve the necessary Shari'ah compliance issues.[49] If IFIs, however, decide to make the reference or seek the advice from the SAC, the ruling or advice provided by the SAC shall be binding on them.[50]

The second function of the SAC is to make rulings on Shari'ah questions referred to it either by the court or arbitrator. This is perhaps its most important and, at the same time, most contentious function. Section 56 of the CBMA makes it mandatory for the court or arbitrator to refer Shari'ah questions in Islamic finance disputes to the SAC for ascertainment.[51] Section 57 of the CBMA clarifies that the rulings made by the SAC shall be binding on the court or arbitrator.[52] This function of the SAC relates to the manner in which Islamic finance disputes are to be resolved. It clearly demarcates the roles that the court and SAC have in adjudicating Islamic finance disputes. In other words, any question which necessitates Shari'ah determination, must be resolved by the SAC. The role of the court is to apply the ruling onto the facts and decide the case. It seems as if sections 56 and 57 allow for the judicial functions of the court to be appropriated by the SAC which is, after all, a committee housed by the agency under the Executive Branch of Government. Would this be a fair characterization of the SAC's functions? In order to have a clear understanding of the SAC's role in the adjudication of Islamic finance cases, there is a need to consider recent judicial decisions on the matter.

The adjudication of Islamic finance disputes by the courts

In 2012, the Court of Appeal delivered a landmark judicial decision in the case of *Tan Sri Abdul Khalid Ibrahim v Bank Islam Malaysia Berhad*.[53] The appellant/plaintiff (Khalid) entered into a *bai bithaman ajil* (BBA) financing facility agreement with the respondent/defendant, Bank Islam Malaysia (BIM). On 10 May 2007, Khalid filed a High Court suit against BIM on the ground that the BBA facility was not Shari'ah compliant and, therefore, BIM breached the license issued under section 3 of the Islamic Banking Act 1983.[54] On 24 May 2007, BIM also filed a separate suit in the High Court against Khalid for breach of terms of the BBA facility and asked for the recovery of money owed by Khalid. Approximately a year later, the High Court consolidated both suits into one in which Khalid was the plaintiff and BIM was the defendant.

On 13 June 2011, BIM made an application to the High Court to refer the questions in relation to Shari'ah compliance of the BBA facility to the SAC of BNM for ascertainment. Khalid objected to this application and argued that sections 56 and 57 of the CBMA, which had been used as the basis of BIM's application, were unconstitutional. On 13 July 2011, Zawawi Salleh J (as he then was) referred the question concerning the constitutionality of sections 56 and 57 to the Federal Court for its determination. Interestingly, the Federal Court declined to consider the matter saying that the High Court should have decided first if there were any Shari'ah questions to be considered before referring the matter to the Federal Court. Because of that, the Federal Court remitted the case back to the High Court. Consequently, Zawawi Salleh J heard BIM's application and concluded that there were Shari'ah questions which merited the referral to the SAC for its ruling. Khalid then appealed to the Court of Appeal. One of the main grounds of the appeal was that sections 56 and 57 are unconstitutional because they enable the SAC to usurp the functions of the court in ascertaining Shari'ah.

The Court of Appeal held that the test for determining whether the impugned sections are unconstitutional was to examine if the Parliament was empowered to enact these sections. The court concluded that Article 74(1) of the Federal Constitution clearly empowered the Parliament to make laws on any matters mentioned under Federal List (List 1) of the Ninth Schedule of the Federal Constitution. Item 4(k) of the List 1 provides: 'Civil and criminal law and procedure and the administration of justice, including: … (k) ascertainment of Islamic law and other personal laws for purposes of federal law'.[55] CBMA, the legislation which contains the impugned sections, is clearly a federal law and there is no doubt that the Parliament, by virtue of Item 4(k) of the List 1, was empowered to enact sections 56 and 57. Responding to Khalid's point that the SAC had usurped the judicial function of the court, the Court of Appeal cited article 121(1) of the Federal Constitution which provides that the courts 'shall have such jurisdiction and powers as may be conferred by or under federal law'.[56] In other words, sections 56 and 57 (federal law) have taken away the court's power to ascertain Shari'ah for the purpose of Islamic finance. That function has been given to the SAC.

Is this a judicial function? The Court of Appeal was of the view that it is not. The court's position was that the role of the SAC is more akin to that of 'a statutory expert'.[57] The court stated:

> The duty of the SAC is confined exclusively to the ascertainment of the Islamic law on financial matters or business. The judicial function is within the domain of the court, ie, to decide on the issues which the parties have pleaded. The fact that the court is bound by the ruling of the SAC under s. 57 does not detract from the judicial functions and duties of the court in providing a resolution to the dispute(s) which the parties have submitted to the jurisdiction of the court. In applying the SAC ruling to the particular facts of the case before the court, the judicial functions of the court to hear and determine a dispute remain inviolated. The SAC, like any other expert, does not perform any judicial function in the determination of the ultimate outcome of the litigation before the court, and so cannot be said to usurp the judicial functions of the court. Hence, s. 56 and s. 57 are valid and constitutional.[58]

How did the court come to this conclusion? The court claimed that the SAC does not violate the court's judicial function as the SAC only makes a ruling on

Shari'ah questions. The ultimate decision in the case rests with the court. That would be an acceptable argument but only if the court is free to decide the case without having to apply the Shari'ah rulings issued by the SAC. If the SAC decides that the BBA facility is Shari'ah compliant, then that ruling, which the court is bound to accept, will certainly have a direct impact on the ultimate outcome of the litigation. Therefore, the court, at least in theory, gets to be the one who makes a final decision but, there is no doubt that the scope of its decision becomes foreseeable in the circumstances where it has no choice but to accept and enforce the ruling made by the SAC. This arrangement becomes even more unusual when the statutory expert in question, the SAC, is set up under BNM which is an agency of the Executive Branch of Government (Ministry of Finance).

The court's claim that the SAC is like any other expert is also problematic. It is a basic common law norm that an expert evidence (opinion) provided by either a gazetted expert such as the SAC or expert that comes under preview of the Evidence Act 1950 (Malaysia) should not be binding on the court.[59] The court should be able to hear evidence from both parties' experts. While it is true that the party appointed experts are likely to present opinions which are in favour of the appointing party, the credibility and quality of their evidence is normally established through cross-examination. The court is also not under the obligation to accept expert opinions if the court is of the view that their opinions are not credible. The SAC has two characteristics which differentiates it from a typical expert witness. First, the SAC's ruling (opinion) cannot be cross-examined nor challenged by the parties. Second, the SAC's ruling is final and binding on the court. These SAC's unique characteristics lead to a following question. Is an opinion of a statutory expert, which has a binding effect on the court, tantamount to appropriation of the judicial power of the court?

As it has already been indicated, the Court of Appeal, in this case, decided that it does not. However, in 2017, the Federal Court, the Malaysian apex court, delivered its decision in *Semenyih Jaya Sdn Bhd v Pentadbir Tanah Daerah Hulu Langat*.[60] This was not an Islamic finance case. Nevertheless, one of the issues raised in the case is relevant to this discussion. The court was asked to decide whether section 40D of the Land Acquisition Act 1960, which allowed two assessors (a government valuer and a private valuer) to conclusively determine the amount of compensation payable to a person whose land has been acquired by the government, is unconstitutional in view of article 121 of the Federal Constitution. The Federal Court unanimously decided that 'the judicial power of the court resides in the Judiciary and no other as is explicit in art 121(1) of the Constitution'.[61] The court also said that the 'discharge of judicial power by non-qualified persons (and not by judges or judicial officers) or non-judicial personages render the said exercise ultra vires art 121 of the Federal Constitution in the judge and not the assessors'.[62] The Federal Court concluded that section 40D, which made the decision of the assessors final and binding on the parties and the judge, was in contravention with article 121(1) of the Federal Constitution and, therefore, it had to be struck down. The court held that the judge should not have 'merely rubber-stamped the decision of the assessors'.[63] A similar observation was made again in 2018 in the case of *Indira Gandhi Mutho v Pengarah Jabatan Agama Islam Perak*,[64] where the Federal Court stated that

> the jurisdiction of the High Courts cannot be truncated or infringed. Therefore, even if an administrative decision is declared to be final by a governing statute, an aggrieved party is not barred from resorting to the supervisory jurisdiction of the court.[65]

Will these two Federal Court decisions have any effect on the Court of Appeal decision in *Tan Sri Khalid's* case? The constitutional issues raised in these cases are similar. How different is the SAC from the statutory assessors under section 40D of the Land Acquisition Act 1960? Both seem to be external bodies created by statutes whose decisions are final and binding on the court. They purportedly act as statutory experts with the aim of giving the court expert opinions. But, as the Federal Court indicated, the finality of assessors' decision and the judge's inability to question their judgment is tantamount to infringement of the judicial functions of the court. The court function cannot be reduced to that of rubber-stamping whatever is decided by the statutory experts such as the SAC. Therefore, it is submitted that the above Federal Court decisions indeed could have damaging implications on the constitutionality of sections 56 and 57 of the CBMA. As of the time of writing this chapter, it has been reported that a nine-member Federal Court bench is going to deliver its decision on the constitutionality of sections 56 and 57 of the CBMA, in the case of *Kuwait Finance House (M) Bhd v JRI Resources Sdn Bhd*.[66] It remains to be seen, however, if the Federal Court will be prepared, to apply the same reasoning as it did in *Semenyih Jaya* and *Indira Gandhi*.

Another line of reasoning that the Federal Court could consider is to look at the practicality and benefits that sections 56 and 57 provide. What is the alternative if these two sections were to be repealed? Perhaps going back to the beginning where the courts will have a full autonomy to adjudicate and make rules on Shari'ah questions. The experience of the courts prior to enactment of sections 56 and 57 is informative here. One such case was briefly mentioned earlier namely the High Court judgment in *Arab-Malaysian Finance Bhd v Taman Ihsan Jaya Sdn Bhd & Ors*.[67] Same as in *Tan Sri Khalid's* case, the issue raised was in relation to Shari'ah compliance of the BBA financing facility. But, at that time, the CBMA was not in force and the referral of Shari'ah questions to the SAC for ascertainment was at a discretion of the judge. Abdul Wahab Patail J (as he then was), decided not to refer the Shari'ah question to the SAC and instead came up with Shari'ah ruling on his own. He held that the BBA is not Shari'ah compliant because, *inter alia*, it is permissible only under *Shafi'* school of thought.[68] Other schools of thought (*Maliki, Hanbali*, and *Hanafi*) have categorically rejected it and, according to the learned judge, an Islamic banking product which is offered to all Muslims, irrespective of which school of thought they belong to, must be permissible by all recognized schools of thought.[69]

Therefore, the learned judge declared that the BBA facility does not comply with Shari'ah since, among other things, it does not comply with other schools of thought. This decision has been widely criticized as an inaccurate representation of Shari'ah position on the matter.[70]

The judgment was also strongly criticised by the Court of Appeal in *Bank Islam Malaysia Berhad v Lim Kok Hoe & Anor (and 8 Other Appeals).*[71] Raus Sharif JCA (as he then was) delivering the judgment of the court stated:

> … we do not think the Religion of Islam is confined to the four mazhabs alone as the sources of Islamic law are not limited to the opinions of the four imams and the schools of jurisprudence named after them. As we all know, Islamic law is derived from the primary sources i.e., the Holy Quran and the Hadith and secondary sources. There are other secondary sources of Islamic law in addition to the jurisprudence of the four mazhabs. In this respect, it is our view that judges in civil court should not take upon themselves to declare whether a matter is in accordance to the Religion of Islam or otherwise. As rightly pointed out by Suriyadi J (as he then was) in *Arab-Malaysian Merchant Bank Bhd v Silver Concept Sdn Bhd* [2006] 8 CLJ 9 that in the civil court 'not every presiding judge is a Muslim, and even if so, may not be sufficiently equipped to deal with matters, which ulamak take years to comprehend'. Thus, whether the bank business is in accordance with the Religion of Islam, it needs consideration by eminent jurists who are properly qualified in the field of Islamic jurisprudence.[72]

The decision in *Taman Ihsan Jaya* and the subsequent setting aside of it in *Lim Kok Hoe* are believed to be the reasons for the enactment of sections 56 and 57 of the CBMA. Since the enactment of these provisions, the SAC has full responsibility in pronouncing Shari'ah rulings and the issue seems to be resolved. Sections 56 and 57 have been welcomed by Islamic finance practitioners and Shari'ah scholars. But, the customers and legal scholars are cautious given that fact that the court, a constitutionally guaranteed administer of justice, has been side-lined on this. This concern has also been shared by some members of the judiciary. For example, Hamid Sultan Abu Backer JC (as he then was) in *Majlis Amanah Rakyat v Bas Bin Ali,*[73] made the following remarks by way of *obiter*:

> The common notion that the Islamic jurists or the Shariah Advisory Boards were the sole arbiter for determining whether a shariah financial instrument is shariah compliant is flawed. The court is the supreme body to decide what is right and what is wrong in a given circumstance, and hence, is the final decision maker to decide whether a contract or an Islamic product based on Murabaha, Bay al Inah or Mudarabah principles as the case may be is valid or otherwise.[74]

As far as the lower courts are concerned, they seem to have been fully complying with sections 56 and 57. This can be seen from two very recent High Court decisions involving Islamic finance disputes. On 13 February 2018, the High Court delivered a judgment in *Bank Kerjasama Rakyat Malaysia Bhd v MME Reality & Management Sdn Bhd*.[75] In this case, the customer of the bank challenged the Shari'ah compliance of the *bai inah* (sale and buy back) financing facility. The customer argued that the facility was not valid as it contradicted the SAC's published rulings on *bai inah*. The SAC's rulings[76] stipulated that a valid *bai inah* contract must not, among other things, contain a repurchase of the asset clause in it and the sequence of the component contracts (Asset Purchase Agreement and Asset Sale Agreement) must be correct. The court made a reference to the SAC's published rulings and found that the *bai inah* facility contravened both of these conditions. Azizah Nawawi J applied the SAC's ruling on the Shari'ah questions posed to her and decided that the facility was rendered void. The judge concluded by saying 'I am therefore of the considered opinion that all SAC Rulings must be complied with'.[77] An alternative scenario would be that the learned judge ignores the SAC's rulings and instead makes a decision on the facts of the case or based on the views of invited expert witnesses. But, that would most certainly be in contravention of sections 56 and 57 of the CBMA.

On 21 February 2018, the High Court in *Sigur Ros Sdn Bhd v Maybank Islamic Berhad*,[78] again recognized the role of the SAC in the adjudication of Shari'ah questions. The plaintiff disputed the validity of the security documents on the ground that they were not in compliance with 'Broad Shariah Principles' and/or 'Broad Murabahah Requirements'. Mohamad Shariff Hj Abu Samah JC rejected the plaintiff's submission stating:

> In this case, the Plaintiffs' dispute of the validity of the security documents governing the Financings does not raise any triable issue as it is lacking in precision for failing to identify any express law, guidelines or Shariah Advisory Council resolutions with which the security documents might be alleged to be noncompliant. Instead, the Plaintiffs appear to have taken it upon themselves to set out (in paragraphs 6A and 6B of the ReAmended Statement of Claim) their own guidelines which they have loosely defined as "Broad Shariah Principles" and "Broad Murabahah Requirements". The so-called "Broad Shariah Principles" and "Broad Murabahah Requirements" are not in reference to any issued guidelines, rulings, or resolutions of the Shariah Advisory Council.[79]

It is obvious from this case that the court is only willing to accept the SAC's rulings pertaining to Shari'ah questions on Islamic finance.

From this brief examination of some of the latest cases on Islamic finance, it is apparent that the Malaysian courts judiciously follow the adjudication process envisaged by sections 56 and 57 of the CBMA. Clearly this process entails an abdication of the courts power over Shari'ah questions to the SAC. This also happens to be the major factor that fuels the concern that sections 56 and 57 could be declared as unconstitutional by the Federal Court in the near future. Nevertheless, the level of certainty in the adjudication of Islamic finance disputes that sections 56 and 57 brought could be the risk worth taking. The system appears to work. The courts seem to have little concern about referring Shari'ah questions to the SAC and following its rulings. In fact, one gets an impression by looking at some of the latest Islamic finance decisions that the courts are grateful that they do not need to dwell upon Shari'ah questions any more.

Alternatives to litigation

An inherent risk of litigating Islamic finance disputes is that the final outcome of litigation could convert an Islamic finance facility into a conventional one. When, for instance, the court is not interested in finding whether *murabahah* financing facility is Shari'ah compliant but rather whether it complies with the conventional laws governing the facility, then the purported *murabahah* becomes akin to a conventional loan agreement.[80] While this scenario is unlikely in Malaysia as long as sections 56 and 57 of the CBMA are in force, it is worth exploring if there are some other viable alternatives to litigation. It has been argued that a number of Alternative Dispute Resolution (ADR) mechanisms exist. Unlike litigation which inevitably leads to a win-lose situation, ADRs facilitate a win–win situation where parties obtain an amicable resolution of their dispute and ensure the ongoing relationship.[81] The most common ADR mechanisms are mediation and arbitration. The following section explores what are the prospects of these two mechanisms being used in the resolution of Islamic finance disputes in Malaysia.

Mediation

Mediation is a structured and interactive process where a neutral third party is appointed to help the disputing parties bridge their differences and come to an amicable settlement. Mediation can be conducted voluntarily between the parties devoid of any court assistance or court-annexed mediation where the court's involvement is necessary. For some reason, mediation has not been a popular choice in Islamic finance disputes. This is perhaps because IFIs feel that they can easily obtain a summary judgment in their favour against the defaulting parties. This belief is justified as the courts in Malaysia have been rather quick in treating all defaulters alike, even though, from the Islamic point of view, no two defaulters should be presumed to be alike without a detailed analysis of the reasons for their default. Therefore, the only way for IFIs to consider mediation seriously is if the court mandates it through a formalized court-annexed mediation.

In 2010, the then Chief Justice of Malaysia, Tun Zaki bin Azmi, issued the Practice Direction No. 5 of 2010 (Practice Direction on Mediation) in which he directed the judges of the High Court, Sessions Court and Magistrates to encourage the litigating parties, at the pre-trial case management stage, to opt for court-annexed mediation.[82] In 2011, the Kuala Lumpur Court Mediation Centre (later renamed into the Court-Annexed Mediation Centre Kuala Lumpur) was established at the Kuala Lumpur Court Complex to facilitate the court-annexed mediation. In 2012, the then Chief Justice Tan Sri Arifin bin Zakaria, reported that court-annexed mediation was already producing very good results and commented:

> Mediation now forms a core component in our judicial system. It provides an alternative to parties to resolve their dispute without going through the trial process. Mediation has been practised at all levels of courts including at the appellate level. At the Federal Court, 2 cases had been mediated last year while at the Court of Appeal, a total of 13 cases were settled through mediation. During the same period, 2,276 cases at the High Court and 4,347 cases at the subordinate courts were mediated. Out of all these cases, 50% were successfully settled through mediation.[83]

In 2016, Mediation Division of the Federal Court was set up to, among other things, establish a mediation centre at every state court and to regulate the operation of the mediation centres.[84]

Essentially, court-annexed mediation is a service provided by the judiciary, free of charge, as an alternative to a trial. Since the court-annexed mediation is free and parties have nothing to lose by attempting to mediate their dispute, the court is authorised to order it to the parties as part of the litigation process. A court-ordered mediation requires the parties and their lawyers to commit to the mediation process. The mediation can be conducted either by a judge or by an external mediator agreeable by both parties. If the mediation is conducted by a judge, the judge hearing the case and ordering the mediation should not be the mediating judge, unless agreed by the parties.[85] If the mediation is successful, the mediating judge should record the consent judgment as agreed to by the parties. If the mediation fails, then the case will revert to the original judge to hear and complete the case. The parties are also at liberty to appoint any other mediator of their choice.[86] If the mediation conducted by an external mediator is successful, the mediation outcomes should be provided in a written settlement agreement and the parties must record the terms of the settlement as a consent judgment. The litigating parties are required to report to the court on the progress of mediation not later than one month from the date the case is referred to mediation. All mediations must be completed not later than three months from the date the case is referred for mediation, unless prior approval for an extension was obtained from the court. It is important to note that any party is free to withdraw from mediation at any time if the party does not wish to continue.

Court-annexed mediation has a number of advantages over litigation. It is a much quicker process than litigation. As seen above, the parties are required to reach a settlement within three months of the commencement of mediation. Court-annexed mediation is free, although if the parties chose an external mediator, a fee will need to be paid. These fees are likely to be much less compared to the costs associated with a full trial before the court. Court-annexed mediation is less formal as the normal court rules and procedure are ignored. The parties' attention is focused on their needs and interests rather than their strongly held positions and arguments. The parties are free to discuss issues which may not be legally relevant and all disclosures, admissions, and communications made during mediation are confidential and privileged. The mediator cannot be compelled to divulge the information or records obtained in mediation in any judicial proceedings. Court-annexed mediation also preserves relationships, business or personal. Unlike litigation which is an adversarial process with win-lose outcomes, mediation is collaborative with win-win outcomes. Since there are no losers in mediation, the outcomes of mediation tend to be better and more readily accepted than the ones in litigation.

Can the court-annexed mediation be a viable solution for Islamic finance disputes? While a judge-led mediation is possible, the second option where the mediation is conducted by an external mediator could be better. The choice should be left to the parties. But, before the choice is made, the parties should analyse the nature of their dispute first and develop questions which the mediator would need to address. If the questions are of legal or procedural nature, then perhaps judge-led mediation would be a good choice. If the questions are pertaining to Shar'ah compliance, then the parties should appoint an external mediator who is knowledgeable in Shari'ah and Islamic finance. It has been suggested by some commentators that the court should identify experts in Islamic finance with the help of the SAC.[87] That may not be necessary. To let the parties identify and choose their own mediator could be the best choice. Why is there a need to have a list of experts who can mediate? And why the SAC needs to advise the court on who shall be on that list? In fact, one of the main criticisms addressed against the SAC is the monopoly which it holds when it comes to Shari'ah pronouncements. The SAC is the only authority on Islamic finance matters whom the BNM, court, arbitrators, and IFIs have no choice but to obey. The SACs views are final and they cannot be questioned. There are times when the views of a particular Shari'ah scholar are different from the views of the SAC members and the views of the latter always prevail.[88] This disregard of the views of other scholars, who may be as or more competent than those who sit on the SAC, is not encouraged in Islam. In fact, Islam encourages the plurality of thought, although such views must have a solid basis in Islamic jurisprudence. Any approach where the views of one Shari'ah scholar or a particular group of Shari'ah scholars is promoted as the only correct interpretation of Shari'ah, to the exclusion of views of all other Shari'ah scholars, is simply not correct.

The Ombudsman for Financial Services (OFS), formally known as Financial Mediation Bureau, is another institution which offers mediation to financial consumers as an alternative to litigation to settle disputes with IFIs. In October 2016, the OFS was appointed as an official operator of the Financial Ombudsman Scheme by BNM.[89] All financial institutions in Malaysia, including IFIs, are required to be members of the OFS. Financial consumers may lodge a complaint to the OFS, free of charge, pertaining to any Islamic financial services or products, developed, offered, or marketed by any member institution not exceeding the monetary limit of RM250,000, *takaful* claims not exceeding RM10,000, unauthorized transaction through the designated payment instruments (internet banking, mobile banking, ATM) not exceeding RM25,000, and unauthorized use of cheques not exceeding RM25,000. The OFS does not have jurisdiction to hear complaints exceeding the above stated monetary limits, or complaints on general pricing and product features.[90] In 2017, the OFS received 8,797 complaints and enquiries.[91] It registered 1,327 disputes out of which 1,237 were resolved.[92] Furthermore, 50 per cent of those disputes were resolved through amicable settlement.[93] It should be noted that the final outcome of the OFS is only binding on the member institution. The complainant, the financial consumer, may seek other ADR mechanisms or go to the court if the outcome of mediation conducted by the OFS is not satisfactory.

Arbitration

Arbitration, like mediation, is a form of an alternative dispute resolution mechanism conducted by a neutral third party. Arbitration is also similar to litigation as the parties are required to make their submissions before an arbitrator. The arbitrator will adjudicate the submissions and make a decision. The arbitrator's decision will usually be binding on the parties. While in litigation the parties cannot choose the judge who will be litigating their dispute, in arbitration, the arbitrator or the panel of arbitrators is appointed by the parties. An advantage of having an arbitrator appointed by the disputing parties is that the parties are more likely to accept the decision of the person they appointed. Furthermore, if the dispute is pertaining to Shari'ah questions, the parties are able to appoint an arbitrator who is knowledgeable in Shari'ah and Islamic finance. There is an argument that a 'blank page arbitrator' could be a better choice because the decision will be made based on the evidence submitted by the parties and not based on arbitrator's personal beliefs.[94] If that is the case, then how different is an arbitrator from a judge? There may be times, just like in litigation, when an arbitrator will need to make a decision pertaining to certain Shari'ah questions which go beyond the scope of the agreement. If the arbitrator lacks the necessary knowledge and expertise in Shari'ah, then he or she would have to rely on expert witnesses. Experts may give different views which is not uncommon. In that case, the arbitrator would be in a dilemma as to which view to adopt. All this could be avoided if the arbitrator possesses the required knowledge and expertise in Shari'ah.

One of the most significant advantages of arbitration over litigation and mediation is the enforceability of the arbitral awards in the 159 states which are signatories to the Convention on the Recognition and Enforcement of Foreign Arbitral Awards (also known as the New York Convention).[95] The New York Convention requires the courts of any member state to recognize and enforce arbitral awards made in other member states. Article 5 of the Convention, however, provides some exceptions where the recognition and enforcement of the award may be refused. For example, enforcement may be denied if an arbitral party can demonstrate that 'the award deals with a difference not contemplated by or not falling within the terms of the submission to arbitration, or it contains decisions on matters beyond the scope of the submission to arbitration'.[96] Therefore, if the parties' agreement states that Shari'ah shall be the governing law, and the arbitrator, for some reason, refuses to respect the parties' choice of law, the award is unlikely to be recognized and enforced under the New York Convention.[97] This provision should be a reminder to arbitrators that any departure from Shari'ah, in the circumstances where the parties have expressed their desire to have their agreement arbitrated in a Shari'ah compliant manner, places the recognition and enforcement of the award at risk.

Having an arbitral award Shari'ah compliant and, at the same time, internationally recognized and enforced is the ultimate aim of dispute resolution in Islamic finance. It seems that this aim is best achieved through a hybrid type of arbitration which will have features of both Islamic arbitration and commercial arbitration. The two may not be necessarily the same. Schwing has identified four key areas where Islamic arbitration differs from conventional commercial arbitration, namely: the agreement to arbitrate, the choice of governing law, the selection of arbitrators, and the enforcement of the award.[98]

First, agreement to arbitrate, which forms the basis of the commercial arbitration, does not find its basis in the classical Islamic jurisprudence. The arbitration used to be considered only when disputes arose. It was not common for the arbitration clause to be included in the actual agreement. The reason for that was perhaps the belief that having such a clause in the agreement could inadvertently encourage the parties to seek arbitration for trivial matters which can be solved through a simple negotiation. Arbitration was always viewed as the last option. Nevertheless, modern commercial agreements and prevailing trade practices are more complex than they used to be in the early years of Islam. Arbitration clauses have become a necessity. Therefore, the contemporary Muslim scholars have allowed arbitration clauses to be included in the commercial agreements under the Islamic principles of *ibahah* (permissibility) and *urf* (custom).[99]

Second, designating Shar'ah as the governing law in the agreement seems as a natural choice for any devout and observing Muslim but this may not be the case for arbitration. Commercial arbitration has not always been keen on having Shari'ah as the governing law.[100] Shari'ah tends to be seen by the Western scholars as vague and undefined. This is not surprising as Shari'ah, for the most part, is uncodified. There is an ongoing debate among the Muslims scholars on whether Shari'ah should be codified or not.[101] It is likely that that codification of Shari'ah could limit its scope and stifle its development. Shari'ah is meant to be developing through *ijtihad* (scholarly legal reasoning) so that it can remain relevant to the needs of the society at any time and any place. What may appear to be an acceptable solution in one place and time may not be the case in another place and time. Islam also welcomes the plurality of thought. It is quite common that something which is permissible under one *mazhab* (school of thought) may not be under another.[102] This, however, creates a level of uncertainty for arbitration. Despite that, arbitration tribunals nowadays are more open to the possibility of having Shari'ah as the governing law.[103] In fact, as mentioned earlier, an arbitrator's refusal to arbitrate according to the law chosen by the parties may invalidate the arbitrate award.

Third, the criteria for the selection of arbitrators in Shari'ah is not different from the criteria required for the appointment of judges. The traditional requirements for the appointment of a *qadi* (judge) are the following: male, Muslim, mature, wise, knowledgeable in Shari'ah, of good character, impartial, and not blind, deaf, or mute.[104] These prescriptive conditions are in contrast to a cardinal principle of commercial arbitration that provides the autonomy to the parties to appoint an arbitrator of their choice. If there is an arbitration tribunal, as is the case for most international arbitrations, then both disputing parties will be allowed to select their own arbitrator and their arbitrators will appoint a third one who will serve as a chair of the tribunal.

Fourth, the enforcement of an arbitral award is not certain or clear-cut. Arbitration awards are recognized and enforceable in all 159 signatory states to the New York Convention. One of the situations where the award may not be recognized and enforced, as explained above, is when it contains matters which are beyond the scope of the submission to the arbitration. Another common situation is if the award contravenes the public policy of the country where the award is sought to be enforced. Given that Shari'ah is viewed and interpreted differently in dissimilar countries, there is a fear that courts in some countries, especially Islamic countries, may refuse to accept the arbitrator's interpretation of Shari'ah in the arbitration award on the ground that the award is contrary to the public policy of that country. One example could be an arbitral award in which an arbitrator has recognized the validity of a certain Islamic finance product such as *bai inah*, could be rejected in countries where *bai inah* is not considered to be Shari'ah compliant.

Considering the differences between Islamic and commercial arbitration, one may conclude that some kind of hybrid version of arbitration, which will have the features of both, would be an ideal solution for Islamic finance disputes. One such framework of arbitration is claimed to have been provided by the Asian International Arbitration Centre (AIAC), formally known as Kuala Lumpur Regional Centre for Arbitration (KLRCA).[105] In 2012, KLRCA introduced i-Arbitration Rules (latest version is i-Arbitration Rules 2018), which was the first of its kind anywhere in the world.[106] The Rules consist of two parts. Part I contains provisions on Shari'ah compliance while Part II reproduces United Nations Commission on International Trade and Law (UNCTRAL) Arbitration Rules 2010, and in case of any inconsistency between the two, Part I shall prevail.[107] It is believed that the underlying objective of the Rules is to facilitate Islamic arbitration but one which will not be devoid of international recognition and enforcement.

The Rules begin with a model arbitration clause which should be included in a contract if the parties would like their dispute to be arbitrated in accordance with the Rules. The model arbitration clause states: 'Any dispute, controversy or claim arising out of or relating to this contract, or the breach, termination or invalidity thereof shall be settled by arbitration in accordance with the AIAC i-Arbitration Rules'.[108] In addition to the model clause, the parties are also advised to specify the seat of arbitration, the language to be used, the substantive law that governs the contract, and a provision requiring mediation if the parties wish to conduct mediation before they proceed with arbitration. If the arbitration clause has not been included in the agreement, the arbitration under the Rules may also be chosen after the dispute has arisen by concluding the following agreement: 'The parties hereby agree that the dispute arising out of the contract dated … shall be settled by arbitration under the AIAC i-Arbitration Rules'.[109]

One of the most notable provisions of the Part I is Rule 11 which provides the procedure for the reference to Shari'ah Advisory Council or a Shari'ah expert. Rule 11 provides that the arbitral tribunal (a sole arbitrator or panel of arbitrators) may refer any Shari'ah questions arising from the contract to the relevant Council or Shari'ah expert. This is a discretionary power given to the arbitral tribunal if there is a need to make such reference. If the arbitral tribunal has required expertise, as one would expect from an arbitrator deciding an Islamic finance dispute, then the reference is not necessary. This provision, when considered on its own, seems to be fine. However, a problem may arise if the parties have chosen Malaysian law as the governing law of their contract. As has been explained earlier, sections 56 and 57 of the CBMA make such a reference to the SAC mandatory and the ruling binding on the arbitral tribunal. Therefore, if, for example, one of the parties is not Malaysian, and the governing law is Malaysian law, then the SAC's ruling on the Shari'ah compliance, which may not be in line with the party's *mazhab* and the religious view, will nevertheless be mandatory on the arbitral tribunal and the parties. This problem may seriously cripple Malaysia's and the AIAC's prospect of becoming a forum for settlement of international Islamic finance disputes. One way to eliminate this problem would be to repeal the parts of sections 56 and 57 which make any reference to arbitration. One may appreciate the need for consistency and certainty, and the role played by the SAC in the context of litigation, but that argument becomes obsolete in arbitration. The decisions of the arbitral tribunal have no precedential effect.

Arbitration of Islamic finance disputes in Malaysia, and more specifically, in the AIAC has not been a success story. It has been reported that Malaysian IFIs prefer litigation over arbitration. One study found that most of IFIs in Malaysia have a 'credit policy' not to include arbitration clauses in their agreements and instead opt for litigation.[110] This is understandable. IFIs, like most other corporations, prefer certainty. Litigation provides certainty of outcomes. The judicial decisions and now the role played by the SAC in the litigation, provides the kind of certainty that corporations including IFIs cannot get in arbitration. Another study conducted an informal discussion with one of the AIAC panellist for Islamic banking and finance cases and found that only two cases have been arbitrated under the AIAC Rules.[111] Schwing has raised a legitimate concern regarding the AIAC's panel of arbitrators available for Islamic finance disputes.[112] He found that there are only four members of the AIAC panel of arbitrators who are experts in Islamic finance. Schwing also questioned the Shari'ah compliance of the Rules. If certain aspects of the Rules are found not to be Shari'ah compliant, the enforcement of the award in other countries could be jeopardized for the earlier mentioned reasons. Shari'ah compliance of some of the provisions of the Rules is, to say the least, debatable.[113] All of the above could be some of the reasons for a poor take up rate of arbitration.

Conclusion

This chapter examined the use of litigation and the possible alternatives in the form of mediation and arbitration that would be most suitable to resolve Islamic finance disputes in Malaysia. The key finding is that for any dispute resolution mechanism to be suitable for Islamic finance disputes, it must fulfil two criteria. First, it must be Shari'ah compliant. Second, it must produce an outcome which will be recognized and enforced. For Malaysia, all the three mechanisms (litigation, mediation, and arbitration) appear to have fulfilled both requirements. The choice will then have to be left to the parties depending on their specific needs. IFIs would most likely find litigation most suiting provided sections 56 and 57 remain the law. Consumers would likely prefer court-annexed mediation as it gives them the bargaining power that they would otherwise not have in litigation. And the parties in cross-border Islamic finance contracts would prefer arbitration which would allow them to choose the law and arbitrators of their choice and so facilitate a smooth and easy enforcement of the award. Nevertheless, the parties should be aware of the inherent weakness that each of the three mechanisms have, and hopefully this chapter will contribute to such awareness.

Notes

1 See ICD-Thomson Reuters (Islamic Finance Development Report 2017) www.icd-ps.org/ accessed 30 May 2018.
2 See Islamic Finance Country Index 2017 (Global Islamic Finance Report 2017).
3 Malaysia International Financial Centre in collaboration with Islamic Corporation for the Development of the Private Sector (Islamic Finance in Asia: Reaching New Heights Report 2017), www.mifc.com/index.php?ch=28&pg=72&ac=188&bb=uploadpdf accessed 30 May 2017.
4 See Ng Min Shen, 'Malaya Remains Lead in Islamic Finance' (*The Malaysian Reserve*, 5 April 2018) https://themalaysianreserve.com/2018/04/05/malaysia-remains-lead-in-islamic-finance/ accessed 30 May 2018.
5 Ibid.
6 For more details, see Mohd Zakhiri Md Nor, Ani Munirah Mohamad and Hakimah Yaacob, 'The Development of Islamic Finance in Malaysia' in Adnan Trakic and Hanifah Haydar Ali Tajuddin (eds), *Islamic Banking and Finance: Principles, Instruments and Operations* (2nd edn, Malaysian Current Law Journal 2016) 601–617.
7 The Central Bank of Malaysia.
8 [2002] WL 346969 (QB Com Ct, 13 February 2002).
9 [2004] EWCA Civ 19.
10 For more details, see Chapter 4.

11 In Malaysia, the word 'Shari'ah' is spelled 'Syariah'. The author, however, will retain 'Shari'ah' spelling throughout the chapter for the consistency and easy reference.
12 See List I (Federal List), Ninth Schedule of the Federal Constitution.
13 See List II (State List), Ninth Schedule of the Federal Constitution.
14 See, for example, Syariah Criminal Offences (Federal Territories) Act 1997 which contains offences, such as wrongful worship, false doctrine, sexual intercourse out of wedlock etc.
15 List II (State List), Ninth Schedule of the Federal Constitution states that the Shari'ah courts 'shall have jurisdiction only over persons professing the religion of Islam'.
16 Some have argued that companies or incorporated entities may be considered as 'Muslims' for specific purposes, such as payment of *zakat* (obligatory almsgiving or religious tax). For further discussion, see Tun Abdul Hamid Mohamad and Adnan Trakic, 'Critical Appraisal of the Companies' Obligations to Pay Zakat in the Malaysian Context' (2013) 10 ICCLR 375.
17 KL High Court Civil Suit No S3–22–101–9. The case was not reported and the court did not deliver a written judgment. The case was cited in Norhashimah Mohd Yasin, 'Legal Aspects of Islamic Banking: Malaysian Experience' in Salman Syed Ali and Ausaf Ahmed (eds), *Islamic Banking and Finance: Fundamentals and Contemporary Issues* (Islamic Research and Training Institution 2007) 225.
18 Art 121 (1A) states: 'the courts referred to in Clause (1) (civil courts) shall have no jurisdiction in respect of any matter within the jurisdiction of the Syariah courts' (emphasis added).
19 See Elsa Satkunasingam, 'Jurisdiction over Islamic Banking in Malaysia: Challenges of Maintaining the Status Quo' in Adnan Trakic and Hanifah Haydar Ali Tajuddin (eds), *Islamic Banking and Finance: Principles, Instruments and Operations* (2nd edn, Malaysian Current Law Journal 2016) 783–798.
20 List II of the Federal Constitution. *Zakat* is a form of alms-giving treated as obligatory on Muslims who meet *nisab* (criteria of wealth). *Fitrah* is a smaller charitable contribution required to be paid by Muslims normally in the month of *Ramadhan* (month of fasting). *Baitulmal* is an institution (treasury) which collects *zakat* and *fitrah* and distributes it to the needy.
21 Ibid.
22 See *Bank Kerjasama Rakyat Malaysia Bhd v Emcee Corporation Sdn Bhd* [2003] 1 CLJ 625, 628 as per Abdul Hamid Mohamad JCA (as he then was):

> As was mentioned at the beginning of this judgment the facility is an Islamic banking facility. But that does not mean that the law applicable in this application is different from the law that is applicable if the facility were given under conventional banking. The charge is a charge under the National Land Code. The remedy available and sought is a remedy provided by the National Land Code. The procedure is provided by the Code and the Rules of the High Court 1980. The court adjudicating it is the High Court. So, it is the same law that is applicable, the same order that would be, if made, and the same principles that should be applied in deciding the application.

See also *Arab-Malaysian Merchant Bank Bhd v Silver Concept Sdn Bhd* [2006] 8 CLJ 9.
23 See Tun Abdul Hamid bin Haji Mohamad, 'Cadangan Mewujudkan Bahagian Mu'amalat di Mahkamah Tinggi' (in Malay) www.tunabdulhamid.my. Summary of the findings and the reasons could also be found in 'Interlink/interface between common law system and Shariah rules and principles and effective dispute resolution mechanism' (28–29 September 2009) www.tunabdulhamid.my accessed on 5 June 2018.

24 See Tun Abdul Hamid Mohamad and Adnan Trakic, 'The Shari'ah Advisory Council's Role in Resolving Islamic Banking Disputes in Malaysia: A Model to Follow?' in Adnan Trakic and Hanifah Haydar Ali Tajuddin (eds), *Islamic Banking and Finance: Principles, Instruments and Operations* (2nd edn, Malaysian Current Law Journal 2016) 520.
25 S 27 of the CBMA.
26 S 60 of the CBMA.
27 Ss 59 and 73 of the CBMA.
28 www.bnm.gov.my/guidelines/05_shariah/02_Shariah_Governance_Framework_2010 1026.pdf accessed 31 May 2018.
29 S 283(b) of the IFSA clarifies that every guideline, direction, circular or notice made under the repealed Acts shall be deemed to have been standards made under a corresponding provisions in IFSA and shall continue to remain in force.
30 IBA contained 60 sections while IFSA has 291 sections.
31 S 28(1) of the IFSA.
32 S 29 read together with s 2 of the IFSA clarify that 'person' refers to an Islamic financial institution as well as the responsible director, officer, or a member of a Shari'ah Committee of an institution.
33 S 28(5) of the IFSA.
34 See ss 30–36 of the IFSA.
35 See Tun Abdul Hamid Mohamad and Adnan Trakic, 'The Shari'ah Advisory Council's Role in Resolving Islamic Banking Disputes in Malaysia: A Model to Follow?' in Adnan Trakic and Hanifah Haydar Ali Tajuddin (eds), *Islamic Banking and Finance: Principles, Instruments and Operations* (2nd edn, Malaysian Current Law Journal 2016) 513.
36 S 16B of the repealed Central Bank of Malaysia Act 1958.
37 Ibid. Unlike the courts, the rulings made by the SAC were binding on the arbitrators. It is unclear why there was this discrepancy.
38 [2009] 1 CLJ 419. A more detailed discussion of the case is available in the later part of the chapter.
39 [2009] 6 CLJ 22.
40 Ibid, [32]–[35].
41 The respective representatives were invited by the High Court in *Mohd Alias Ibrahim v RHB Bank Bhd & Anor* [2011] 4 CLJ 654 as *amicus curiae*. For more details on their submission in this case, see [26]–[30].
42 S 51 of the CBMA.
43 S 100(f) of the CBMA.
44 S 53 of the CBMA.
45 www.sacbnm.org/?page_id=3351 accessed 26 July 2018.
46 S 54 of the CBMA.
47 S 52 of the CBMA.
48 Ss 55 and 57 of the CBMA.
49 S 55 of the CBMA.
50 S 57 of the CBMA.
51 If the SAC has already published its ruling on a particular Shari'ah issue, then the court or arbitrator is obliged to follow it. If the ruling is not available, then the SAC will deliberate on the issue and make the ruling.
52 S 57 of the CBMA.
53 [2013] 1 CLJ 436 (*Tan Sri Khalid*).
54 S 3 of the Islamic Banking Act 1983 required that the business conducted by the licensed institutions must be in accordance with the religion of Islam. In 2013, the Act has been repealed and replaced with Islamic Financial Services Act 2013. S 28 is an equivalent section in the new Act.
55 See Item 4(k) of the List 1 of the Ninth Schedule, Federal Constitution.

56 Art 121(1) of the Federal Constitution.
57 [2013] 1 CLJ 436, 446.
58 Ibid.
59 Malaysian law recognizes two types of experts, gazetted expert which is a creature of statute, and experts that come under the purview of ss 45 and 49 of the Evidence Act 1950 (Malaysia). See Augustine Paul, *Evidence: Practice and Procedure* (Malayan Law Journal, 2003) 448.
60 [2017] 3 MLJ 561 (*Semenyih Jaya*).
61 Ibid. 593.
62 Ibid. 597.
63 Ibid.
64 [2018] 3 CLJ 145 *(Indira Gandhi*).
65 Ibid. 173.
66 Hafiz Yatim, 'Nine-member Bench to Rule if Shariah Council Decision Binds Civil Court' (*Malaysiakini*, 27 August 2018) www.malaysiakini.com/news/440593 accessed 28 August 2018.
67 [2009] 1 CLJ 419 (*Taman Ihsan Jaya*).
68 There are four recognized schools of thought among Sunni Muslims, namely *Shafi'*, *Maliki*, *Hanbali*, and *Hanafi*.
69 [2009] 1 CLJ 419, 446.
70 See Tun Abdul Hamid Mohamad and Adnan Trakic, 'The Adjudication of Shari'ah Issues in Islamic Finance Contracts' (2015) 26 JBFLP 39, 55; Fakihah Azahari, 'Islamic Banking: Perspectives on Recent Case Development' (2009) 1 MLJ xci, xcv.
71 [2009] 6 CLJ 22 (*Lim Kok Hoe*).
72 Ibid. 37.
73 [2009] 2 CLJ 433.
74 Ibid. 434.
75 [2018] 6 CLJ 381.
76 See SAC Resolution on *Condition for Validity of Bai' Inah Contract* (16th meeting dated 11 November 2000 and 82nd meeting dated 17 February 2009) www.sacbnm.org/wp-content/uploads/2018/03/72.E.pdf accessed 7 August 2018.
77 [2018] 6 CLJ 381, 396.
78 [2018] 1 LNS 220.
79 Ibid, [31].
80 Potter LJ, delivering a unanimous decision of the English Court of Appeal in *Shamil Bank of Bahrain EC v Beximco Pharmaceuticals Ltd* [2004] 4 All ER 1072, [54], made the following observation:

> having chosen English law as the governing law, it would be both unusual and improbable for the parties to intend that the English court should proceed to determine and apply the Sharia'a in relation to the legality or enforceability of the obligations clearly set out in the contract.

81 See, for example, Umar A Oseni and Abu Umar Faruq Ahmad, 'Towards a Global Hub: The Legal Framework for Dispute Resolution in Malaysia's Islamic Finance Industry' (2016) 58 *International Journal of Law and Management* 48, 50. Also in litigation parties have no control over the appointment of judges litigating their dispute, the disposal of cases could take long time, and litigation could also be very costly.
82 See Practice Direction No 5 of 2010 (Practice Direction on Mediation) www.malaysianbar.org.my/index.php?option=com_docman&task=doc_details&gid=2720&Itemid=332 accessed 10 August 2018.

83 See 'Speech by Tan Sri Arifin bin Zakaria, Chief Justice of Malaysia, at the Opening of the Legal Year 2012 (14 January 2014)' www.malaysianbar.org.my/speeches/speech_by_tan_sri_arifin_bin_zakaria_chief_justice_of_malaysia_at_the_opening_of_the_legal_year_2012_14_jan_2012.html accessed 13 August 2018.

84 www.kehakiman.gov.my/en/about-us/chief-registrars-office/division-pkpmp/mediation-division accessed 10 August 2018.

85 See Annexure A (Judge-Led Mediation) of the Practice Direction No. 5 of 2010. It may not be wise to have the judge hearing the case to be the mediating judge even if the parties agree to that. This may find fault with the principle of mediator impartiality and neutrality. It may also prejudice the hearing as the information obtained during mediation should remain confidential. See Choong Yeow Choy, Tie Fatt Hee, and Christina Ooi Su Siang 'Court-Annexed Mediation Practice in Malaysia: What the Future Holds' (2016) 1 *University of Bologna Law Review* 271, 281.

86 See Annexure B (Mediation by Any Other Mediator) of the Practice Direction No. 5 of 2010.

87 Umar A Oseni and Abu Umar Faruq Ahmad, 'Towards a Global Hub: The Legal Framework for Dispute Resolution in Malaysia's Islamic Finance Industry' (2016) 58 *International Journal of Law and Management* 48, 54.

88 For example, in the High Court case of *Kuwait Finance House (Malaysia) Bhd v JRI Resources Sdn Bhd* [2016] 10 CLJ 435, one of the issues was in relation to Shari'ah compliance of *ijarah* (leasing) agreement concluded by the parties. One of the Shari'ah expert witnesses submitted that the agreement did not comply with Shari'ah but, later, he was overruled by the SAC who ruled otherwise. As mentioned earlier, this case has been appealed before the Federal Court and the decision is yet to be made.

89 S 138 of the IFSA provides for the establishment of the 'financial ombudsman scheme'.

90 A detailed list of matters which fall outside the OFS's jurisdiction is available at its website www.ofs.org.my/en/scope accessed 13 August 2018.

91 See Ombudsman for Financial Services Annual Report 2017, 3. www.ofs.org.my/file/files/OFS-AR2017-lowres.pdf accessed 13 August 2018.

92 Ibid.

93 Ibid.

94 KC Lye, 'Panel Discussion and Question and Answer Session' (Workshop on Dispute Resolution and Insolvency in Islamic Finance: Problems and Solutions, National University of Singapore, September 2013) 44–45.

95 www.uncitral.org/pdf/english/texts/arbitration/NY-conv/New-York-Convention-E.pdf accessed 14 August 2018.

96 Art V(1)(c) of the New York Convention.

97 Mel Andrew Schwing, 'The KLRCA I-Arbitration Rules: A Shari'a-Compliant Solution to the Problems with Islamic Finance Dispute Resolution in Singapore and Malaysia?' (2017) 34 *Journal of International Arbitration* 425, 447.

98 Ibid, 439.

99 The principle of *ibahah* is based on the following maxim: 'The general norm in regards to things is that of permissibility' (*Alaslu filashyaa' al Ibadah*). See Umar Oseni, 'Islamic Finance Arbitration: Integrating Classical and Modern Legal Frameworks', in A Trakic and HHA Tajuddin (eds.), *Islamic Banking and Finance: Principles, Instruments and Operations* (2nd edn, Malaysian Current Law Journal, 2016) 553. *Urf* is a well-known secondary source of Islamic law. See Muhammad Hashim Kamali, *Principles of Islamic Jurisprudence* (2nd edn, Ilmiah Publishers 2009) 283–296.

100 See, for example, arbitration award of The Right Hon. Lord Asquith of Bishopstone in the *Matter of an Arbitration between the Petroleum Development (Trucial Coast) Limited and His Excellency Sheikh Shakhbut Bin Sultan Bin Za'id, Ruler of Abu*

Dhabi and its Dependencies (1952) 1 *International Comparative and Law Quarterly* 247 (part 2). See also *Saudi Arabia v Arabian American Oil Company* 27 ILR 117 (1963).

101 See Najmaldeen K Kareem Zanki, 'Codification of Islamic Law Premises of History and Debates of Contemporary Muslim Scholars' (2014) 4 *International Journal of Humanities and Social Sciences* 127.

102 See, for example, *bai inah* arrangement (sale with immediate repurchase) in Islamic finance. Three classical schools of thought in Islam, *Hanafi*, *Maliki* and *Hanbali* prohibit the practice of *bai inah*. Only *Shafi'* school of thought, to which Malaysia belongs, allows it. Most of the Middle East Shari'ah scholars are of the view that *bai inah* is not allowed because of its fictitious nature which is meant to legalese interest. For further details, see Shaharuddin A, 'The Bay' al-'Inah Controversy in Malaysian Islamic Banking' (2012) 26 *Arab Law Quarterly* 499.

103 For more details on the possibility of having Shari'ah identified as the governing law in Islamic finance agreements, see Chapter 3 of this book.

104 Mel Andrew Schwing, 'The KLRCA I-Arbitration Rules: A Shari'a-Compliant Solution to the Problems with Islamic Finance Dispute Resolution in Singapore and Malaysia?' (2017) 34 *Journal of International Arbitration* 425, 445.

105 www.aiac.world/ accessed 17 August 2018.

106 Hereinafter referred to as 'the Rules'.

107 R 1(3) of the AIAC i-Arbitration Rules 2018.

108 See AIAC i-Arbitration Rules 2018.

109 Ibid.

110 Hakimah Yaakob, 'Arbitration – Consistent with the Spirit of Islamic Banking? The Benefits and Challenges of Arbitrating in Islamic Banking and Finance Disputes' (Asia Pacific Regional Arbitration Group Conference, Kuala Lumpur Regional Centre for Arbitration (KLRCA) 9–10 July 2011). This study involved a survey of 10 Islamic banks and 12 Takaful operators in Malaysia.

111 Umar A Oseni and Abu Umar Faruq Ahmad, 'Towards a Global Hub: The Legal Framework for Dispute Resolution in Malaysia's Islamic Finance Industry' (2016) 58 *International Journal of Law and Management* 48, 56.

112 Mel Andrew Schwing, 'The KLRCA I-Arbitration Rules: A Shari'a-Compliant Solution to the Problems with Islamic Finance Dispute Resolution in Singapore and Malaysia?' (2017) 34 *Journal of International Arbitration* 425, 455.

113 Ibid, 452–456.

7 Settlement of Islamic finance disputes in the Kingdom of Saudi Arabia

Aishath Muneeza and Zakariya Mustapha

Introduction

The Kingdom of Saudi Arabia (KSA) is an independent Arab country located in the western flank of Asia, comprising a greater portion of the Arabian Peninsula.[1] Occupying a total land size of about 2,150,000 square kilometres, the country is the second and fifth largest in the Arab world and Asia respectively.[2] With a population of more than 32 million people (2016),[3] petroleum is the backbone of the KSA's economy. The Kingdom of Saudi Arabia is run by an absolute monarchical system of government based on Islamic theocracy.[4] While declaring the Holy *Qur'an* and the *Sunnah* (Traditions) of Prophet Muhammad as the country's constitution, its Basic Law[5] enshrines the King's power to be bound only by the provisions of Shari'ah. Therefore, an Islamic system of law and justice administration, coupled with royal decrees, the KSA addresses a variety of disputes on diverse subject matters among the citizens of the Kingdom and expatriates alike.[6]

A dispute encompasses disagreement and or argument that may impede peoples' ability to deal with their own affairs. Disputes are an inevitable component of human dealings that arises as circumstance dictates without being restrained by time and place, whether the parties concerned are prepared for it or not. Disputes, unless tackled in an appropriate manner, could escalate into a conflict with negative ramifications that may lead to disappointment of all concerned. The need for settlement procedures of dispute in any dealing is therefore necessary, so that disputing parties can have recourse to a settlement forum in order to avoid matters degenerating. Such a forum might have been agreed on in the contractual agreement or in the absence of such agreement, the default provisions of law will apply. Whatever may be the dimension of a dispute, its settlement is always sought primarily in order to ascertain and apportion rights and responsibilities of the parties concerned according to the agreement and the law.

A dispute may pertain to one or more subject matters and more often than not arises in the context of a particular jurisdiction so that it is addressed by local laws of the jurisdiction concerned. This chapter therefore discusses the settlement of Islamic finance disputes in the context of Saudi Arabia. Islamic finance is a financial system that involves the provision and formulation of financial services and products according to the dictates of Shari'ah or Islamic law. As a matter of business and commerce, Islamic finance will inevitably involve disputes of various types. Accordingly, the settlement of Islamic finance disputes requires a forum where Shari'ah issues would be taken into consideration in the resolution of such matters. By law, the financial system of the country is governed by national finance laws and regulations which are underpinned by the Shari'ah. Thus, regardless of whether Islamic finance disputes are to be settled by litigation or arbitration in the KSA, Shari'ah-compliance in the processes and procedures would be paramount and cannot be over-emphasized.

Legal systems and sources of law in the Kingdom of Saudi Arabia

The principal source of law in Saudi Arabia is Shari'ah, obtained from the holy *Qur'an* and the *Sunnah* (teachings and/or the traditions of the Prophet Muhammad). The country is an exception among most present-day Muslim countries in that there is no codification of the Shari'ah, thus giving leverage to judges to utilize independent and unfettered legal reasoning in the determination of matters and reaching decisions.[7] The effect of this supposed vacuum would seem to be watered down with recent official initiative of inaugurating book on legal precedent aimed at establishing legal guide on judicial principles.[8] In terms of jurisprudence, the country shows marked preference for and officially follows *Hanbali* School and its principles. The country's judiciary is epitomized by a Shari'ah court system encompassing *qadis* (judges) and lawyers that constitute a section of the *ulama* or the Islamic scholars of the Kingdom.[9] Another major source of law is Royal decree, otherwise known as 'regulations' instead of 'laws' for the reason that they are subsidiary to the Shari'ah. The Royal decrees are issued to complement the application of Shari'ah in certain areas like corporate, labour and commercial laws.[10] It is for this reason that such decrees form the governing law for both conventional and Islamic banking and finance being commercial activities in the KSA.[11]

It should be noted that the Kingdom of Saudi Arabia has no written constitution in the modern notion and form of the word. It rather has the Basic Law which was issued in 1992 by King Fahd bin Abdulaziz Al-Saud as the extant governing law, equivalent to constitution. This piece of law is fundamental in the country's legal system in that it enunciates the government's responsibilities and rights. Other significant provisions of this law include the sections that officially declare *Islam* as the state religion while the *Qur'an* and *Sunnah* as the constitution. The Basic Law also stipulates the Kingdom must protect people's rights in accordance with Shari'ah, establishes judicial independence and founds the process of dispensation of justice on rules of Shari'ah in accordance with the teachings the *Qur'an*, the *Sunnah* and regulations issued by the King, as long as they are not in conflict with the *Qur'an* and the *Sunnah*.[12]

Prior to the Basic Law, the expression 'Saudi law' had emerged alongside the development of the Saudi legal system. It started to be used in the middle 1960s during the time that the Kingdom underwent a widespread transformation and reforms via the introduction of a number of regulations and laws, even though the country had been formally unified into a kingdom as early as 1932. Before the 1960s, few laws were enacted and the existing laws then were largely subjugated to the reasoning of individual judges, as well as ministerial or governmental circulars and decrees issued by the king with respect to specific matters.[13] To a very large extent, Saudi Arabia is thought of as a country where the law of the land is only the Shari'ah, particularly by people that are not familiar with the country's legal system. However, contrary to this perception, 'Saudi law' as a term encompasses much more than the Shari'ah, in that it incorporates Shari'ah, royal decrees and regulations that are modifications upon some existing legislations within the domain of the principles of Shari'ah. Therefore, while making or issuing regulations and royal decrees, Saudi Arabian 'legislators' only assume the responsibilities of ensuring conformity with Shari'ah while keeping up with modern political, economic and social interest of the Kingdom.

In this regard, one major predicament of the Saudi legislators and scholars is the regulation of forbidden undertakings under Shari'ah, particularly where such undertakings are crucial in advancing modern economic development, such as certain banking undertakings involving interest (*riba*) which the Shari'ah vehemently prohibits.[14] The 1966 Banking Control Law for instance demonstrates how the Saudi legislators handle such forbidden undertakings under Shari'ah. Thus, the law simply remains silent on interest charged by banks, because enshrining it in the law is an express infringement of Shari'ah, which for all intent and purpose is the constitution of the country. Notwithstanding, it is deducible that the law has only allowed for the pragmatic control of such undertakings.[15] Be that as it may, interests in practice are undeniably charged in public expenditures, particularly in non-domestic or international transactions involving banks financing. Therefore in practice, the prohibition of interest is unenforceable provided that the parties have, out of their own volition, agreed to observe their own agreement. To such extent, if a dispute involving the government arises in the course of such transactions, a semi-government tribunal known as Board of Grievances (to be discussed subsequently) is the proper forum for settlement. Interestingly, the Board cannot uphold interest provisions in any agreement and/or transaction. This is a clashing point between economic and religious interests of Saudi Arabia, which leads some people to support allowing interest for economic development as opposed to the well-known religious prohibition as well as state policy against any form of interest.[16]

Legal framework for Islamic finance in the KSA

Islamic banking and finance denotes a banking and finance system based on Islamic law (the Shari'ah). It is a banking and finance system that follows Shari'ah rules on transactions (*fiqh muamalat*). It is, in other words, a Shari'ah-compliant banking and finance that is ethical in accordance with the dictates of Shari'ah,[17] aimed at realizing the objectives of Shari'ah (*maqasid al-Shari'ah*) in all contractual, commercial and financial dealings.[18] Interest (*riba*) and other unethical dealings such as involving gambling, liquor, speculations and excessive uncertainty (all repugnant to and prohibited by Shari'ah) have characterized conventional banking and finance. Rules of Shari'ah against such dealings, coupled with the critical roles assumed by banks financing services in the modern economy, prompted the development and proliferation of the Islamic equivalents of banking and financing as well as capital market and fund management.[19]

Saudi Arabia has a relatively well-defined and assured funds regime that positioned it to be home to a greater number of Islamic investment funds that are based in the Gulf Cooperation Council (GCC). Additionally, in terms of issuance of *sukuk* (Islamic equivalent of bond) and the volume of Shari'ah-compliant structured financings, the country is a global market and one of the fastest growing in that regard. In terms of regulations, the country's financial sector is regulated by a legal framework that comprises of various laws.

More so, in seeking to provide an assured legal regime, new regulations were introduced between 2012 and 2013 as part of a reform aimed at enhancing the country's finance, real estate, mortgage and Islamic funds industries. The regulations were also meant to simplify the procedures of foreign arbitral awards enforcement and local judgments.[20] Thus, pursuant to the reforms, laws were specifically enacted for organized activities of financial institutions including Islamic banks, commercial banks and specialized bank. These laws are in addition to the central bank laws, insurance laws and other laws for financing and regulating capital market activities such as securities and stock exchange. Besides, regulations are already put in place that provide for the legal fundamentals of the country's economic, commercial, political and social governance.[21] In essence, Islamic finance practice has been provided for by relatively sufficient laws that confer it with clear legality and validity of its products and services. This is ensured not only to modern regulatory standards but also in a manner that is to a large extent amenable to the *Shari'ah*. Accordingly, the practice of Islamic finance is overseen by prudent regulators and its dispute resolution mechanisms are established by decisive regulations.

Consequently, the Islamic finance industry in Saudi Arabia has developed and matured, accounting for about two-thirds of bank financing in the country.[22] The country is considered the biggest Islamic finance market. It is home to the world's largest Islamic bank, Al-Rajhi Bank,[23] as well as the Islamic Development Bank (IDB) which is a key body among Islamic banking institutions globally.[24] In addition, there are over 12 commercial banks that are licensed and operate in the country. Out of this number, four are established as full-fledge Islamic banks or Shari'ah-compliant banks while the rest are conventional banks that mostly provide a combination of conventional and Islamic banking services and products.[25] On the whole, the practice of Islamic finance in Saudi Arabia is a composite of several financial operations. While Islamic banking is a major component thereof, there are *takaful* (Islamic insurance), *sukuk*, mutual funds and other Islamic capital market operations where some of these activities are undertaken by financial institutions including banks.[26]

Regulating Islamic finance and settlement of Islamic finance disputes

The principal regulator of the banking and finance industry in Saudi Arabia is the Saudi Arabian Monetary Authority (SAMA).[27] Established in 1952, pursuant to the SAMA Charter, via royal decrees number 30/4/1/1046 and 30/4/1/1046,[28] SAMA is the Central bank of the country that regulates and oversees the operations of banks and other financial institutions accordingly. The major legislation for regulating banking business and operations in Saudi Arabia is the Banking Control Regulation, promulgated via Royal Decree No. M/5 of 1966. This law is administered by SAMA in carrying out its mandate of overseeing banking operations. Moreover, SAMA regulates and supervises *takaful* institutions and their operations. The Law on Supervision of Co-operative Insurance Companies 2003, enacted through Royal Decree No. M/32, designates SAMA as regulator and supervisor of *takaful* business. This is in addition to Implementing Regulations 2003 and several other regulations issued and published by SAMA.

Another important body in the regulation of financing transactions and investment funds is the Capital Market Authority (CMA). Established in 2003, following the enactment of the Capital Market Law via royal decree number M/30, the CMA regulates the issuance of *sukuk* and capital market operations in all ramifications under the Capital Market Law. *Sukuk* investments in the Kingdom comprise governmental and private entities' issuance by both Islamic and conventional banks and financial institutions.

It is noteworthy that Saudi Arabian laws and regulations allow the operation of conventional banks and financial institutions along with Islamic ones. Therefore, all the banks and financial institutions licensed to operate in the country are subject to the same regulatory and supervisory requirements under the authority of SAMA or CMA, depending on the type of institution and/or financing transaction. For instance, the SAMA regulates Islamic banks in the same manner it regulates conventional banks, as are Islamic insurance, mutual funds and capital market operations by their respective regulators. Also, by these laws and regulations, no local bank could be identified as 'Islamic' since, in theory, all banking and financing activities within the country have been deemed Shari'ah-compliant.[29] So, identifying a bank as such implies that others, not so identified, are not Shari'ah-compliant. This could not be tenable in a country where Shari'ah is the grundnorm. Therefore, there is no any special or preferential regulatory treatment of Islamic financial products or extra support for Islamic banks and financial institutions.[30] Notwithstanding, Islamic banking and finance businesses are witnessing rapid development and advancement in the country.[31]

Islamic finance disputes: nature and dimension

In the course of usual and routine business and operational activities of Islamic financial institutions, disputes are bound to arise therefrom. These disputes may concern local Islamic finance transaction where all parties involved are local.

Such disputes could be between individuals and corporate entities or simply between corporate and related entities that are parties to such transactions and at local level. The dispute may involve the question of determining the rights and obligations of parties arising out of banker–customer relationship or any form of contractual client-services and financing arrangements. Occasionally, the transaction may be international where parties of different nationalities would be involving. For instance where a foreign financial institution offers Shari'ah-compliant product targeting investors in the Saudi Arabia or the GCC but using documentation that is governed by a law other than Saudi law.[32] Depending on dispute resolution provision in the documentation or agreement (if any), in the event of dispute under such circumstances, it may be resolved by either litigation or arbitration including any of the known alternative dispute resolution mechanisms. While participants and investors in some Islamic finance jurisdictions such as Malaysia and, until recently, Saudi Arabia, favour litigation, in other jurisdictions they tend to opt for arbitration for the resolution of Islamic finance disputes.

Kingdom of Saudi Arabia court approach to settlement of Islamic finance disputes

Dispute resolution in Islamic finance is a topic of peculiarities depending on the applicable laws of finance and legal system of a jurisdiction. However, a common denominator to all of Islamic finance dispute resolution issues is upholding Shari'ah-compliance, as the transaction from which the dispute emanates. This is because, as Islamic finance follows Shari'ah, it is a fundamental requirement that it should be Shari'ah-compliant in all its ramifications.[33] Accordingly, article 48 of the Basic Law obliges the courts to

> apply the rules of *Shari'ah* in the cases that are brought before them, in accordance with the precepts contained in the Quran and the Sunnah, and regulations decreed by the ruler which do not contradict the Quran and the Sunnah....

In adherence to this requirement, it is essential that the practice and procedures before all forums that handle Islamic finance dispute be Shari'ah-compliant. This is because being a Shari'ah-compliant transaction implies the settlement of disputes arising from such transaction in accordance with Shari'ah.[34] It appears that Shari'ah-compliance of Islamic finance practice and disputes relating to it has been unarguably envisaged by the fact that Shari'ah is the principal law of Saudi Arabia.

Under the judicial system of the country, there are several avenues for the settlement of a variety of disputes including Islamic finance disputes. These consist of Shari'ah Courts alongside self-governing statutory tribunals and quasi-judicial committees which entertain subject-matter specific cases. Under article 49 of the Basic Law, the Shari'ah courts are regular courts of general jurisdiction to deal with all kinds of disputes. They are under the Ministry of Justice and they are hierarchical in structure. The self-governing judicial body is mainly the *Diwan al-Mazalim* or Board of Grievances which is a statutory body established for specific subject matter concerning certain royal decrees. It is directly answerable to the King. The quasi-judicial committees are established to also handle certain matters under some royal decrees such as banking and finance, commercial and labour matters under respective ministries. In this respect, there is the Committee for Banking Disputes and other similar committees, which function subject to and under finance ministry's direct control.[35] It should be noted that litigation is a popular mechanism for the settlement of banking disputes in the Saudi Arabia, as such the practice and procedure adapted by these judicial and quasi-judicial bodies or any other tribunal in the country are meant to be in accordance with rules of Shari'ah (being the law of the land) or at least devoid of elements repugnant to the Shari'ah. Accordingly, all matters of procedure and evidence in any cause of action would be deemed Shari'ah-compliant as well.[36]

The Shari'ah Courts

The hierarchy of Shari'ah Courts consist of a Shari'ah Courts of First Instance and a Court of Appeal. With litigation as the preferred mechanism of dispute resolution, the Shari'ah Courts would appear to be the first and most important point of call for Islamic finance dispute resolution in Saudi Arabia. The courts are staffed by personnel who are qualified judges and lawyers that form part of the country's *ulama* (the religious leaders). The courts entertain civil matters based on monetary value of a claim, the subject of a dispute. Accordingly, the Shari'ah Court of First Instance which has jurisdiction over a dispute or claim worth up to 20,000 Saudi Arabian Rial.[37] This includes disputes in Islamic finance. Appeal against decision of Shari'ah Court of First Instance is provided for to be pursued at a Shari'ah court that is higher in hierarchy, i.e. the Court of Appeal. An appeal can be made to the Court of Appeal and from there to a Supreme Judicial Council. The Court of Appeal usually entertains appeals without necessarily reversing the decision of the lower trial court (Shari'ah Court of First Instance). The Court rather acts on the appeal by either upholding the decision of the lower court or by returning it to the trial court along with its comment for retrial. The lower court judge may maintain his decision. On second appeal and only then, the Court of Appeal will annul and override the initial decision and order another judge of the lower court to re-examine the matter.[38] The Court of Appeal is thus not an appellate court in the technical sense of the phrase since it does not examine cases on their merits but rather refer them back to the same or different lower courts for re-trial. Where the Court of Appeal upholds the decision of the Shari'ah Court of First Instance, an aggrieved party can appeal to the Supreme Judicial Council. The Supreme Council is the apex body in the country's judicial system and its decision is final and binding on all concerned.[39]

The Board of Grievances

The Board of Grievances or *Diwan al-Al-mazalim* is a specialist tribunal or judicial body established to handle matters pertaining to specific royal decrees. Established as an administrative judicial body by its 1982 re-establishment law, the Board of Grievances stands on an equal footing with the Shari'ah Court System. However, unlike the Shari'ah Courts which are under the Ministry of Justice, the Board of Grievances is directly under and answerable to the King. Following judicial reform in 2008, the Board of Grievances enjoys more jurisdiction than it did at its inception. The reform, necessitated by the desire for a robust system of judicial dispute settlement for a more liberalized country, saw the transformation of the Board not only in terms of jurisdiction but its membership and composition of the judicial personnel that staff it.[40]

Originally, the Board of Grievances used to have jurisdiction only in matters where claims were made against the Saudi government. This used to be the Board's sole jurisdiction. It was, however, subsequently upgraded and granted broader jurisdictions to consider many other types of commercial disputes. Importantly, Islamic finance disputes come before the Board among matters within its commercial jurisdiction. For the purpose of exercising commercial jurisdiction, one-third of the judicial officers or judges of the Board are dedicated to commercial disputes.[41] Usually, the remedies granted by the Board include monetary damages and order of attachment which works like a freezing injunction for the preservation of defendant's property during the period of proceedings. Additionally, the Board may uphold a claimant's plea to recover legal and any expert cost or fees. Likewise, the Board at its discretion can grant costs to its judgment creditor generally where a claim is found to be vexatious.[42] The Board of Grievances is hierarchically structured for appeal and precedent, with a First Instance Circuit, ascending to Circuit of Appeal and at the apex the Board of Appeal Circuit.[43] The Board of Appeal is the topmost authoritative body within the structure of the Board of Grievances.[44] A party that is not satisfied with the decisions of Board of Grievances can appeal to the King as final appeal lies to the King in all matters.

The Committee for Banking Disputes

Quasi-judicial bodies and specialist tribunals are established by government at times in the form of committees under some ministries to handle disputes relating to specific royal decrees.[45] Such committees form part of the judicial dispute settlement mechanism in Saudi Arabia. For example, in banking and finance disputes, there is the Saudi Arabian Monetary Agency's (SAMA) Committee of Banking Disputes (CBD), under the auspices of the Saudi Ministry of Finance. The Committee of Banking Disputes is established and governed by the Regulation of the Committee for Banking Disputes issued via Royal Decree No. 8/729 of 1987.[46]

The Committee has jurisdiction only in banking and financing disputes. These encompass disputes arising from and out of Shari'ah-compliant banking and financing. The Committee had wielded wide-ranging powers in the determinations of the issues it handles, so much so that its exact status as a judicial body and the extent of its authority were doubted and questioned by other judicial bodies. Therefore, Royal Decree no. 3744 was issued in 2012 which introduces certain changes in its operations and clarified its status as a competent judicial body. Accordingly, the Committee is conferred with very wide enforcement and sanctioning powers that can be exercised when issuing decisions. These include placing restrictions on a debtor party in dealing with banks or governmental bodies, freezing of accounts and a travelling embargo among others.

With an alternate member for the purpose of rotation among its judges, the Committee requires a quorum of three members with one of them being a Shari'ah scholar. In addition to the legal qualifications required of all the judges, each of them must have reasonable financial dealings experience. Proceedings before the Committee involves hearing disputes based on parties' assertions in their statement of claims and defence as well as the details of the agreement they initially entered into. As is the tradition with judicial bodies, the Committee reaches its decisions by a voting majority. Further, as part of the reform, the Royal Decree No. 3744 introduced an appellate body of the Committee known as Committee of Appeal for Banking Disputes and Violations. This Appeal Committee hears appeals against the decisions of the Committee for Banking Disputes and Committee for Resolution of Violation of the Banking Control Law. For the purpose of appeal, parties to a dispute at the Banking Dispute Committee have 30 days after a decision to lodge an appeal to the Appeal Committee. Otherwise the right of appeal lapses. Decisions of the Appeal Committee are not appealable in any other forum in Saudi Arabia.[47]

The courts as well as the tribunals are guided by rules of evidence and procedure as laid down by the Shari'ah are only codified by royal decrees.[48] For the purpose of enforcement and execution of ruling or judgment, the King or whomever he deputizes shall be responsible to do so as the competent and appropriate authority under article 50 of the Basic Law. This is applicable to all sanctions and decisions within the country.

Arbitration in KSA Islamic finance disputes

Generally in Saudi Arabia, arbitration was not as popular as litigation until the enactment of the Law of Arbitration via Royal Decree No. M/46 of April 2012. This Law repealed the entire Law of Arbitration of 1983 which hitherto governed arbitration practices in the country.[49] The Saudi authorities, however, did not issue corresponding Implementing Regulations for the 2012 Arbitration Law until May 2017, which then brought the Arbitration Law into force on 9 June 2017. The promulgation and coming into force of the Implementing Regulations is a significant development for dispute resolution through arbitration in the country as it reinforces the principal legislation (the 2012 Arbitration Law) by providing clarification on several of its provisions. Generally, before 1983, the attitude of regulators to both individual and institutional arbitration was not favourable and could not create the right environment for it to develop.[50] It was nonetheless under these circumstances that the 1983 law was promulgated. Subsequently, certain deficiencies arose that warranted its repeal in 2012.[51] The new law therefore appears to have remedied most of the deficiencies identified in the former law, such as being silent on arbitrating body's seat, rules of delivering awards, processes of notification and communications between the parties and the arbitrating body as well as with third parties.[52]

Accordingly, the 2012 Law of Arbitration provides a framework for more flexible commercial arbitration, including banking and finance disputes. The Law establishes and promotes arbitration as a strong alternative dispute resolution mechanism in Saudi Arabia.[53] Generally, arbitration is voluntary, however, regulators can recommend it as compulsory in certain cases. So, depending on the nature of the dispute, arbitration in Saudi Arabia can be either voluntary or compulsory. It is apparent that the wisdom behind compulsory arbitration seems to be to avoid inconsistencies and possible clashes between Saudi Law and Shari'ah on the one hand and between Saudi Law and other Saudi traditions on the other hand. This may be the reason for limiting the Shari'ah courts' jurisdiction in certain matters that are known to be generally controversial in the Kingdom.[54]

Incorporating international best practices, the Arbitration Law establishes a new and more efficient practice of arbitration. Examples of such practices the Arbitration Law provides include allowing parties the leverage to agree on arbitration by integrating into their contracts industry-standard arbitration clauses and refer to rules of arbitration institutions.[55] These rules comprise the Rules of the London Court of International Arbitration (LCIA), the Rules of Dubai International Arbitration Centre (DIAC) and the Rules of the International Chamber of Commerce (ICC).[56] Where parties have not agreed on a specific arbitration rule that will govern their contract, then the default procedure provided by the Arbitration Law will be applied.[57] Arbitrators must be odd in number and are bound by the choice of law of the parties.[58] One provision which particularly facilitates best practice in international arbitration is international parties' freedom to choose arbitration seat and language where the fundamental contracts are not in Arabic. In addition, an arbitrator is required to possess a university degree in Islamic law or Shari'ah. Where a panel is made up of more than an arbitrator, it is sufficient for the panel chairman to have such a degree. This standard is specially established for arbitrating disputes such as those of Islamic finance and others that are more of domestic nature.

The procedure of a domestic arbitral award is as follows. First, the award must be handed down by the deadline agreed to by the parties, otherwise it must not exceed one year from the arbitration commencement date. This is subject to the power of the tribunal for further extension by six months and the ability of the parties to opt for a longer duration. To overturn an award, a party needs to file an application for annulment within 60 days at the competent court. Grounds for invalidating an arbitral award are limited and include non-existence of the agreement or its negation, lack of capacity of either party to conclude a contract at the time of agreement, appointing an arbitrator not in accordance with agreement.[59] Importantly, no party may argue or raise the issue of an award violating Shari'ah or public policy. Such arguments or issues can only be raised by the court *suo motu*. Additionally, an appellate court would not consider the merit of a dispute in deciding whether to uphold or annul an arbitral award. Such a decision is appealable which bestows some degree of confidence and certainty in process of arbitration. Unless invalidated through the procedure laid out by the law as highlighted, an arbitral decision once issued becomes a *res judicata* and remains enforceable.[60]

For the purpose of implementation, the award in practice is enforced with the intervention of a court of law by issuing a court order to that effect. Before the enforcement and execution of an award, the court has to verify and ensure that the defendant in the matter has been validly notified of the award; that it is not contrary to Islamic law and public policy in Saudi Arabia; that it is not in conflict with any judgment handed down by a court or other relevant authorities, and that the court has jurisdiction in the subject matter of the dispute.[61]

Enforcement of foreign arbitral award in KSA

Saudi Arabia is a signatory to the New York Convention on Recognition and Enforcement of Foreign Arbitral Awards. Therefore, this means that arbitral awards handed down outside the country are enforceable in the country as well. Application for enforcement of foreign judgment is evaluated based on two criteria. First, the jurisdiction that issues the award or judgment will enforce Saudi courts' judgments reciprocally. Second, consistency with Shari'ah as applied and enforced in Saudi Arabia. This is to uphold the Islamic prohibition of interest and other practices in conventional banking, financing and insurance that are considered unethical and repugnant to the Shari'ah.[62]

Conclusion

Saudi Arabia is generally an epitome of Islamic finance being a Muslim economy that has the largest concentration of Islamic funds and assets in the world. The country is an embodiment of Islamic finance in terms of banking, insurance and most significantly *sukuk* and its prospects have been attracting investors to it. The country as such serves as a global Islamic finance hub. This chapter presented a general discussion on the legal system of Saudi Arabia in relation to the practice of Islamic finance and the way related disputes can be settled. In this regard, judicial approach to Islamic finance dispute settlement and arbitration were examined. The practice of Islamic finance and its dispute settlement mechanism have been aligned with the law of the land, i.e. the Shari'ah or Islamic law. Facilitated by an enabling environment and/or legal regime, the Islamic finance industry in Saudi Arabia has recorded growth, development and significant prospects through innovative state interventions. Also, backed by a robust judicial system, Saudi laws have ensured the stability and growth of the country's economy, largely through Shari'ah-compliant financing and funds administration. The bottom line validity of all Islamic finance transactions as well as settlement of dispute arising therefrom is Shari'ah compliance. Accordingly, regular reforms carried out in line with modern economic developments sustains the industry but in tune with Shari'ah. The reforms, largely legal, facilitate and enhance the ease of undertaking Islamic finance business particularly with respect to legality of products and dispute settlement as highlighted in this chapter. The reforms ultimately ensure the establishment and operation of appropriate mechanisms, judicial, semi-judicial and non-judicial for settlement of Islamic finance dispute.

Notes

1 Formerly, the area comprising present day Saudi Arabia consisted of four historic regions that were distinct and separate: Hijaz, Najd, Al-Ahsa (Eastern Arabia) and Asir (Southern Arabia). See Al-Rasheed Madawi, *A Most Masculine State: Gender, Politics and Religion in Saudi Arabia* (Cambridge University Press 2013) 65.
2 Royal Embassy of Saudi Arabia Washington, DC 'About Saudi Arabia: Facts and Figures' www.saudiembassy.net/about/country-information/facts_and_figures/ accessed 30 September 2017.
3 http://worldpopulationreview.com/countries/saudi-arabia-population/ 30 September 2017.
4 Marshall Cavendish, *World and Its Peoples: The Arabian Peninsula* (Marshall Cavendish Corporation 2007) 78. NB: Theocracy is a form of government by divine guidance or by representatives who are believed to be divinely guided. In theocracy, God is considered the supreme ruler of the state and religion plays the central role in governing. In most theocracies, the state's legal system is based on religious law. Saudi Arabia is a leading Islamic theocracy in the world today. See Encyclopaedia Britannica, *Theocracy Political System*, www.britannica.com/topic/theocracy accessed 3 June 2018. See also SB Boyle, *What is a Theocracy* (Crabtree Publishing Company 2013) 1.
5 Promulgated via Royal Order No. (A/91) 1 March 1992.
6 Gerhard Robbers, *Encyclopedia of World Constitutions*, (Infobase Publishing 2007) vol. 1, 791.
7 Some authors claim that the lack of codification of the application of the *Shari'ah* coupled with judges' unfettered power not to be bound by any judicial precedent, make the scope, content and interpretation of the law difficult to predict in Saudi Arabia. See for instance Peter W Wilson and Douglas Graham, *Saudi Arabia: The Coming Storm* (M. E. Sharpe Inc. 1994) 201 and Jan Michiel Otto, *Sharia Incorporated: A Comparative Overview of the Legal Systems of Twelve Muslim Countries in Past and Present* (Leiden University Press 2010) 161–162.
8 Judicial precedent is due to take its shape within the Saudi Arabian judicial system with the inauguration of a Book of Judicial Principles and Legal Precedents for courts in the country. 'Issuing precedents and judicial principles is a fixed policy of the Ministry of Justice, until we reach the point where full legal disclosure is achieved,' reiterated the Saudi Justice Minister and chairman of the Supreme Judicial Council, Walid Al-Samaani, at inauguration of the said book early in January 2018. This development affirms Saudi authorities' commitment to ensuring a judicial practice in tune with modern forms and standards in line with the country's drive towards liberalization. See 'Saudi Justice Minister Inaugurates Book on Legal Precedents' *Arab News*, 5 January 2018, available at www.arabnews.com/node/1219391/saudi-arabia accessed 20 August 2018.

9 Jan Michiel Otto, *Sharia Incorporated: A Comparative Overview of the Legal Systems of Twelve Muslim Countries in Past and Present* (Leiden University, Press 2010) 161–162.
10 Christian Campbell, *Legal Aspects of Doing Business in the Middle East* (Yorkhill Law Publishing 2007) 265.
11 It is on record that, as a governance instrument in KSA, the promulgation of such royal decree might have been initiated by the Royal Decree issued by King Abdulaziz (otherwise known as Ibn Saud) that came into effect on 23 September 1932 thus, unified the two Kingdoms of Hijaz and Najd to mark the official creation of the Kingdom of Saudi Arabia www.britannica.com/place/Saudi-Arabia/The-Kingdom-of-Saudi-Arabia, accessed 30 September 2017. In addition, tribal law and or traditional customary practices constitute a significant source of law in the Saudi system of governance. For an apt exposition on the sources of law in Shariah, see Mohammad Hashim Kamali, *Principles of Islamic Jurisprudence*, (The Islamic Texts Society 2003) 22–258.
12 Mohd Zakhiri Nor, 'Settling Islamic Finance Disputes: The Case of Malaysia and Saudi Arabia', in Vernon Valentine, *et al.*, (ed.) *Mixed Legal Systems, East and West* (Routledge Taylor & Francis Group 2016) 268.
13 Examples of laws issued in that period and still in effect: The Banking Control Law of 1966, the Companies Law of 1965 and the Law of Commercial Agency of 1962.
14 See MA El-Gamal, *Islamic Finance Law, Economics and Practice* (Cambridge University Press 2006) 46–63.
15 Abdulrahman Yahya Baamir, *Shariah Law in Commercial and Banking Arbitration: Law and Practice in Saudi Arabia* (Ashgate Publishing Limited 2010) 7.
16 Thus, the issue leads to the emergence of two schools of thought inside Saudi authorities about the prohibition of banking interest as a state policy. The disagreement has invariably spread to the whole society as a row between a conservative group who resists any initiative aimed at reform in that respect against a modernist group, who supports modernization and liberalism about the issue for the purpose of economic development. The latter group advocates for arbitration in such cases, notwithstanding policies and societal values of the Kingdom. See Abdulrahman Yahya Baamir, *Shariah Law in Commercial and Banking Arbitration: Law and Practice in Saudi Arabia* (Ashgate Publishing Limited 2010) 170.
17 M Iqbal and P Molyneux, *Thirty Years of Islamic Banking: History, Performance and Prospects* (Palgrave Macmillan Ltd 2005) 17.
18 MA Choudhury, 'Development of Islamic Economic and Social Thought,' in MK Hassan and MK Lewis (eds.), *Handbook of Islamic Banking*, (Edward Elgar Publishing Ltd 2007) 34–35.
19 Ayub Mohammed, *Understanding Islamic Finance*, (John Wiley & Sons Ltd 2007) 64.
20 Nabil Issa and James Stull, 'Saudi Arabia, Steady Growth Amidst New Regulations' in Sasikala Thiagaraja *et al.* (eds.) *The Islamic Finance Handbook: A Practitioner's Guide to the Global Markets*, (John Wiley & Sons Pte. Ltd) 423.
21 The 2012 and 2013 reforms in the legal system of Saudi Arabia were largely influenced by the country's desire to modernize and keep up on best practices in the economic, social and political spheres of modern state. The reform brought about fundamental changes in the Saudi law to facilitate the development of the country in many aspects while projecting a liberalized image of itself, to be reckoned with, in the twenty-first-century world. See Mohd Zakhiri Nor (n 10).
22 The two-thirds comprise the following: 38 per cent approximately is offered by Islamic banks while 28 per cent is offered by conventional banks' Islamic windows. This is according to the '2016 Fitch Ratings' Report: Saudi Arabia Islamic Banks Dashboard'. See generally Reuters, *Fitch: Islamic Banking is Dominant in Saudi Arabia*, 2 February 2016, www.reuters.com/article/idUSFit947384 accessed 3 November 2017.

23 Al-Rajhi Bank had over $84.2 billion worth of assets as at end of the year 2016 with presence in over three other countries – Al-Rajhi Bank, https://en.wikipedia.org/wiki/Al-Rajhi_Bank accessed 3 November 2017.

24 Established in 1973, the Islamic Development Bank (IDB), headquartered in Jeddah, Saudi Arabia, was the first multiparty intergovernmental development agency that was set up on Islamic scale in order to serve member countries and help them finance public projects.

25 For instance, the National Commercial Bank of Saudi (NCB) which has declared its plan to convert to full-fledge Islamic bank, has over $120 billion in assets, two-thirds of which is Shari'ah-compliant – 2016 Fitch Ratings Report, (n 19). See also Philip Molyneux and Munawar Iqbal, *Islamic Banking and Financial Services in the Arab World*, (Palgrave Macmillan 2005) 156.

26 Ibrahim Warde, *Islamic Finance in the Global Economy* (Edinburgh University Press 2010) 6.

27 The present name Saudi Arabian Monetary Authority (SAMA) was effected in 2016. Previously, it was known as Saudi Arabian Monetary Agency which was also abbreviated as SAMA. This change was to depict a more accurate translation of its Arabic name.

28 Saudi Arabian Monetary Authority (SAMA), *Historical Preview* www.sama.gov.sa/en-US/About/Pages/SAMAHistory.aspx accessed 3 November 2017.

29 Hisham Al-Homoud, *Banking Overview in Saudi Arabia*, Al-Tamimi & Co., October – November 2012 www.tamimi.com/en/magazine/law-update/section-7/october-november-1/banking-overview-in-saudi-arabia.html accessed 3 November 2017.

30 When it comes to regulations, the issues of interest (*riba*) and ethical concerns are factors often considered so that Islamic financial institutions are treated differently from the conventional ones. While this is true in some advanced Islamic finance jurisdictions, it is worthy of note however, that at present, regulators in emerging jurisdictions have laid Islamic financial institutions open to an equivalent degree of control, regulations and conditions that are applicable to the interest-based conventional ones. To some extent, this puts the Islamic financial institutions at a disadvantage in comparison with the conventional ones. See Iqbal, Munawar, and Molyneux, Philip, *Thirty Years of Islamic Banking: History, Performance and Prospects* (Palgrave Macmillan Ltd 2005) 163.

31 2016 Fitch Ratings' Report, (n 20).

32 The growth of the Islamic finance globally would usually be characterized by the growth of transactions that could inevitably result in disputes, particularly where the underpinning contract for such transaction involves trans-border operations – Jonathan Lawrence *et al.*, *Resolving Islamic Finance Dispute*, Legal Insight, September 2013 www.klgates.com/resolving-islamic-finance-disputes-09-19-2013/ accessed 3 November 2017.

33 SA Bello, *et al.*, 'Jurisdiction of Courts Over Islamic Banking in Nigeria and Malaysia', (2015) 1 (3) *Journal of Islam, Law and Judiciary* 70; HR Abdul-Nasser and Umar Oseni 'Dispute Resolution in the Islamic Banking Industry of Tanzania: Learning from other Jurisdictions' (2016) vol. 9 (1) *International Journal of Islamic and Middle Eastern Finance and Management* 125.

34 HR Abdul-Nasser and Umar Oseni (n 33).

35 Mohd Zakhiri Nor (n 12) 271.

36 Thus, *Shari'ah* being the law of finance and commerce in Saudi Arabia, it supposedly therefore governs all bank financing activities and operations. This implies *Shari'ah*-compliance of all such financing activities and operations. This is a rider to the fact that no Islamic bank is tagged 'Islamic' in its corporate name as doing so would imply that other banks are not just conventional but 'non-Islamic' or 'non-*shari'ah*-compliant'. See Christian Campbell, *Legal Aspects of Doing Business in the Middle East* (Yorkhill Law Publishing 2009) 268–269.

37 Royal Decree No. M/21 – Law of Procedure before Shariah Courts 2000 art 31B.
38 Royal Decree No. M/21 – Law of Procedure before Shariah Courts 2000 arts 187–191.
39 Royal Decree No. M/78 – Law of Judiciary 2007 art 9.
40 Christian Campbell, *Legal Aspects of Doing Business in the Middle East* (Yorkhill Law Publishing 2009) 268–269.
41 Resolution 19 of Council of Ministers – Procedural Rules before the Board of Grievances 1989 arts 14 and 39.
42 Fenwick Elliot, *The Saudi Board of Grievances*, (2014) 11 *International Quarterly*, www.fenwickelliott.com/research-insight/newsletters/international-quarterly/11/saudi-board-grievances accessed 20 November 2017.
43 Law of the Board of Grievances 1982 art 6 and Resolution 19 of Council of Ministers – Procedural Rules before the Board of Grievances 1989 arts 18, 35 and 40.
44 In 2007, some Royal Decrees were made by King Abdullah bin Abdulaziz to reform the Saudi judiciary where a new court system was introduced that divests the Board of Grievances of commercial jurisdiction and confers same on a new commercial division of the Shari'ah court. This reform is yet to be implemented in practice. See Jan Michiel Otto, *Sharia Incorporated: A Comparative Overview of the Legal Systems of Twelve Muslim Countries in Past and Present* (Leiden University Press 2010) 161–162.
45 It was through the instrument of Royal Decrees that King Abdulaziz, founder of the modern Saudi Arabian Kingdom, set up the basis of the current justice system for all citizens after he united the country early in the 1930s, an issue that deserved priority attention for proper settlement of dispute and grievances. See John L Esposito and Emad El-Din Shahin (ed.), *The Oxford Handbook of Islam and Politics* (Oxford University Press 2013) 9–11.
46 Mohd Zakhiri Nor, (n 12) 271.
47 King and Spalding, *Recent Legal Development in Saudi Arabia* www.lexology.com/library/detail.aspx?g=84306b89-e5a2-424d-89c2-2574e7ceeb62 accessed 20 November 2017.
48 Rules of Procedure before the *Shari'ah* Courts are governed by Law of Procedure before the *Shari'ah* Courts – Royal Decree No. M/21, 19 August 2000, while same before the Board of Grievances are governed by Procedural Rules before the Board of Grievances – Council of Ministers Resolution No. 190, 19 June 1989.
49 Abdulrahman Baamir and Ilias Bantekas, 'Saudi Law as *Lex Arbitri*: Evaluation of Saudi Arbitration Law and Judicial Practice', (2009) vol. 25 (2) *Arbitration International* 239–270.
50 The attitude of Saudi regulators towards international arbitration for instance, developed in three stages: first, when the Saudi authorities did not oppose arbitration, particularly for its international affairs. Thus, the government used it to settle the dispute of Al-Buraimi Oasis (Wahat Al-Buraimi) in 1955. The agreement was concluded in Jeddah between Saudi and the Britain which acted for the rulers of Oman and Abu Dhabi. This arbitration had not impacted significantly on the legal system of the KSA. Second, was when the KSA government began to perceive arbitration as a danger to its sovereignty as a nation. This commenced in 1958 as epitomized by the ARAMCO award and changed the Saudi authorities' attitude to international arbitration for some decades. Third, when the attention of Saudi authorities turned to attract investment from foreigners and started with the initial oil boom of 1970s and continues until now. See generally Abdulrahman Yahya Baamir, *Shariah Law in Commercial and Banking Arbitration: Law and Practice in Saudi Arabia* (Ashgate Publishing Limited 2010) 95–96.
51 Abdulrahman Baamir and Ilias Bantekas (n 49).
52 S Saleh, *Commercial Arbitration in the Arab Middle East: Shari'ah, Syria, Lebanon and Egypt* (2nd edn, Heart Publishing 2006), especially Chapter 20, 290–325.

53 M Albejad, *Arbitration in Saudi Arabia* (1st edn, Institute of Public Administration 1999) 30.
54 Ibid, 51. For instance, disputes in relation to tobacco and its products, as well as musical gadgets have to, by regulatory recommendation, be mandatorily referred to arbitration. Abdulrahman Yahya Baamir (n 47) 117–118.
55 Royal Decree No. M/34 – Law of Arbitration 2012 arts 4 and 5.
56 King and Spalding, *Recent Legal Development in Saudi Arabia*, www.lexology.com/library/detail.aspx?g=84306b89-e5a2-424d-89c2-2574e7ceeb62 accessed 20 November 2017.
57 Law of Arbitration 2012 art 15.
58 Law of Arbitration 2012 art 13.
59 Law of Arbitration 2012 art 50.
60 Law of Arbitration 2012 art 52.
61 Law of Arbitration 2012 art 55.
62 Clifford Chance, *A Guide to Doing Business in the Kingdom of Saudi Arabia* https://financialmarketstoolkit.cliffordchance.com/content/micro-facm/en/financial-markets-resources/resources-by-type/guides/doing-business-in-the-kingdom-of-saudi-arabia/_jcr_content/parsys/download/file.res/.pdf accessed 23 November 2017.

8 Settlement of Islamic finance disputes in the United Arab Emirates

Nor Razinah Binti Mohd Zain and Rusni Hassan

Introduction

The concept of Islamic finance was considered as a wishful dream almost three decades ago. Today, more than 300 Islamic financial institutions are operating around the globe. By 2020, Islamic finance assets are estimated to reach $3.2 trillion in value.[1] Their clientele are not confined to citizens of Muslim countries only, but are spread over Europe, the United States of America and the Far East. Muslims now have the opportunity to invest their financial resources in accordance with the ethics and philosophy of Islam. At the same time, Islamic finance offers an alternative for the customers of conventional finance.

The first thorough studies devoted to the establishment of Islamic financial institutions (referred to hereafter as 'Islamic Banks') appeared in the 1940s. Although Muslim owned banks were established as early as in the 1920s and 1930s, they adopted similar practices to conventional banks. In the 1940s and 1950s, several experiments with small Islamic Banks were undertaken in Malaysia and Pakistan. The first great success was the establishment of an Islamic Bank in the Egyptian village of Mit Ghamr, in 1963. Other successes include the establishment of the Inter-Governmental Islamic Development Bank in Jeddah in 1975 and a number of Islamic Banks, such as the Dubai Islamic Bank, the Kuwait Finance House and the Bahrain Islamic Bank in the 1970s and 1980s. In South East Asia, Malaysia became the first country that introduced Islamic finance with the establishment of Bank Islam Malaysia Bhd. in 1983. Commercial banks have also realized the potential of this new field, and a number of major worldwide institutions have adopted Islamic banking and finance as a significant mechanism for diversified growth.

Legal framework for Islamic finance

The legal system of UAE

In championing Islamic finance in the Gulf region, United Arab Emirates (UAE) stands out as a country that has the largest Islamic finance markets in the world. While competing with countries, such as Saudi Arabia and Malaysia, the value of UAE market is 24.4 per cent or 494.5 billion UAE dirhams (equivalent to US$134.59 billion) according to the UAE's Central Bank.[2] The strength of Islamic finance in the UAE depends on the strong legal system that the country offers.

Prior to 1971, there were seven separate emirates in the geographical area of the UAE. They are known as Abu Dhabi, Dubai, Sharjah, Ummal-Qawain, Ajman, Fujairah and Ra's Al Khaimah. The modern history of the UAE began in 1971, following independences from the British and six of the seven separate emirates (Abu Dhabi, Dubai, Sharjah, Ummal-Qawain, Ajman, and Fujairah) agreed and unified to form a country. The last emirate of Ra's Al Khaimah entered the UAE in 1972. The birth of this new country was accompanied with the promulgation of Provisional Constitution of 1971. The Provisional Constitution of 1971 is structured from the Constitution of Kuwait that was originally based on the Constitution of Egypt. The UAE accepted their Provisional Constitution with certain amendments as their main constitution in July 1996.[3] The main capital of UAE is established in Abu Dhabi and Dubai.[4] As a federation, the Constitution of UAE allocates primary authority to the central federal government for certain matters, such as the defence and armed forces, protection and security, finances and taxes.[5] The central federal government has the authority to govern matters relating to banking and finance. The emirates have jurisdictions to legislate in all matters that are not assigned to the central federal government.[6]

Generally, the UAE utilizes the civil legal system by the codification of the constitution and legislation important to their legal practice. As a federation, the UAE implements two systems in relation to its legal structures. First, there is a federal judiciary in which the Federal Supreme Court stands as the highest authority of judiciary.[7] Second, there is a local judicial department that exists at the level of local government. The Ministry of Justice has responsibility to oversee the courts and prosecution departments in the entire UAE, appointment of judges, licencing of lawyers, legal experts and translators. All of the seven emirates choose to maintain their rights to either join the Federal Judiciary or maintain their own local judicial systems. Such right is stipulated clearly in Article 105 of Constitution of UAE. The local courts can be transformed into the federal judiciary based on request from the emirates. The emirates of Sharjah, Ajman, Fujairah, and Ummal-Qawain are among the earliest emirates that choose to join the Federal Judiciary.[8] Currently, there are only two emirates (i.e. Dubai and Ra's Al Khaimah) that still maintain their own local judiciaries. At their local level, the judicial authorities are Dubai courts in Dubai and Ras Al Khaimah Courts in Ras Al Khaimah. They have jurisdiction in all matters that are not conferred to the Federal Judiciary as stipulated in the Constitution of UAE.

Except for Ras Al Khaimah that does not have the Court of Cassation, all the emirates of UAE have three main structures of courts that consist of (i) Court of First Instance; (ii) Court of Appeal; and (iii) Court of Cassation.[9] Article 105 of the Constitution of UAE and the existing federal laws allow the jurisdiction of a local court (in all or part) at the local level to make a reference of the case to the Court of First Instance at the federal level. However, this is only allowed for the local court's jurisdiction and not vice versa.[10] Once the reference is made, federal laws are applicable to the case. In relation to appeals, the federal laws provide the circumstances that the appeals can be made to the federal courts as against the judgments made by the local courts. However, some disputes[11] can only be judged by the Federal Supreme Court[12] at the federal level and cannot be referred to the local court at the emirate's level. A specific law, of Federal Law No. 11 of 1973, is provided to govern the judicial relations between the emirates, such as for (i) exchange of criminal information; (ii) execution of judgments by courts, arbitrators and official writs; and (iii) extradition of fugitives.[13]

The position of Shari'ah in UAE

The Constitution of UAE stipulates that Shari'ah is a principal source of legislation in the UAE.[14] At the same time, the supremacy of the Constitution of UAE is recognized by virtue of Article 151. The provisions of the Constitution of UAE prevail over other existing constitutions of the emirates. The Constitution of UAE also takes precedence over all other legislations issued by the emirates. In an event of conflict between the legislations and the Constitution of UAE, such inconsistency is treated as null and void.[15] However, the legal inconsistency may be brought in front of the Federal Supreme Court to be resolved. The Constitution of UAE does not make any reference to any specific Islamic school of legal thought that the UAE will follow. This means that there is no one special Islamic school of legal thought under the laws, and all schools of Islamic thought are equally treated. Taking this position as an advantage, the legal opinions from the Islamic school of legal thought can be applied in a flexible manner. There are basically four main Islamic schools of legal thought that are available in the region, namely Malikis, Hanafis, Shafi'is, and Hanbalis. Based on the practices of the people, the Maliki school of legal thought prevails in Abu Dhabi and Dubai. Hanbali school of legal thought is predominant in Sharjah. Additionally, Shafi'i school of legal thought is applied in Dubai and Sharjah. In commercial transactions, majority of courts in UAE recognize the application of Mejella which is derived from Hanafi school of legal thought.[16]

Shari'ah is ranked as a high source for legislations in the UAE. Even though, Shari'ah has a high position under the Constitution of UAE, Shari'ah is placed as one of the sources of legislations in the UAE. In the absence of any written legislation, Shari'ah can be referred by the Courts to fill up the gaps.[17] Generally, the judges are bound to uphold the legislated laws of the emirates and the federal laws as conferred by the UAE. In relation to financial matters, the Courts still have to look at the business contractual practice that was agreed between the contracting parties. This means the status of Shari'ah as the principal source of legislations does not disturb the enforcement of the existing and applicable laws. As long as a certain principle is allowed under the legislation, such principle can still be practised even though it may be in contradiction with Shari'ah. For an example, it is clear that under the Shari'ah that interest or usury (*riba*) is prohibited. This legal position is enshrined through Article 204 of Federal Law No. 5 of 1985 (UAE Civil Code).[18] In addition, Article 714 of the UAE Civil Code specifies that a provision relating to interest or benefit that goes beyond what is agreed in a contract of loan is void and unenforceable.[19] By virtue of this Article 714, a simple interest is allowed in the operation of conventional banking system.

Before 1970s, the economic and financial transactions were primarily conducted by conventional banks. At this time the first Islamic bank (Dubai Islamic bank) was still at the stage of infancy. By virtue of Decision No. 14/9 that was issued on 28 of June 1981 by the Constitutional Department of the UAE Federal Supreme Court, charging of interest in banking operations was allowed based on the reason of necessity (*daruriyyah*) of economic existence in the UAE and public interest (*maslahah*).[20] The said decision led to the introduction of Federal Law No. 18 of 1993 (UAE Commercial Code) that separates the operation of civil transaction law over commercial transaction. While commercial transaction are governed under the UAE Commercial Code, civil transactions continue to be governed under the UAE Civil Code. In support of the commercial operation of conventional banks in the UAE, the UAE Commercial Code allows conventional banks to charge certain interest and such interest must be paid. For example:

i Article 76 of UAE Commercial Code states that

> A creditor shall have the right to demand interest on a commercial loan in accordance with the rate stipulated in the contract. If the rate of interest is not stipulated in the contract it shall be calculated in accordance with the rate prevailing in the market at the time of the transaction on condition that in this case it shall not exceed (12%) per cent, until full settlement is made.[21]

ii Article 77 of UAE Commercial Code stipulates that 'Where the contract stipulates the rate of interest and the debtor delays payment, the delay interest shall be calculated on basis of the agreed rate until full settlement'.[22]

iii Article 88 of UAE Commercial Code reads that

> Where the commercial obligation is a sum of money which was known when the obligation arose and the debtor delays payment thereof, he shall be bound to pay to the creditors as compensation for the delay; the interest fixed in Articles (76) and (77), unless otherwise agreed.[23]

iv Article 90 of UAE Commercial Code explains that 'Interest for delay of payment of commercial debts shall accrue on mere maturity of such debts, unless it is otherwise provided for by law or agreement'.[24]

v Article 409 (3) of UAE Commercial Code states that 'The borrower shall be bound to repay the loan and its interest to the bank within such time limits and according to such conditions as are agreed'.[25]

Islamic banks in the UAE

In relation to Islamic banking and finance in UAE, there is a specific law that is applicable to Islamic banks and other Islamic financial institutions, such as branches of Islamic foreign banks and Islamic development banks. The referred law is Federal Law No. 6 of 1985. By virtue of Article 4 of Federal Law No. 6 of 1985, with a cross reference to the Union Law No. 10 of 1980, the Islamic banks are allowed to '(i) carry on for its own account commercial or industrial activities or (ii) acquire, own or trade in goods …; and (iii) acquire immovable property for its own account …'.[26]

Simultaneously, Islamic banks are exempted from applying interest-based transactions in their operations.[27] Even though, the UAE Commercial Code and UAE Civil Code are applicable to Islamic banks, the Federal Law No. 6 of 1985 provides that in the event of inconsistency of existing laws with the nature of the Islamic banks, the Islamic banks have

> the right to carry on all or part of banking, commercial, financial and investment services and operation … to engage in all types of services and operations practiced by banks and referred to in Union Law No. 10 of 1980 … also have the right to establish companies … provided that activities of the latter are in conformity with Islamic Shari'ah Law.[28]

This indicates that the Islamic banks have all the necessary rights and means to ensure that their banking operation and products are in compliance with Shari'ah, as long as they are not contravening any existence laws of the UAE.

Moreover, all the Islamic banks established in the UAE are bound to follow their articles and memorandums of association, and 'a commitment to abide by the provisions of the Islamic Shari'ah Law, and conduct their activities in accordance therewith'.[29] By having such provisions, the Islamic banks (including the foreign Islamic banks and development banks) are required to follow the existing laws of UAE and the principles of Shari'ah. Failure to do so is a contradiction to the Federal Law No. 6 of 1985 and would directly go against the article and memorandums of association of the Islamic banks in the UAE. Additionally, as bound by the ethical stance of the Islamic banking industry in the UAE, Islamic bankers in the UAE must have high morals and Islamic awareness to ensure the Shari'ah compliance of their banks' operations and products.

All banks that exist in the UAE are bound to follow the regulatory policies, directions as provided by the UAE Central Bank by virtue of provisions codified in the Federal Law No. 10 of 1980. The Federal Law No. 10 of 1980 covers the operation of UAE Central Bank, the existence of monetary system and the organization of banking. The UAE Central Bank has responsibility in ensuring the operations of both Islamic and conventional finance are in accordance to the existing laws of UAE. Once a bank satisfies the necessary requirements, a licence to operate is issued to it by the UAE Central Bank.

Based on Article 3 of Federal Law No. 6 of 1985, Islamic banks have several rights. These rights are: (i) to carry on all or part of banking, commercial, financial, and investment services and operations; (ii) to engage in all types of services and operations practised by banks and referred to in the Federal Law No. 10 of 1980, and (iii) to conduct operations and services for the Islamic bank's own account or for or in partnership with a third party; and (iv) to establish companies and participate in enterprises provided that the activities of the latter are in conformity with Shari'ah. Such provision provided under Article 5 of Federal Law No. 6 of 1985 for the establishment of a Higher Shari'ah Authority. Nevertheless, such kind of establishment has never been created in practice.

Islamic banks (including the foreign Islamic banks and development banks) are required by virtue of Article 6 of Federal Law No. 6 of 1985 to appoint at least three Shari'ah scholars as their Shari'ah Supervision Authority or SSA. The SSA is responsible to make sure that the Islamic banks' operations and products meet the principles of Shari'ah at their highest degree. Based on the practices of the Islamic banks in the UAE, the SSB has responsibility to review Islamic banks' financial products or any relevant issue that is related to the said banks' operations. After critical analysis and evaluation, members of SSB may pass a fatwa or an Islamic resolution demanding Shari'ah compliance for the financial products or issues. Once the SSB's approval is obtained, Islamic banks may offer the financial products or settle the issue accordingly. Additionally, the Islamic banks in the UAE are required to adhere to the high standards of the international setting bodies, such as Accounting and Auditing Organisation for Islamic Financial Institutions (AAOIFI) and Islamic Financial Services Board (IFSB). Since their participation in these international setting bodies is on voluntary basis, it is observed that their adherence to stipulations set out by international bodies varies from one Islamic bank to another.

International financial centres of the UAE

With globalization of Islamic banking and finance, countries that offer Islamic finance are competing to become the best global centre of Islamic finance.[30] Examining the market of Islamic finance in the Middle East, Khan and Bhatti observed that:

> The Middle East is the mainstream of Islamic banking and finance. Islamic financial institutions are making individual and collective efforts to develop a wide array of innovative, customer-oriented and competitive products and services to their clientele. It is their core objective to get strong hold over the indigenous oil-wealth and discourage its outgoing to financial institutions in the European and Western world. Recent market developments suggest that the Islamic banking and finance industry is a big success and enjoys a very strong regional support. An increasing number of conventional financial institutions in the Middle Eastern markets are converting their operations either fully or partially on Islamic lines....[31]

The UAE stands among the main frontiers of Islamic finance in the global market. It becomes pertinent for the UAE to have international financial centres, especially to boost their economy through the progressive development of trades, banking, and finance.

Supported by a stable economy, the geographical position of UAE in the Middle East and Africa, and close trading relationship with the Western countries, the UAE has high potential to be the global centre of Islamic finance. As a part of their legislative strategy, the UAE opens a small but yet significant channel for the application of Common Law in the country.[32]

Motivated with such intentions, the Dubai International Financial Centre (DIFC) was established in 2004. Additionally, the Abu Dhabi Global Market (ADGM) was introduced in 2013. These two offshore financial free zones are also introducing new legal centres in UAE. They offer the Common Law based legal system. By having two offshore jurisdictions within the UAE, investors and traders have choices to go for the best legal services that they can get. This also encourages healthy competition between DIFC and ADGM in offering their best legal services. With the establishment of DIFC and ADGM, the UAE has introduced the practice of common law to the public, while maintaining the civil legal system. In parallel, Shari'ah is maintained as the main primary source of legislation. According to Strong and Himber, the DIFC has more flexibility in offering legal services and thus they seem more attractive in comparison to ADGM.[33]

Both DIFC and ADGM are established on the back of the Federal Law No. 8 of 2004 that acknowledged their status as the financial free zones in the UAE. The Federal Decree No. 15 of 2013, Cabinet Resolution No. 4 of 2013 and Abu Dhabi Law No. 4 of 2013 are other relevant legislations that can be referred in relation to ADGM. Meanwhile, DIFC is based on the Federal Decree No. 35 of 2004. DIFC has a vision to become a global financial hub and 'to promote growth and development of financial services within the UAE by providing world-class infrastructure and business opportunities'[34] Even though both of DIFC and ADGM[35] are developed to become international offshore financial free zones, their main difference can be traced from their legal structures.

The primary legislation of ADGM can only be enacted by a specific board of directors. The members of the said board are appointed by the Abu Dhabi Executive Council. Later, the ADGM's secondary legislations can be promulgated based on their primary legislation. The regulations of ADGM cover three authoritative bodies that are known as: (i) the ADGM registration authorities; (ii) the ADGM financial services authority; and (iii) the ADGM court. Meanwhile, the DIFC's primary and secondary legislations are enacted by the Ruler of Dubai. There are three main centre bodies under the DIFC; they are: (i) DIFC administrative authority; (ii) Dubai Financial Services Authority; and (iii) Dispute Resolution Authority (DRA). By having the common law-based regulations and legal system, the DIFC offers a legal constructive channel for the investors and traders to have their preferred choice of jurisdiction that extends to cover their businesses, transactions and contracts, and also dispute resolution forum. All these legal services are carried out based on common law, instead of civil law.

Settlement of Islamic finance disputes

With the introduction of DIFC and ADGM, the UAE manages to formulate a modern and mixed legal system in the country. Uniquely, they have two sets of legal systems i.e. common law and civil law, within which Shari'ah stands as a primary source of law by virtue of Article 7 of Constitution of UAE. In relation to the settlement of Islamic finance dispute, there are three main dispute resolution mechanisms that can be referred to within the mixed legal system of the UAE. The first method is litigation. The second method is arbitration, and the third method is reconciliation.

Litigation is a process of taking a legal action by one party (i.e. Plaintiff) by suing another party (i.e. Defendant) for certain disputed facts through a legal representative or counsel before the recognized judiciary body or court that was established by the state. In failure of denying the purported legal action, a judgment can be passed upon the party that has been sued. According to Chayes, litigation is similar to adjudication where it is understood as 'a process for resolving disputes among private parties which have not been privately settled'.[36] Meanwhile, arbitration can be understood as 'the referral of a dispute to one or more impartial persons for a final and binding determination'.[37] The term reconciliation sometimes is used interchangeably with conciliation. The reconciliation happens when 'an impartial party facilitates discussion between the parties, provides advice on the substance of the dispute, makes proposals for settlement or actively contributes to the terms of any agreement'.[38] In a matter of structure, the identified dispute resolution processes in the UAE can be divided into:

- i The authoritative legal body or court: which refers to the litigation process in the federal civil courts of the UAE;
- ii The court annexed dispute resolution process: which refers to the reconciliation process that attached to the federal civil courts of the UAE;
- iii The institutional dispute resolution: which refers to the common law-based dispute resolution processes as offered in DIFC and ADGM. They can be divided into litigation, and arbitration;
- iv The regional dispute resolution: which refers to dispute resolution processes in certain emirates of the UAE; and,
- v The organizational dispute resolution: which refers to dispute resolution processes that are offered by certain commercial organizations in the UAE. They are divided into arbitration, and reconciliation.

It seems that there is no possibility of a clash between the legal systems since the cases that are brought within one of the legal systems must accordingly follow the legal structures as provided under the UAE's laws. Moreover, even though there is no clear law stipulated that a case cannot be brought again through another legal system, it is a part of a legal and ethical practice in the UAE to avoid such situation. This means if a case is brought by using the civil legal system, it is impertinent to bring it again under the common law legal system.

Dispute resolution under the UAE's Civil Law

Basically, all litigation proceedings in the UAE's civil courts depend on the written pleadings of the disputing parties i.e. the plaintiff and the defendant. Such pleadings are supported with documentary evidence,[39] without any emphasis on oral hearing. In the UAE's civil courts, the cases are decided by the sitting judges based on their merits and not based on the certain standard of proof (such as the balance of probability) as applied under the common law courts. The final decision to resolve the dispute is based on the discretion of the judge who hears the case. Arabic language is the main language used before these courts. If the documentary evidence is written in English or other languages, it must be translated to Arabic language for court reference.

It is highlighted here that the majority of disputes that are brought before the courts are based on contractual agreements between the disputing parties, which cover either commercial contracts or finance contracts. In relation to the legal enforceability of a contract, the courts will not impose other or further meaning to the terms of the contracts, unless the contract is not clear.[40] Thus, as far as the Shari'ah elements of the contracts issued by the Islamic banks, the courts do not evaluate them unless there is lack of clarity and ambiguity to what had been agreed by the disputing parties. According to Khan, the judges may not necessarily be specialists in commercial matters.[41] They can call court-appointed experts be in commercial matters (such as in finance, accounting or other technical matters) to provide expert opinions to assist the judges to reach the correct decision for the cases.

As a part of the UAE's court annexed dispute resolution process, any commercial disputes must be referred to an established reconciliation committee in resolving a dispute. This established committee is known as the Reconciliation and Settlement Committee (RSC) and is appointed by the Ministry of Justice by virtue of the Federal Law No. 26 of 1999. The disputing parties are usually heard by the RSC in person to understand the root of the dispute. If the reconciliation process by the RSC fails, then the disputing parties may file a legal claim in the Court of First Instance. If the resolution is reached, the RSC will record a settlement and the parties will officially enter a legally binding settlement agreement. However, the procedure to refer to RSC is not established in Dubai and Ras Al Khaimah. In Dubai, they have their own court annexed process which is known as the Centre for Amicable Resolution of Disputes.[42] That centre was established in April 2002 and deals with disputes relating to commonly owned property, debt (at the maximum of AED 50,000), and disputes that were agreed to be settled before the centre. Apart from this centre, there are also other regional dispute resolution centres, such as Sharjah International Commercial Arbitration

Centre[43] and Ras Al Khaimah Centre of Reconciliation and Commercial Arbitration.[44] The Sharjah International Commercial Arbitration Centre was established based on Amiri Decree No. 6 of 2009 issued by His Highness Sheikh Dr Sultan bin Mohammad Al Qassimi the member of Supreme Council and Ruler of Sharjah. Ras Al Khaimah Centre of Reconciliation and Commercial Arbitration was established under Ras Al Khaimah Chamber of Commerce and Industry by virtue of Amiri Decree No. 17 of 2008.

Specifically focusing on Islamic banking and finance, the International Islamic Center for Reconciliation and Arbitration (IICRA) was established with the cooperative efforts made by the government of the UAE, the Islamic Development Bank, and the General Council of Islamic Banks and Financial Institutions. The IICRA was founded in 2005 but initiated operations in 2007.[45] The IICRA can be considered as an organizational initiated dispute resolution process, with the objective to attain a Shari'ah compliance resolution to any Islamic finance disputes. Under the IICRA, the dispute resolution process takes place between the Islamic banks and their clients or any third party through arbitration or reconciliation. The IICRA is established as a non-profit international organization with legal and independent personality. The disputing parties that choose the IICRA in resolving their dispute have option to go for arbitration or reconciliation. While the ruling issued by the ICCRA's Arbitration Panel has a binding and mandatory effect to both of the disputing parties, the decision made through the reconciliation is only binding upon the parties after their voluntary entry into a valid agreement.

Depending on the arbitration rules as provided under the UNCITRAL model law on International Commercial Arbitration[46] and with certain modification to suit the UAE laws, the IICRA stands out in comparison to other centres of dispute resolution with an aim to reach a Shari'ah compliance resolution between Islamic banks and their clients or other third party. Moreover, the award made by the IICRA's Arbitration Panel received recognition from the signatories' members of New York Convention of 1958 on the Recognition and Enforcement of Foreign arbitrators' judgments. The said award also can be enforced within the UAE through the courts and their laws.[47] They also offer certificates and trainings for arbitrators specializing in dispute resolution in Islamic finance.[48]

Another organizational initiated dispute resolution process can be traced from the Dubai International Arbitration Centre or DIAC.[49] The said centre was first established in 1994 by the Dubai Chamber of Commerce and Industry and known as the Centre for Commercial Conciliation and Arbitration. The DIAC can also be considered as a regional dispute resolution centre that operates within Dubai. Focusing to resolve disputes among the business players locally and internationally in the UAE, the DIAC offers an arbitration process at affordable rates. Among the DIAC's services are: (i) facilities in conducting commercial arbitration process; (ii) promoting arbitration process; and (iii) providing training to arbitrators with exposure to the international practice of arbitration.

The DIAC arbitration rules come into effect based on Dubai Decree No. 11 of 2007. The said decree replaced the Rules of Commercial Conciliation and

Arbitration of Dubai Chamber of Commerce and Industry No. 2 of 2004. Based on the DIAC arbitration rules, the provisions do not prevent any reference of Islamic finance dispute from being made to the DIAC. Thus, the alternative dispute resolution service by DIAC may be considered by the Islamic banks in resolving disputes with their customers. Their process in resolving disputes is apparently based on Civil Law since the DIAC is tied down to follow the UAE Civil Procedure Code, as stipulated under Federal Law No. 11 of 1992.

Dispute resolution under the UAE's Common Law

Article 121 of the UAE Constitution was amended in 2004 to authorize the federal government exclusively in relation to 'the order and the manner of establishing Financial Free Zones and the boundaries within which they are exempted from having to apply rules and regulations of the Union'.[50] Federal Decree No. 35 of 2004 was adopted on 27 June 2004 to establish the financial free zone in Dubai. In accordance with that decree, Federal Law No. 8 of 2004 was promulgated on 14 March 2004 to establish the international financial free zones.[51]

Article 3 of Federal Law No. 8 of 2004 exempts the financial free zones from all federal, civil, and commercial laws. However, the financial free zones are not exempted from following federal criminal laws (such as the Federal Law No. 4 of 2002 on the criminalization of money laundering, and the UAE Penal Code). At the same time, the financial free zones must accordingly follow all the required constitutional provisions of the UAE. Article 7 (3) of Federal Law No. 8 of 2004 authorizes financial free zones to create its own legal and regulatory framework to cover all civil and commercial matters. However, they are still subjected to follow all the international treaties that the UAE is a signatory member.[52] A wide flexibility is given to the financial free zones in emphasizing their legal personality.[53] They are also authorized to enter into any memorandum of understanding and cooperation (MOU) with any similar entities.[54]

The main references for dispute resolution under the UAE's common law depend on the legal services offered under the international financial centres of DIFC and ADGM. The legal services are not limited to commercial matters per se but may also include Islamic finance disputes.

Under the DIFC, there are three independent authoritative bodies that support the growth of the DIFC. These independent bodies are known as Dubai International Finance Centre, Dubai Financial Services Authority, and Dispute Resolution Authority.[55] The Dispute Resolution Authority or DRA has the responsibility to administer justice and legal excellence within the DIFC. Under the DRA, there are four main components which are DIFC Courts, DIFC Arbitration Institute, DIFC Wills and Probate Registry, and Academy of Law. In relation to settlement of Islamic finance disputes, the primary components of DRA are the DIFC Courts and DIFC Arbitration Institute.

The DIFC Courts are an independent judicial authority that deal with legal matters arising in the DIFC. They are based on common law judicial system, and their proceedings are conducted in English. At their earlier establishment, the jurisdiction of the courts was limited to the geographical area of the DIFC only. Later on, the Dubai Law No. 16 of 2011 was legislated and allows the DIFC courts to hear either local or international cases to resolve commercial disputes. However, such resolution can only be done with consent from all the parties involved. By following the Convention on the Recognition and Enforcement of Foreign Arbitral Awards or New York Convention 1958, the DIFC Court also has the jurisdiction to recognize and enforce foreign arbitral awards.[56] At the local level, the jurisdiction of DIFC Court is extended to recognize and enforce domestic arbitral awards which are decided within the Emirate of Dubai. Furthermore, a judgment made by the DIFC Court is recognized by the onshore courts of Dubai and can be enforced outside the DIFC. This may be carried out by virtue of Dubai Law No. 12 of 2004. In comparison to the UAE's civil courts, the DIFC Courts have only two levels of courts in their structure. They are (i) the Court of First Instance with one sitting judge, and (ii) the Court of Appeal that comprises with at least three judges. The DIFC's Court of First Instance may deal with legal disputes involving:

1 Civil or commercial cases and disputes involving the DIFC, any of the DIFC's bodies or any of the DIFC's establishments;
2 Civil or commercial cases and disputes involving the DIFC, any of the DIFC's bodies or any of the DIFC's establishments;
3 Objections filed against a decision made by the DIFC's bodies, which are subject to objection in accordance with the DIFC's laws and regulations;
4 Any application over which the Courts have jurisdiction in accordance with the DIFC's laws and regulations.[57]

The DIFC's Court of Appeal may deal with legal disputes involving:

1 Appeals filed against judgments and awards made by the Court of First Instance;
2 Interpretation of any article of the DIFC's laws based upon the request of any of the DIFC's bodies or the request of any of the DIFC's establishments provided that the establishment obtains leave of the Chief Justice....[58]

The decision made by the DIFC's Court of Appeal is considered as the final judgment or award and no further appeal is allowed. In relation to the settlement of Islamic finance disputes, they tend to treat them similarly with other commercial disputes or disputes arise from contracts. No compulsory reference can be made to any Shari'ah committee in resolving any related Shari'ah issues in the Islamic finance disputes. However, the DIFC courts may call them before the court as a part of expert opinion. In resolving disputes arising from Islamic finance contracts, there is still no clear position from DIFC courts.

As a common law-based court, the judges may take a similar approach as followed in Islamic *Investment Company of the Gulf (Bahamas) Ltd v Symphony Gems N.V. & Ors*[59] and *Shamil Bank of Bahrain EC v Beximco Pharmaceuticals*

Ltd & Ors.[60] The incorporation of Shari'ah must be sufficiently identified within the contract' terms and the parties are agreed to be bound by it. Those cases are not bound to be followed by the DIFC's courts. Instead of focusing on existence of conflict of laws, the DIFC courts may give emphasis on the party autonomy in allowing application of Shari'ah. Moreover, such application must not be in contradiction to the UAE's existing laws, while upholding the Shari'ah as one of the sources of the said existing laws. Different from the Court's position in *Shamil Bank's case*, Shari'ah is not foreign under the UAE's legal system and may receive a high appreciation in resolving Islamic finance disputes. Thus, the DIFC courts may apply Shari'ah compliance resolutions to Islamic finance disputes. This is also advantageous in upholding DIFC as the international financial centre.

The DIFC also offers alternative dispute resolution in resolving Islamic finance disputes. The alternative dispute resolution as offered by the DIFC is mainly focused on arbitration. The early legal reference can be made to DIFC Law No. 8 of 2004, which was later replaced by DIFC Law No. 1 of 2008 and amended further by DIFC Law No. 6 of 2013. By having the DIFC Law No. 1 of 2008,[61] all legal limitations in choosing DIFC as the legal sitting for alternative dispute resolution is removed. Additionally, the alternative dispute resolution (especially arbitration) is not bound to follow the civil procedure as stipulated in the Federal Law No. 11 of 1992. A wide flexibility can be seen from the DIFC No. 1 of 2008 where it is substantially derived from UNCITRAL Model Law, the English Arbitration Act 2006, and some parts of Japanese and German arbitration laws. Under DIFC, the DIFC Arbitration Institute was established under the DRA. Later on, a collaboration was concluded between the DIFC and London Court of International Arbitration or LCIA[62] to establish the DIFC-LCIA arbitration centre. The DIFC-LCIA arbitration centre is operated by virtue of its Constitution by the DIFC Arbitration Institute.[63] According to Blanke, he observes that:

> In light of the wording of Articles 8(5)(a) and (b) of Law No. (7) of 2014, it is not entirely clear to what extent the Arbitration Institute is meant to dispense arbitration services itself and will not be confined to the promotion of the profession and practice of arbitration within the DIFC only. Too little is presently known to allow any meaningful assessment of the true scope of duties and powers of the Arbitration Institute … the role of the DIFC-LCIA, which – to date at least – has been widely recognized as the dedicated arbitration centre of the DIFC.[64]

The DIFC-LCIA arbitration centre offer several types of alternative dispute resolution processes. The disputing parties may choose any of the alternative dispute resolution processes available, such as arbitration, mediation, adjudication, expert determination and other ad hoc alternative dispute resolution proceedings. The arbitration rules that they refer to are almost similar with the LCIA's arbitration rules.[65] There are also specific mediation rules that the parties need to follow if they refer their dispute with the said centre.[66] The Islamic banks may also refer any of their Islamic finance disputes with their customers at the DIFC-LCIA arbitration centre. However, both parties must agree to such alternative dispute resolution processes.

Under separate legislations of the ADGM, they provide the common law-based courts with ADGM Courts, Civil Evidence, Judgments, Enforcement and Judicial Appointments Regulations 2015 as enacted on 11 December 2015, and subject to the ADGM Courts Procedure Rules as enacted on 30 May 2016.[67] The ADGM courts are structured as (i) the Court of First Instance, and (ii) the Court of Appeal. The courts' structures are similar with the DIFC's. Unlike the DIFC courts, the ADGM courts are bound to follow the UAE's existing laws, Abu Dhabi laws, and their own established legislations.[68] The ADGM courts only entertain legal disputes that are of commercial or civil nature.[69] Thus, any Islamic finance dispute is treated similar to other commercial or civil cases. Similar with the DIFC courts, there is no specific Shari'ah authority that the ADGM courts may refer to in relation to Shari'ah issues. However, the judges of ADGM courts are not restrained from calling any Shari'ah scholars for their expert opinions.[70]

The establishment of alternative dispute resolution process under the ADGM are available but still are at their infancy stage. The ADGM enacted their Arbitration Regulations 2015 on 17 December 2015 and derived such establishment based on the UNCITRAL Model Law. The Arbitration Regulations 2015 provides the details in conducting arbitral proceedings, the recognition of awards, and enforcement of arbitral awards within the ADGM.[71] In evaluating the said regulations on arbitration, Gaffney said:

> A pervasive pro-arbitration approach has been taken in the Regulations: there is limited scope for court intervention in the arbitral process; tribunals have the power to consider and decide disputes concerning their jurisdiction; and the grounds for challenging an arbitral award are limited to narrow circumstances with no review of the merits of the dispute. The Regulations are also intended to ensure that tribunals constituted within a ADGM are independent of, and impartial as between, the parties, must respect due process and must ensure equal treatment of the parties.[72]

Recently, the ADGM established its own Arbitration Centre which may begin operation by the first quarter of 2018. According to Ahmad Al Sayegh, the ADGM Chairman:

> The ADGM arbitration centre will be available to all parties seeking to have their arbitration case heard, or mediation held in the centre. We have intended for the centre to be inclusive and to serve the needs of the whole business community in this region and internationally.[73]

In extending the legal services of ADGM courts and ADGM arbitration centre, the ADGM concluded a Memorandum of Understanding or MOU with Ras Al

Khaimah International Corporate Centre in 2017.[74] By having such MOU, any business entities that registered with the said Corporate Centre may bring their disputes before the ADGM courts or make a reference to the ADGM Arbitration Centre. The MOU can also be seen as an effort to extend the jurisdiction of ADGM courts or the ADGM Arbitration centre based on voluntary participation from the disputing parties themselves. So far, there is no clear position from ADGM on their tendency to refer to other alternative dispute resolution processes, except for arbitration. In comparison to the DIFC-LCIA arbitration centre, the ADGM arbitration centre is still new in establishment, with low flexibility in the implementation of the awards. The awards issued by the ADGM arbitration centre may be enforced before the ADGM courts.

The processes of alternative dispute resolution under the ADGM arbitration centre and DIFC-LCIA arbitration centre are not attached or annexed to their respective courts. This means, the disputing parties may choose to go directly to litigate their dispute or to arbitrate or reconcile their dispute through those centres. Even though, both of the DIFC and ADGM courts are established based on common law, there is no clear provision or case that showed the judgment made by any of the said courts may be imposed or enforced by the other courts. It indicates that once the judgment is made by the ADGM courts, it is not necessary for the DIFC courts to enforce their judgment or vice versa.

There is a similar treatment traceable both in the DIFC-LCIA arbitration centre and the ADGM arbitration centre (based on their Arbitration Regulations 2015) for the Islamic finance disputes. It seems that as long as the position of Shari'ah is clearly provided in the stipulated contract, the disputing parties are obliged to follow their own concluded contracts, unless for any contradictory evidence. Moreover, Shari'ah is not foreign before the ADGM, similar to the DIFC. Even though ADGM stands to follow its own legislations, it is still bound to follow the Constitution of UAE that regards Shari'ah as one of the sources of laws in the UAE. Thus, the judges have significant roles in determining the approaches that they want to adopt in dealing with Islamic finance disputes, as in the *Shamil Bank's* case.[75] Instead of depending too much of previously decided cases in different courts, the DIFC and ADGM courts can have a fresh start by appreciating the Shari'ah in resolving the Islamic finance disputes. Moreover, the DIFC-LCIA and ADGM arbitration centres have a wide flexibility of procedures that allow the disputing parties to decide on the dispute resolution processes.

Decided awards and their enforcements

The decision made by the courts is binding upon the disputing parties as it is, regardless whether it is decided in the UAE's civil courts, DIFC courts, or ADGM courts. Once the dispute happens (especially in the absent of a clear dispute resolution clause in the concluded contract), the disputing parties may choose which court they want to refer to if they opt for litigation process. If they go for the UAE's civil court, then the dispute will be decided based on the

UAE's civil law. Even though the laws are silent on the referral made by the parties from civil court to the DIFC court or ADGM court, it is a well-established legal practice that once a dispute is resolved by one court with their specific system and laws, such dispute will not be entertained by a different court with different system and laws. The judges have the rights to refuse entertaining such requests, and acknowledge the already decided judgment. This is important to avoid double jeopardy from one similar dispute.

When it comes to the resolutions decided by the institutional or organizational dispute resolution centres, the disputing parties once they agreed to the resolution, they eventually have to conclude an agreement for such resolution. Such agreement may be entered as an end result from alternative dispute resolution processes (such as from reconciliation and mediation). If one of the disputing parties fails to fulfil the said agreement, a reference can be made to the courts. The same goes to the awards made through arbitration. The concluded agreement made in the DIFC-LCIA arbitration centre may be enforced by the DIFC courts or onshore courts of Dubai. While the concluded agreement made in the ADGM arbitration centre maybe enforced by the ADGM courts or any other onshore courts that have stipulated MOU with them.[76] Up to now, there is an absence of MOU in bridging the DIFC courts and ADGM courts or those respective arbitration centres.

In the enforcement of foreign arbitration awards, it is a clear position that the UAE has already ratified the New York Convention in August 2006. As a result, the UAE is bound to enforce foreign arbitral awards from the member states that are also ratified by the New York Convention. However, the foreign arbitral awards may be ordered to be enforced in the UAE's court on the same conditions as stipulated by the existing laws of the foreign country for the enforcement of similar awards issued in the UAE. The UAE also entered into bilateral reciprocal treaties with several countries to enforce judgements or awards.[77] The enforcement order maybe applied to the Court of the First Instance based on the required jurisdiction which can be the UAE's civil courts or DIFC courts or ADGM courts.

The enforcement of the foreign arbitral awards may also be challenged before the UAE's civil courts if it goes contrary to the verification grounds provided under Article 235 (2) of Federal Law No. 11 of 1992. They are:

a That the state's courts are not authorized to examine the litigation in which the decision or the order has been delivered and that the foreign courts which have delivered it are authorized therewith according to the international rules of the judicial jurisdiction decided in their law.
b That the decision or the order has been delivered from an authorized court according to the law of the country in which it has been issued.
c That the litigant parties, in the action in which the foreign decision has been delivered, have been assigned to attend and have been properly represented.
d That the decision or the order has acquired the power of the decided order according to the law of the court which delivered it.

Table 8.1 List of treaties entered into by the UAE for the enforcement of judgment or awards

International treaty	*Participating countries*
Convention on the Recognition and Enforcement of Foreign Arbitral Awards or New York 1958	159 signatory members, such as Afghanistan, Algeria, Angola, Antigua and Barbuda, Armenia, Austria, Bahamas, Bangladesh, Belarus, Benin, Bolivia, Botswana, Brunei, Burkina Faso, Cambodia, Canada, Central African Republic, Chile, Colombia, Comoros, Croatia, Cyprus, Denmark, Dominica, Ecuador, Estonia, Finland, Gabon, Germany, Greece, Guinea, Haiti, and the UAE
Riyadh Arab Agreement for Judicial Cooperation 1983 or Riyadh Convention	Algeria, Bahrain, Djibouti, Iraq, Jordan, Kuwait, Lebanon, Libya, Mauritania, Morocco, Oman, Palestine, Qatar, Saudi Arabia, Somalia, Sudan, Syria, Tunisia, the UAE, and Yemen
Convention on Judicial Assistance, Recognition and Enforcement of Judgments in Civil and Commercial Matters 1992 or Paris Convention 1992	Paris and the UAE
GCC Convention 1996	GCC countries (including the UAE)
Legal and Judicial Cooperation Agreement 2000	The Arab Republic of Egypt and the UAE
Convention on Judicial Assistance in Civil and Commercial Matters 2004	The Republic of China and the UAE

e That it does not conflict with a decision or an order delivered previously from a court in the state nor does it include what breaches the morals or the public order therein.[78]

Under the DIFC and ADGM laws, the grounds of objection in enforcing the foreign arbitral awards are limited. Such grounds may include existence of fraud, the enforcement is contrary to the UAE's public policy, and the court may transgress the principles of natural justice by allowing the enforcement. Regardless of the grounds of objection, the burden of proof will be held by the disputing party that makes such objection. In relation to resolution of Islamic finance disputes, it is necessary for the awards and their enforcement must be consistent with Shari'ah compliance, without having any element of interest, gambling or speculation. The given interest per annum as a part of the awards as exists under the DIFC laws or the UAE's civil laws should not be applicable to the resolution's awards and enforcement of Islamic finance disputes.

Conclusion

Based from the legal landscape of the UAE, it is significant to observe that there are a variety of dispute resolution channels that can be referred to in resolving Islamic finance disputes. These dispute resolution channels operate within with mixed legal systems, i.e. common law and civil law. The existence of such dispute resolution channels is important to support the expansion and growth of the UAE's Islamic banking and finance industry. The availability of dispute resolution channels including courts helps investors either local or international to come and expand their businesses in the UAE.

Nevertheless, it is important to highlight that Shari'ah compliance is supposed to be the end result for every Islamic finance dispute. By following the laws of the UAE's, DIFC's and ADGM's, it is a stipulated right for the sitting judge to call for Shari'ah scholars as expert witnesses to give their opinions relating to the Islamic finance dispute. Such position is rather loose when it goes to alternative dispute resolution processes between the disputing parties since they may agree or not agree to refer to Shari'ah scholars in reaching a Shari'ah compliance resolution.

It is acknowledged that professional arbitrators or experts of reconciliation or mediators have their own experiences in dealing with the Islamic finance disputes. However, it is pertinent to deal with Shari'ah compliance with care and certainty. Therefore, it is encouraged for the Government of the UAE to properly acknowledge and establish the Higher Shari'ah Authority as provided under Article 5 of Federal Law No. 6 of 1985. The Higher Shari'ah Authority can be a sole reference in reaching Shari'ah compliance resolution in every Islamic finance dispute, regardless of the dispute resolution channels that the disputing parties referred to. This is necessary to ensure certainty in Shari'ah compliance resolution. Thus, the UAE's civil courts, DIFC courts, ADGM courts, and other available arbitration and reconciliation centres may refer directly to the Higher Shari'ah Authority to ensure Shari'ah compliance in every Islamic finance dispute.

As a matter of requirement, it is also important to ascertain the qualifications of the Higher Shari'ah Authority. The sitting judges may call experts from the Higher Shari'ah Authority to assist them in reaching a rightful and Shari'ah compliant decision for Islamic finance disputes. The emphasis on achieving a Shari'ah compliance resolution should also be enshrined through trainings for arbitrators, experts in reconciliations and mediators. By having such a body, it is believed that UAE would become a leader in promoting Shari'ah compliance resolution for Islamic finance disputes, not only locally but also globally.

Acknowledgements

The authors would like to thanks all the contacted lawyers and legal firms of the UAE who replied and shared their valuable knowledge and experiences with us.

Notes

1 'Islamic Finance Assets Forecast to be worth $3.2trn by 2020' (*Arabian Business*, 7 August 2016) www.arabianbusiness.com/islamic-finance-assets-forecast-be-worth-3-2trn-by-2020-641156.html accessed 30 July 2018.
2 Amjad Ali Khan, 'United Arab Emirates' (*The Law Reviews*, November 2017) https://thelawreviews.co.uk/edition/the-islamic-finance-and-markets-review-edition-2/1150803/united-arab-emirates accessed 30 July 2018.
3 The Official Portal of the UAE Government, 'Constitution of UAE' (as adopted in July 1996) https://government.ae/en/about-the-uae/the-constitution-of-the-uae accessed 30 November 2017.
4 The Constitution of UAE, art 9.
5 The Constitution of UAE, arts 120 and 121.
6 The Constitution of UAE, arts 116 and 122.
7 The Constitution of UAE, arts 94 to 109 provide the general principles of the existing systems. The details of the laws are left to the discretions of the local judiciaries.
8 The Official Portal of the UAE Government, 'The Federal Judiciary' https://government.ae/en/about-the-uae/the-uae-government/the-federal-judiciary accessed 30 November 2017.
9 Bashir Ahmed, 'United Arab Emirates' (Afridi & Angell, 2010/2011), http://afridi-angell.com/items/limg/disputeresolution_vol. 11.pdf accessed 30 November 2017.
10 The Official Portal of the UAE Government, 'The Federal Judiciary' https://government.ae/en/about-the-uae/the-uae-government/the-federal-judiciary accessed 30 November 2017.
11 The Constitution of UAE, art 99.
12 The Constitution of UAE, art 96.
13 Federal Law No. 11 of 1973 of UAE.
14 The Constitution of UAE, art 7.
15 The Constitution of UAE, art 151.
16 Samir Saleh, *Commercial Arbitration in the Arab Middle East: A Study in Shari'a and Statute Law* (London, Graham & Trotman Limited 1984), 343.
17 Federal Law No. 5 of 1985 (UAE Civil Code), art 1 of Section 1 stipulates that:

> Legislative provisions shall be applicable to all matters dealth therein, in letter and context. In presence of an absolutely unambiguous text, there is no room for personal interpretation. In the absence of a text in this Law, the judge shall adjudicate according to Islamic Shari'a taking into consideration the choice of the most appropriate solutions in the schools of Imam Malek and Imam Ahmad Ben Hanbal and, if not found there, then in the schools of Imam El Shafe'i and Imam Abou Hanifa, as the interest so requires. Where no solution is found, the judge shall decide according to custom, provided it is not incompatible with public policy and morals. In case the custom is restricted to a specific Emirate, it shall be effective therein.

18 Federal Law No. 5 of 1985 (UAE Civil Code), art 204 states that 'If the subject matter of the disposition or the consideration thereof is money, its amount and type must be specified without any increase or decrease in the value of that money at the time of payment having any effect'.
19 Federal Law No. 5 of 1985 (UAE Civil Code), art 714 states that 'If the contract of loan provides for a benefit in excess of the essence of the contract otherwise than a guarantee of the rights of the lender, such provision shall be void but the contract shall be valid'.
20 Andrew MacCuish and Sai Dandekar, 'United Arab Emirates: Applicability and legal entitlement to interest under UAE law' (*Mondaq*, 9 August 2016) www.mondaq.com/x/517384/Contract+Law/Applicability+And+Legal+Entitlement+To+Interest+

Under+UAE+Law accessed 30 July 2018; Al-Tamimi, 'Islamic Finance: A UAE Legal Perspective' (Dubai Chamber 2018) http://web.dubaichamber.ae/LibPublic/Islamic%20finance%20a%20UAE%20legal%20perspective.pdf accessed 30 July 2018.

21 Federal Law No. 18 of 1993 (UAE Commercial Code), art 76.
22 Federal Law No. 18 of 1993 (UAE Commercial Code), art 77.
23 Federal Law No. 18 of 1993 (UAE Commercial Code), art 88.
24 Federal Law No. 18 of 1993 (UAE Commercial Code), art 90.
25 Federal Law No. 18 of 1993 (UAE Commercial Code), art 409 (3).
26 Federal Law No. 6 of 1985, art 4.
27 Union Law No. 10 of 1980, art 96 (e).
28 Federal Law No. 6 of 1985, art 3.
29 Federal Law No. 6 of 1985, art 1.
30 David Bassens, Ben Derudder and Frank Witlox, 'Searching for the Mecca of finance: Islamic financial services and the world city network' [2010] Area 42, no. 1, 35–46.
31 M Mansoor Khan and M Ishaq Bhatti, 'Islamic Banking and Finance: On Its Way to Globalization' [2008] Managerial Finance vol. 34 (10), 708–725.
32 Damien P Horigan, 'The New Adventures of the Common Law' [2009] Pace Int'l L. Rev. Online Companion, vi.
33 M Strong and R Himber, 'The Legal Autonomy of the Dubai International Financial Centre: A Scalable Strategy for Global Free-Market Reforms' [2009] 29 Economic Affairs, 36–41.
34 Dubai International Financial Centre, 'About DIFC' (*DIFC*, July 2018) www.difc.ae/about accessed 30 July 2018.
35 Abu Dhabi Global Market, 'About ADGM' (*ADGM*, July 2018) www.adgm.com/about-adgm/about-adgm/ accessed 30 July 2018.
36 A Chayes, 'The Role of the Judge in Public Law Litigation' [1975] Harv L Rev 89 1281.
37 Hakimah Yaacob, *Alternative Dispute Resolution (ADR): Expanding Options in Local and Cross Border Islamic Finance Cases*, (Kuala Lumpur, ISRA 2012), 53.
38 Mary-Jane Ierodiaconou, 'Conciliation, Mediation and Federal Human Rights Complaints: Are Rights Compromised?' [January 2005], Centre for Employment and Labour Relations Law, Working Paper no. 32, 3–28, 10.
39 Federal Law No. 5 of 1985 (UAE Civil Code), Article 112.
40 Federal Law No. 5 of 1985 (UAE Civil Code), Article 265.
41 Amjad Ali Khan, 'United Arab Emirates' (*The Law Reviews*, July 2018) https://thelawreviews.co.uk/edition/the-islamic-finance-and-markets-review-edition-2/1150803/united-arab-emirates accessed 30 July 2018.
42 Government of Dubai, 'Service Guide' (*Government of Dubai*, July 2018) www.dubaicourts.gov.ae/portal/page/portal/dc/Gess_service_info?_piref292_597916_292_597889_597889.service_code=1595 accessed 30 July 2018.
43 Sharjah International Commercial Arbitration Centre, 'Official Page' (*Tahkeem*, July 2018) www.tahkeem.ae/en accessed 30 July 2018.
44 Ras Al Khaimah Centre of Reconciliation and Commercial Arbitration, 'Articles of Association' (*Rak Chamber*, July 2018) www.rakchamber.ae/data/upload/mainE.pdf accessed 30 July 2018.
45 Islamic Center of International Reconciliation and Arbitration (IICRA), 'About IICRA' (*IICRA*, July 2018) www.iicra.com/iicra/en/page/details/page_id/ee37cbdbcdad1a37ec1e4247382903ff accessed 30 July 2018.
46 UNCITRAL, 'UNCITRAL model law on International Commercial Arbitration' (*UNCITRAL*, July 2018) www.uncitral.org/uncitral/en/uncitral_texts/arbitration/1985Model_arbitration.html accessed 30 July 2018.
47 Islamic Center of International Reconciliation and Arbitration (IICRA), 'Arbitration in IICRA' (*IICRA*, July 2018) www.iicra.com/iicra/en/page/details/page_id/9e554bfdc98a6fd03666b2902e66c496 accessed 30 July 2018.

48 Islamic Center of International Reconciliation and Arbitration (IICRA), 'Arbitration Certificate in IICRA' (*IICRA*, July 2018) www.iicra.com/iicra/en/page/details/page_id/d4ba4be2e85d90e0667529fae4bd03c1 accessed 30 July 2018.
49 Dubai International Arbitration Centre (DIAC), 'Official Page' (*DIAC*, July 2018) www.diac.ae/idias/ accessed 30 July 2018.
50 Constitutional Amendment No. 1 of 2003, 10 January 2004.
51 DFSA Translation, 'Federal Law No. 8 of 2004' (*DFSA*, July 2018) www.difc.ae/files/5314/5449/7480/Federal_Law_No_8_of_2004_English.pdf accessed 30 July 2018.
52 Federal Law No. 8 of 2004, art 5.
53 Federal Law No. 8 of 2004, art 2.
54 Federal Law No. 8 of 2004, art 6.
55 Dubai International Financial Centre, 'About DIFC' (*DIFC*, July 2018) www.difc.ae/about accessed 30 July 2018.
56 UNCITRAL, 'Convention on the Recognition and Enforcement of Foreign Arbitral Awards' (*UNCITRAL*, July 2018) www.uncitral.org/pdf/english/texts/arbitration/NY-conv/New-York-Convention-E.pdf accessed 30 July 2018.
57 Dubai International Financial Centre Courts, 'Court Structure' (*DIFC Courts*, July 2018) www.difccourts.ae/court-structure/ accessed 30 July 2018.
58 Dubai International Financial Centre Courts, 'Court of Appeal' (*DIFC Courts*, July 2018) www.difccourts.ae/court-of-appeal/ accessed 30 July 2018.
59 [2014] EWHC 3777.
60 [2004] 1 Lloyd's Rep 1.
61 Dubai International Financial Centre Courts, 'DIFC Arbitration Law' (*DIFC Courts*, July 2018) www.difc.ae/files/9014/5449/8249/DIFC_Arbitration_Law_2008_0_1.pdf accessed 30 July 2018.
62 LCIA, 'Official Page' (*LCIA*, July 2018) www.lcia.org/ accessed 30 July 2018.
63 Dubai Law No. (9) of 2004, as amended by Dubai Law No. (7) of 2014.
64 Gordon Blanke, 'DIFC introduces Arbitration Institute' (*Kluwer Arbitration Blog*, 4 June 2014) http://arbitrationblog.kluwerarbitration.com/2014/06/04/difc-introduces-arbitration-institute/ accessed 30 July 2018.
65 DIFC-LCIA Arbitration Centre, 'Arbitration Rules 2016' (*DIFC-LCIA*, July 2018) www.difc-lcia.org/arbitration-rules-2016.aspx## accessed 30 July 2018.
66 DIFC-LCIA Arbitration Centre, 'Mediation Rules 2012' (*DIFC-LCIA*, July 2018) www.difc- www.difc-lcia.org/mediation.aspx accessed 30 July 2018.
67 Abu Dhabi Global Market, 'ADGM Legal Framework' (*ADGM*, July 2018) www.adgm.com/doing-business/adgm-legal-framework/?sect=3 accessed 30 July 2018.
68 ADGM Courts, Civil Evidence, Judgments, Enforcement and Judicial Appointments Regulations 2015, art 1 (3).
69 ADGM Courts, Civil Evidence, Judgments, Enforcement and Judicial Appointments Regulations 2015, art 5.
70 ADGM Courts, Civil Evidence, Judgments, Enforcement and Judicial Appointments Regulations 2015, art 71.
71 Arbitration Regulations 2015, art 55.
72 John Gaffney, 'A New Seat is Born: Abu Dhabi Global Market Issues a UNCITRAL-based Arbitration law' (*Al-Tamimi & Co.*, February 2016) www.tamimi.com/law-update-articles/a-new-seat-is-born-abu-dhabi-global-market-issues-a-uncitral-based-arbitration-law/ accessed 30 July 2018.
73 Fareed Rahman, 'ADGM arbitration centre aims to resolve disputes of all parties' (Guld News, 13 September 2017) https://gulfnews.com/business/economy/adgm-arbitration-centre-aims-to-resolve-disputes-of-all-parties-1.2089785 accessed 30 July 2018.
74 Sarah Townsend, 'ADGM signs accord with Ras Al Khaimah on dispute cases' (The National, 16 November 2017) www.thenational.ae/business/economy/adgm-signs-accord-with-ras-al-khaimah-on-dispute-cases-1.676341 accessed 30 July 2018.

75 *Shamil Bank of Bahrain EC v Beximco Pharmaceuticals Ltd & Ors* [2004] 1 Lloyd's Rep 1.
76 International Consultant Legal Office, 'UAE Arbitration Yearbook 2016' (ICLO, 2016) www.iclo.ae/wp-content/uploads/2014/06/UAE-Arbitration-Yearbook-2016.pdf accessed 30 July 2018.
77 Such as through Riyadh Arab Agreement for Judicial Cooperation 1983 and GCC Convention 1996.
78 Federal Law No. 11 of 1992, art 235 (2).

9 Dispute resolution in Islamic finance

The way forward

John Benson, Adnan Trakic and Pervaiz K Ahmed

Introduction

This book seeks to encourage discussion and debate around the most appropriate mechanisms to resolve disputes involving financial contracts within the broad area of Islamic finance. As indicated by the structure of the book, the mechanisms adopted involve issues around the choice of law, and in particular, the adoption of Shari'ah approved processes and jurisdictions. These are important issues given the growth of Islamic financial products, not only in Islamic countries[1] such as Malaysia, Saudi Arabia and the UAEs, but also the rapid growth of such products in major secular countries such as the United Kingdom and the United States of America.

To do justice to the complexities of the issue surrounding dispute resolution in Islamic finance requires considerable knowledge of both dispute resolution mechanisms and Shari'ah law. This is made more complex by the different approaches of countries practicing Islamic finance and the different emphases given to the various forms of dispute resolution. Nevertheless, despite the perceived or actual shortcomings of the prevailing dispute resolution approaches litigation appears to be the preferred mechanism in all of the five countries surveyed in this book. Whilst there may be solid reasons for such a preference, we would contend that alternative dispute resolution mechanisms need to be more closely examined as they would likely lead, in most cases, to more acceptable outcomes and less demand on the financial resources of the parties and the state.

To commence such a discussion and debate, we would normally begin with a detailed review and analysis of the current literature on dispute resolution in Islamic finance. This is a difficult task as the paucity of research in this field does not address such issues. What does exist is case law drawn from a variety of jurisdictions from both secular and Islamic countries. The decisions emanating from such a litigious process do not, however, address the issue of the effectiveness of outcomes and whether courts are equipped to handle such matters.

Given these limitations, this book set out to answer some fundamental questions concerning dispute resolution in Islamic finance. We do not pretend to have all or indeed many of the answers, although we believe the process we have adopted provides some confidence in the development of a basis to such discussions. In particular, it is important to acknowledge the book had its origins in a symposium held in Kuala Lumpur in September 2017 titled 'Dispute Resolution in Islamic Finance: Litigation or Arbitration'. This event allowed for the issue to be comprehensively debated by scholars, senior Malaysian judges, experts in alternative dispute resolution mechanisms and various others who offered their views on these questions. We hope the book does justice to the participants of this important symposium.

Four questions have been addressed by the various authors of the substantive chapters of this book. These were outlined in Chapter 1 but are worth mentioning again in this chapter. These are:

- What are the appropriate ways to settle disputes in Islamic finance and do such approaches vary depending on context and issue?
- What basis in Islamic law exists to support the various dispute settling processes and what are the arguments against the adoption of such processes?
- How ready are Islamic financial institutions to reconsider the ways they currently use to resolve disputes?
- Is there a strong argument, based on Islamic law, for the reform of existing laws and policies governing the way disputes can be, or should be, settled?

Of course, in addressing these questions the contributing authors and the various chapters raise further questions relating to the underpinning issues surrounding dispute settlement in Islamic finance.

Choice of law and effectiveness of dispute settling mechanisms

Prior to a consideration of the way disputes are settled in the case study jurisdictions we need to place the discussions in the context of the choice of law and the effectiveness of prevailing practices in dispute resolution in Islamic finance. Such constructs underpin any analysis of the present state of affairs and any call for reform in Islamic finance dispute settlement.

A choice of law clause (also known as a governing law clause) is a term in a cross-border agreement which names the jurisdiction whose laws will govern the contract. In Chapter 2, Julio Colón explains that there is a widespread practice among many individuals in many countries to enter into agreements which make a clear reference to Shari'ah as the governing law but, at the same time, identify a court of a secular country as the forum for the settlement of any dispute. This leads to a situation where, in case of a dispute, a secular court judge is tasked with making a decision involving the interpretation and application of Shari'ah. Therefore, it comes as no surprise, Colón argued, that a judge in a secular jurisdiction could interpret the contract or its terms in a way which could be devoid of Shari'ah. As a result, a Shari'ah compliant contract, through courts' involvement and interpretation, transforms into a conventional non-Shari'ah compliant contract. For example, the Court of Appeal in *Shamil Bank of Bahrain EC v Beximco Pharmaceuticals Ltd* (*Shamil Bank*) held that, by virtue of the Rome Convention on the Law Applicable to Contractual Obligation 1980 (Rome Convention), the *murabahah* agreement cannot be governed by Shari'ah because the law chosen by the parties must be the law of a country and not a non-state law. The court did, however, point to the possibility of having Shari'ah principles incorporated into the contract as specific black-letter provisions.

One of the central questions that Colón attempts to answer is whether Shari'ah, being a non-state law, could be recognized as the choice of law in Islamic finance agreements. Colón opines that a comparative study of the Rome Convention 1980 and its successor, the Rome I Regulation of 2008, reveals that there may be argument against the reasoning of the court in *Shamil Bank*. He also points out to the Hague Principles on the Choice of Law in International Contracts Text and Commentary of 2015 (Hague Principles), which have been often cited as the authority to say that a non-state law could be the choice of law, although such a view is not all together reassuring either. Colón concludes that while there is a strong argument for Shari'ah to be recognized as the choice of law, there are practical problems that may come with that choice.

One of the ways to overcome this problem is not to choose a court of a secular country as the forum for the settlement of the dispute and instead select a court of a Muslim country which will recognize and enforce the Shari'ah. Or perhaps a more pragmatic solution could be to opt for other alternative dispute resolution mechanisms such as mediation and arbitration.

How effective are these various mechanisms utilized in resolving conflicts? In Chapter 3 Siti Faridah Abdul Jabbar, Suzana Muhamad Said and Asma Hakimah Ab Halim detail these practices and conclude that litigation is not a suitable mechanism for Islamic finance, although they recognize that any dispute settlement procedure must be backed by the court system of a country to ensure financial contracts are enforced. The authors of this chapter argue that arbitration is the way forward and suggest that mandatory arbitration clauses could be inserted into Islamic finance contracts on the proviso that the principles of Shari'ah apply. Mediation was also considered an acceptable mechanism to resolve disputes, although the private nature of this approach may not assist in the overall development of Islamic finance. The authors conclude by pointing out the lack of qualified arbitrators, arbitrators who are experienced in Shari'ah and cross-border enforcement of contracts, will be an important constraint on the use of such alternative dispute resolution procedures.

Key findings from case study jurisdictions

The case study countries include two secular jurisdictions where Islamic finance is rapidly growing (United Kingdom; United States of America) and three Islamic jurisdictions (Malaysia; Saudi Arabia; United Arab Emirates). The first group of countries involves dispute settlement via litigation in the conventional courts, whilst the second group has the potential to set up alternative structures, although this does not appear to be the general case.

Considering the situation in the United Kingdom, in Chapter 4, Maria Bhatti observed that while dispute resolution mechanisms in the Western world (including United Kingdom and United States of America) are 'cognitive and formal', the resolution of disputes in Islam tends to be 'intuitive and informal'. Bhatti argues that *sulh* (Islamic mediation) began to gain prominence in the United Kingdom some 30 years ago with the introduction of Shari'ah Councils; which are informal dispute resolution bodies to which Muslims could refer their Islamic family and personal law disputes to be decided in accordance with Shari'ah. These Councils, however, do not operate under the Arbitration Act 1996 (United Kingdom) and, thus, their decisions are not legally binding. The enforcement of their decisions is dependent on the good will of the parties. This was one of the main reasons why, according to Bhatti, the Muslim Arbitration Tribunal (MAT) was established in 2007. Unlike Shari'ah Councils, the MAT is a formal tribunal which conducts *tahkim* (Islamic arbitration) under the Arbitration Act 1996 and its decisions are binding. Islamic finance disputes, Bhatti claimed, may also be referred to the MAT for arbitration. The establishment of the MAT, however, has been seen by some as an attempt to introduce into the British legal system the interpretation of Shari'ah which may be inconstant with Western values. Bhatti argued that these claims are unfounded as both Shari'ah Councils and the MAT have clearly stated that they only operate within the existing British legal system and that any Shari'ah principle which is inconsistent with the laws of the United Kingdom cannot and shall not be applied. When it comes to arbitration of Islamic finance disputes in the MAT, Bhatti concluded that the Asian International Arbitration Centre i-Arbitration Rules 2018 should be adopted as standardized rules which provide an internationally recognized arbitral procedure as well as compliance with Shari'ah.

The United States of America dispute resolution processes are much the same as in the United Kingdom. As Julio Colón pointed out in Chapter 5 whilst there are various means and procedures for recovery in civil disputes and a range of administrative mechanisms these must be considered within the secular jurisdiction of the country and the desire by government not to engage in interpreting religious principles. Nevertheless, the courts will honour the applicable laws agreed to by the parties and will consider any relevant material. In doing so this may involve considering aspects of non-secular law, although only when such components are 'discoverable and abstract'. Thus, arguments over inconsistent positions, when the first position has been accepted, are rarely permitted; the aim being the protection of the integrity of the legal process. In general, the courts are unwilling to become involved in religious matters, notwithstanding, as Colón pointed out, Islamic financial institutions in the United States are not religious organizations. Colón concluded by arguing that the intent of the parties must be considered and the decisions produced by statutory and arbitration bodies require greater analysis.

In Malaysia the situation is also somewhat similar to the two secular states, although some important distinctions exist as well as some important legal implications for both Conventional and Shari'ah law have arisen. Adnan Trakic discusses these issues in Chapter 6 and concluded that despite having Shari'ah courts as a constitutionally recognized court system, which operates in parallel with the civil (secular) court system in Malaysia, the civil courts have jurisdiction over Islamic finance disputes. The reason behind this, as Trakic explained, is that the laws applicable to Islamic finance agreements are the same as the laws that apply to the conventional counterparts. The major difference between an Islamic and conventional finance agreement is that the former must comply with Shari'ah. To overcome the issue of the civil court judges interpreting and applying Shari'ah, the Malaysian Parliament enacted into law sections 56 and 57 of the Central Bank of Malaysia Act 2009 which made it mandatory for judges and arbitrators to refer Shari'ah questions in Islamic finance disputes to the Shari'ah Advisory Council (SAC) of the Central Bank of Malaysia. The decision made by the SAC is binding on the court and arbitrator.

While sections 56 and 57 ensure that the Shari'ah underlying nature of Islamic finance agreement is determined by Shari'ah experts (i.e. the SAC) and enforced by the court, which is not the case in the secular jurisdictions discussed earlier, the constitutionality of these provisions, as Trakic pointed out, has been questioned. The binding nature of the SAC's decision on the court in the circumstances where the SAC's decision cannot be questioned or cross-examined is, Trakic argued, a matter of concern. At the time of writing this book, a nine-member Malaysian Federal Court sat for the first time to decide whether the impugned provisions are unconstitutional. The decision is yet to be handed down.

Islamic finance disputes, Trakic contended, do not have to be litigated. There are viable alternatives to litigation where both the conventional and Shari'ah aspects of an Islamic finance agreement can be effectively enforced. One of the alternatives, Trakic suggested, is court-annexed mediation which appears to be an attractive solution for domestic Islamic finance disputes. As for cross-border Islamic finance agreements, Trakic proposed that the arbitration in the Asian International Arbitration Centre (AIAC) in accordance with the AIAC i-Arbitration Rules 2018 seems to be a viable alternative to litigation and which is worth exploring further.

The Kingdom of Saudi Arabia and the dispute settlement processes in Islamic finance were discussed in detail in Chapter 7 by Aishath Muneeza and Zakariya Mustapha. The principle source of law in Saudi Arabia is Shari'ah, although the lack of codification allows considerable freedom to judges in reaching decisions. This also provides complications as 'forbidden undertakings' cannot be enshrined in law as to do so may be a breach of Shari'ah. The authors pointed out, however, there is a strong regime of legislation which covers various the various institutions of Islamic finance and the resolution of disputes. Shari'ah compliance has been 'guaranteed' as Shari'ah is the principle law of the country. Disputes can be resolved by litigation or arbitration, although until recently litigation has dominated. Recent changes in the Law of Arbitration and its subsequent implementing regulations now provides a more flexible approach to commercial arbitration and a more efficient practice. Contracts can include the rules of other arbitration institutions such as the London Court of International Arbitration or the International Chamber of Commerce. As Saudi Arabia is a signatory to the New York Convention arbitral awards emanating from outside the country remain enforceable.

Finally, dispute resolution in the United Arab Emirates was considered by Nor Razinah Binti Mohd Zain and Rusni Hassan in Chapter 8. Shari'ah is recognized as a source of law in the UAE Constitution. That however, the authors explained, does not preclude the operation of the conventional finance. Islamic and conventional financial institutions operate in parallel with each other. The UAE courts the authors explained recognize and uphold the Shari'ah underlying nature of Islamic finance agreement not because Shari'ah is a source of the UAE Constitution but because the parties have included Shari'ah compliance in their agreement. The UAE courts are bound by law to enforce what has been agreed to by the parties. The judges adjudicating Islamic finance disputes in any UAE court, including those in the UAEs most famous international financial centres, Dubai International Financial Centre (DIFC) and Abu Dhabi Global Market (ADGM), are, according to authors, unlikely to have the required expertise to decide Shari'ah compliance questions. Therefore, the UAE's laws as well as the laws of DIFC and ADGM, the authors contended, have empowered the judges to call on Shari'ah scholars to give expert evidence in court to assist them in making the Shari'ah rulings. The courts may also, if deemed fit, refer the case to court annexed conciliation and, if it succeeds, the outcome would be recorded as a judgment. If the conciliation is not successful, the case will revert back to court.

Islamic finance disputes may also be resolved, as authors explained, in the International Islamic Centre for Reconciliation and Arbitration (IICRA). The centre offers dispute resolution either through arbitration or conciliation. While arbitral decision are binding, the decisions reached through conciliation are binding only after the parties have recorded it in the form of a valid agreement. Other centres that offer arbitration and mediation for Islamic finance disputes are the DIFC – LCIA (London Court of International Arbitration) Arbitration Centre, and the ADGM Arbitration Centre. The authors asserted that unlike the judges in the UAE courts who are empowered by law to call and hear Shari'ah scholars' opinions on Shari'ah questions, it is less clear as to whether arbitrators are given the same rights as the parties may agree or disagree to call on Shari'ah scholars. To overcome these challenges, the authors suggested that the Government of the UAE establish the Higher Shari'ah Authority which will be the sole reference for all Shari'ah questions faced by the judges and arbitrators in Islamic finance disputes. This, according to the authors, should bring certainty in terms of Shari'ah compliance in Islamic finance disputes. The proposed Higher Shari'ah Authority appears to resemble the centralized Shari'ah Advisory Council (SAC) in Malaysia. The UAE Government may consider exploring the Malaysian experience with the SAC before embarking on the establishment of a similar statutory expert body.

Analysis and future developments

The information and analysis presented in this book allows us to make some tentative answers to the questions posed in Chapter 1 and make some observations on how dispute resolution in Islamic finance is likely to develop from both an Islamic and conventional finance perspective. This is our contribution to the debate and discussion, although we rightly concede that other perspectives have validity and merit. As we concluded in Chapter 1 we hope this exercise will raise the awareness of alternative dispute resolution mechanisms and the key issues that serve to achieve or prevent effective dispute resolution outcomes.

Key questions

1 What are the appropriate ways to settle disputes in Islamic finance and do such approaches vary depending on context and issue?

A variety of approaches exist but in the main these have been dominated by litigation. Of course, it is difficult to be firm about such a conclusion as many disputes may well be settled by arbitration or other alternative dispute resolution mechanisms without becoming part of the public domain. What is the appropriate way of settling disputes in Islamic finance will largely depend on the party's needs and preferences. It appears that Islamic financial institutions prefer litigation as it provides them with certainty, quick summary and default judgments and other various interim reliefs not available with alternative dispute resolution mechanisms, such as mediation and arbitration.

The alternatives to litigation are more likely to result in more favourable results to financial consumers. Mediation, in particular, is promising as it leads to a win-win situation and it preserves the ongoing relationship between the parties. The financial institutions, however, are less likely to submit to mediation voluntarily when they know their chances of winning with litigation are better. This is where a mandatory form of mediation, such as a court-annexed mediation where the parties are asked to try and resolve their disputes amicably, should be considered for Islamic finance disputes. The court annexed mediation introduced in Malaysia has been hailed as a success by the Malaysian judiciary and is worth exploring further. Arbitration, particularly international arbitration, could be an attractive mechanism for cross-border Islamic finance disputes. It enables the parties to have their disputes decided by an arbitrator appointed by them and in accordance with the laws and procedure of their choice. There has been some movement towards arbitration (e.g. Malaysia, UAE, and Saudi Arabia) since changes in legislation and regulation.

Whether litigation or its alternatives are appropriate in the given situation will also depend on the nature of the issue in dispute. For Shari'ah issues, mediation and arbitration may have advantages over litigation due to the parties' autonomy to appoint an arbitrator or mediator who possesses the required knowledge and expertise in Shari'ah. A judge in a civil court may refer to expert evidence submitted by Shari'ah scholars. However, the party appointed expert witnesses (each party may appoint a Shari'ah scholar as an expert witness) are likely to provide conflicting views. The judge deciding the matter would still need to make a decision as to which expert's opinion is more credible. To make such a decision may require a knowledge of Shari'ah on the part of the deciding judge.

Malaysia is probably an exception to the above situation as the judges are required by law to refer Shari'ah questions to the centralized Shari'ah Advisory Council and the Council's decision is final. The Malaysian approach, with its advantages and disadvantages, has been detailed in Chapter 6. If issues in Islamic finance dispute are of non-Shari'ah nature, such as contractual and finance-related issues, then the position of litigation and mediation or arbitration is more levelled. In some cases, going to court may be a preferred pathway especially when the parties are in need of quick interlocutory measures.

2 What basis in Islamic law exists to support the various dispute settling processes and what are the arguments against the adoption of such processes?

Shari'ah recognizes a variety of dispute resolution process, such as *qada* (litigation), *sulh* (negotiation, mediation, and conciliation), *tahkim* (arbitration), and *fatwa al mufti* (expert determination). It is important to note that litigation, mediation, arbitration and other dispute resolution mechanisms in Islam may differ, sometimes significantly, from the conventional dispute resolution mechanisms. The difference stems from the criteria as to who can be appointed as a judge, an arbitrator, or a mediator as well as from the basic principle that the entire process and outcome of the resolution process must be in accordance with the teaching of Islam. As a result, any dispute resolution mechanism, be it litigation or its alternatives, which does not recognize and enforce the Shari'ah underlying nature of an Islamic finance agreement is not acceptable in Islam.

Islamic mediation and arbitration are encouraged in Islam as alternatives to litigation. Shari'ah constantly reminds the parties about the value of an amicable resolution of disputes. For example, in the Qur'an (Chapter 4, verse 35) it is said:

> And if you fear dissension between the two (husband and wife), send an arbitrator from his people and an arbitrator from her people. If they both desire reconciliation, Allah will cause it between them. Indeed, Allah is ever Knowing and Acquainted.

Even though this verse is pertaining to matrimonial disputes, it has been widely used as an authority for the use of alternative dispute resolution mechanisms in a wider context including commercial disputes. Litigation before a competent *qadi* (judge) is an option when the parties are not able to solve their disputes amicably. Therefore, alternative dispute resolution mechanisms like mediation and arbitration in Islam should perhaps be the primary ways of resolving disputes with litigation becoming an alternative.

3 How ready are Islamic financial institutions to reconsider the ways they currently use to resolve disputes?

This is difficult to ascertain as most Islamic financial institutions have appeared ready and willing to defend themselves in courts. The advantages of alternative forms of dispute resolution are numerous including cost, effectiveness and reputation protection. Nevertheless, there are possible downsides and given the power imbalance it may well be the case that institutions have calculated overall that litigation is the most efficient and likely approach to maintaining their position. Litigation provides them with certainty of outcome and fast enforcement through summary judgments. Therefore, it is unlikely that institutions on their own would opt for alternatives such as mediation or arbitration. If overall benefits of the alternatives outweigh possible downsides and this research shows that that could be the case, then other stakeholders should take the initiative to introduce the alternatives processes. The courts could do it through mandatory court-annexed mediation. Alternatively, legislation could be enacted to encourage a greater use of arbitration through, for example, introduction of mandatory arbitration clauses in Islamic finance agreements.

4 Is there a strong argument, based on Islamic law, for the reform of existing laws and policies governing the way disputes can be, or should be, settled?

There is a case that the adoption of alternative dispute resolution processes, which are based on Islamic law, could be seen by the stakeholders, including the parties and governments, as the way forward to settling such disputes. The stakeholders, however, need to be aware that the one size fits all approach may not be the solution. Various jurisdictions and this includes those discussed in this book have differences in terms of their legal system, constitutional structure, and treatment of Islam in their legal system and in the courts. Their ability to offer alternative dispute resolution mechanisms may be limited by factors which are internal to a particular jurisdiction such as infrastructure, expertise and finances. Therefore, the solution to the problem of resolving Islamic finance disputes effectively will have to be devised from within the jurisdiction. Experiences of other jurisdictions may certainly be useful. However, all solutions should be scrutinized and assessed carefully because what works in one country may not work in another. Nevertheless, there is one common factor that every jurisdiction that wishes to formulate an effective dispute resolution mechanism for Islamic finance disputes must consider and that is a religious requirement that the Shari'ah underlying nature of an Islamic finance agreement is recognized and that process and outcome of the Islamic finance dispute is in accordance with the teaching of Islam.

Future developments in Islamic finance dispute resolution

On the basis of the answers to the questions as given above, and discussions with various parties, we would suggest the following three developments or trajectories are likely, although we recognize such conclusions are contestable. First, there will be a shift towards alternative forms of dispute resolution, such as arbitration, with the state providing a clear framework for resolution.

Second, countries, both secular and non-secular, becoming signatories to international conventions and thus allowing those decisions to be recognized for domestic purposes. This appears to work well with bodies such as the New York Convention (Convention on the Recognition and Enforcement of Foreign Arbitral Awards). Supporting legislation may well be needed to ensure enforcement and to ensure that the process is Shari'ah compliant.

Third, considerable development of the pool of potential arbitrators/mediators will need to take place. Such arbitrators will need to work within some form of administrative structure and have the requisite skills to gain the confidence of the parties and to prevent a return to litigation. As with all arbitrators the ability to work with disputing parties and keep them focused on the issues at hand will be essential. In addition, however, they will need to be knowledgeable in both finance and Shari'ah law as well as understand the multitude of issues that can arise in cross border financial disputes.

Whilst the above suggestions are only a starting point we hope they will generate further discussion and rigorous debate. If they do the objectives we have set for this book will have been achieved.

Note

1 Please refer to footnote 10 in Chapter 1.

List of statutes and regulations

Kingdom of Saudi Arabia

Basic Law 1992
Board of Grievances Law 1982
Law of Arbitration 2012
Law of Commercial Agency of 1962
Law of Judiciary 2007
Law of Procedure Before Shariah Courts 2000
Procedural Rules Before the Board of Grievances 1989
The Banking Control Law of 1966
The Companies Law 1965

Malaysia

AIAC i-Arbitration Rules 2018
Arbitration Act 2005
Capital Markets and Services Act 2007
Central Bank of Malaysia Act 2009
Evidence Act 1950
Federal Constitution
Islamic Banking Act 1983
Islamic Financial Services (Financial Ombudsman Scheme) Regulations 2015
Islamic Financial Services Act 2013
Mediation Act 2012
National Land Code 1965
Penal Code
Rules of High Court 2012
Syariah Criminal Offences (Federal Territories) Act 1997
Takaful Act 1984

United Arab Emirates

Abu Dhabi Law No. 4 of 2013
ADGM Arbitration Regulations 2015
Amiri Decree No. 17 of 2008
Amiri Decree No. 6 of 2009

Cabinet Resolution No. 4 of 2013
Constitution of UAE (as adopted in July 1996)
DIFC Law No. 1 of 2008
DIFC Law No. 6 of 2013
Dubai Decree No. 11 of 2007
Dubai Law No. 12 of 2004
Dubai Law No. 16 of 2011
Federal Decree No. 15 of 2013
Federal Decree No. 35 of 2004
Federal Law No. 11 of 1973
Federal Law No. 11 of 1992
Federal Law No. 18 of 1993 (UAE Commercial Code)
Federal Law No. 26 of 1999
Federal Law No. 8 of 2004
Federal Law No. 8 of 2004
Federal Law No. 5 of 1985 (UAE Civil Code)
Rules of Commercial Conciliation and Arbitration of Dubai Chamber of Commerce and Industry No. 2 of 2004
Union Law No. 10 of 1980

United Kingdom

Arbitration Act 1996
Arbitration and Mediation Services (Equality Bill)
Courts and Legal Services Act 1990
Criminal Justice and Public Order Act 1994
Equality Act 2010
Family Law Act 1996

United States of America

12 CFR §204.2
12 USC §1813
12 USC §24
12 USC §29
15 USC §77bbb
26 USC §1031
26 USC §163
Federal Rule of Civil Procedure 12(b)(1)
Tex Civ Pract & Rem Code Ann §171.001
Tex Civ Pract & Rem Code Ann §171.087
US Constitution amendment I

Miscellaneous

1980 Rome Convention on the Law Applicable to Contractual Obligations [1998] OJ (L 177) 34
Convention on Judicial Assistance in Civil and Commercial Matters 2004

Convention on Judicial Assistance, Recognition and Enforcement of Judgments in Civil and Commercial Matters 1992 or Paris Convention 1992

Convention on the Recognition and Enforcement of Foreign Arbitral Awards, June 10, 1958, 21 UST 2517, 330 U.N.T.S. 38

Council Regulation (EC) No 593/2008 of the European Parliament and of the Council of 17 June 2008 on the law applicable to contractual obligations (Rome I) [2008] O.J. (L 177) 6, 10 (EC)

GCC Convention 1996

Hague Principles on Choice of Law in International Contracts Text and Commentary (approved 19 March 2015)

Legal and Judicial Cooperation Agreement 2000 (Egypt and UAE)

Majalla (the civil code of the Ottoman Empire in the late 19th and early 20th centuries)

Riyadh Arab Agreement for Judicial Cooperation 1983 or Riyadh Convention

United Nations Commission on International Trade Law ('UNCITRAL') Rules 2010

List of cases

Affin Bank Bhd v Zulkifli Abdullah [2006] 3 MLJ 67
Ahli United Bank (UK) PLC (Petition No M071001A), Advisory Opinion TSB-A-08(2)R (NYSDTF Taxpayer Services Div April 28, 2008)
Arab-Malaysian Finance Bhd v Taman Ihsan Jaya Sdn Bhd & Ors [2009] 1 CLJ 419
Arab-Malaysian Merchant Bank Bhd v Silver Concept Sdn Bhd [2006] 8 CLJ 9
Bank Islam Malaysia Berhad v Adnan bin Omar KL High Court Civil Suit No S3–22–101–9
Bank Islam Malaysia Berhad v Lim Kok Hoe & Anor (and 8 Other Appeals) [2009] 6 CLJ 22
Bank Islam Malaysia Bhd v Adnan bin Omar [1994] 3 CLJ 735
Bank Kerjasama Malaysia Rakyat Bhd v PSC Naval Dockyard [2008] 1 CLJ 784
Bank Kerjasama Rakyat Malaysia Bhd v Emcee Corp Sdn Bhd [2003] 2 MLJ 408; [2003] 1 CLJ 625
Bank Kerjasama Rakyat Malaysia Bhd v MME Reality & Management Sdn Bhd [2018] 6 CLJ 381
Dato Hj Nik Mahmud bin Daud v Bank Islam Malaysia Bhd [1996] 4 MLJ 295 (High Court), [1998] 3 MLJ 396 (Supreme Court)
El-Farra v Sayyed 226 SW3d 792 (2006)
Filli Shipping Co Ltd v Premium Nafta Products Ltd [2007] UKHL 40
In re Arbitration Between Petroleum Dev (Trucial Coast) Ltd v Sheikh of Abu Dhabi, 1 Intl & Comp L Q 247, 250–251 (September 1951)
In Re Arcapita Bank BSC (C), Bankruptcy Case No. 12-11076 (S.D.N.Y. 6 January 2014)
In re East Cameron Partners, LP, 'Order on Def [s'] Rule 12 Motions', Bankruptcy Case No 08-51207; Adv Proc No 08-05041 (Bankruptcy Court, WDLa 2009) (unpublished order 17 April 2009)
In re East Cameron Partners, LP, 'Sukuk Certificate holders' Mot. (I) to Dismiss Pl ['s] Verified Compl for TRO, Prelim Injunction, & Declaratory J, or in the Alternative (II) for More Definite Statement, 19 December 2008', Bankruptcy Case No 08-51207; Adv Proc No 08-05041 (Bankruptcy Court, WDLa)
In re East Cameron Partners, LP, 'Verified Compl of East Cameron Partners, LP for TRO, Prelim Injunction, & Declaratory J, 16 October 2008', Bankruptcy Case No 08-51207; Adv Proc No 08-05041 (Bankruptcy Court, WDLa)
In re East Cameron Partners, LP, 22 December 2008', Bankruptcy Case No 08-51207; Adv Proc No 08-05041 (Bankruptcy Court, WDLa)
Indira Gandhi Mutho v Pengarah Jabatan Agama Islam Perak [2018] 3 CLJ 145

Islamic Investment Company of the Gulf (Bahamas) Ltd v Symphony Gems NV & Ors [2002] WL 346969 (QB Comm. Ct 13 February 2002)
Jabri v Qaddura 108 SW3d 404 (Tex App—Fort Worth 2003, no pet)
Jacob & Youngs, Inc v Kent, 230 NY 239 (1921).
Jama v Guidance Residential LLC, Civil No 12-77(DSD/JSM) (D Minnesota August 16, 2012)
Kuwait Finance House (M) Bhd v JRI Resources Sdn Bhd [2016] 10 CLJ 435
Malayan Banking Bhd v Marilyn Ho Siok [2006] 7 MLJ 249
Mohd Alias Ibrahim v RHB Bank Bhd & Anor [2011] 4 CLJ 654
Murray v US Department of Treasury 681 F3d 744 (6th Cir 2012)
Nat'l Grp for Commc'ns & Computers v Lucent Techs Int'l, 331 F. Supp. 2d 290, 292 (D.N.J 2004)
National Bank v Matthews 98 US 621 (1878)
National Group for Communications & Computers v Lucent Technologies Intl 331 F Supp 2d 290 (DNJ 2004)
Sanghi Polyesters Ltd (India) v The International Investor KSCS (Kuwait) [2001] CLC 748
Sanghi Polyesters Ltd (India) v Int'l Investor KCFC (Kuwait) [2000] 1 Lloyd's Rep 480
Saudi Basic Indus Corp v Mobil Yanbu Petrochem Co 866 A.2d 1, 7 (Del. 2005)
Saudi Basic Industries Corp v Mobil Yanbu Petrochemical Co 866 A 2d 1 (Del 2005)
Securities and Exchange Commission v Al-Raya Investment Company and Waleed Khalid Al-Braikan as Representative of the Heirs of Hazem Khalid Al-Braikan, et al., Civil Action No 1:09-CV-6533 (NRB) (SDNY)
Semenyih Jaya Sdn Bhd v Pentadbir Tanah Daerah Hulu Langat [2017] 3 MLJ 561
Serbian Eastern Orthodox Diocese v Milivojevich, 426 US 696, 710, 96 SCt 2372, 49 LEd2d 151 (1976)
Shamil Bank of Bahrain v Beximco Pharmaceuticals Ltd & Ors [2004] 2 Lloyd's Rep. 1; [2004] EWCA Civ 19
Sigur Ros Sdn Bhd v Maybank Islamic Berhad [2018] 1 LNS 220
Tan Sri Abdul Khalid Ibrahim v Bank Islam Malaysia Berhad. [2013] 1 CLJ 436
The Investment Dar Company KSCC v Blom Developments Bank SAL [2009] EWHC 3545 (Ch)
Tinta Press v Bank Islam Malaysia Bhd [1986] 1 MLJ 474
United Islamic Society v Masjed Abubakr Al-Seddiq, Inc, No A16–0140 (Mich Ct App August 29, 2016)
Warda v Commr 15 F3d 533 (6th Cir 1994)

Bibliography

'Islamic Finance Assets Forecast to be Worth $3.2trn by 2020' (*Arabian Business*, 7 August 2016) www.arabianbusiness.com/islamic-finance-assets-forecast-be-worth-3-2trn-by-2020-641156.html accessed 30 July 2018.

'Saudi Justice Minister Inaugurates Book on Legal Precedents' (Arab News, 5 January 2018) www.arabnews.com/node/1219391/saudi-arabia accessed 20 August 2018.

Abu Dhabi Global Market, 'About ADGM' (*ADGM*, July 2018) www.adgm.com/about-adgm/about-adgm/ accessed 30 July 2018.

Abu Dhabi Global Market, 'ADGM Legal Framework' (*ADGM*, July 2018) www.adgm.com/doing-business/adgm-legal-framework/?sect=3 accessed 30 July 2018.

Agha O, 'Islamic Finance Dispute Resolution' [2009] *Islamic Finance News* 31.

Ahmed B, 'United Arab Emirates' (Afridi & Angell 2010/2011) http://afridi-angell.com/items/limg/disputeresolution_vol. 11.pdf accessed 30 November 2017.

Akgunduz A, *Introduction to Islamic Law* (IUR Press 2010).

Albejad M, *Arbitration in Saudi Arabia* (1st edn, Institute of Public Administration 1999).

Al-Haj M U, *A Dissertation on the Administration of Justice of Muslim Law* (The Book House 1980).

Al-Homoud H, 'Banking Overview in Saudi Arabia' Al-Tamimi & Co, (October–November 2012) www.tamimi.com/en/magazine/law-update/section-7/october-november-1/banking-overview-in-saudi-arabia.html accessed 3 November 2017.

Ali ERAE, 'Constraints and Opportunities in Harmonisation of Civil Law and Shariah in the Islamic Financial Services Industry' (2008) 4 MLJ i.

Al-Qurashi Z, 'Arbitration under the Islamic Sharia' (2004) 1 TDM www.transnational-dispute-management.com/article.asp?key=4 accessed 3 March 2018.

Al-Rajhi Bank https://en.wikipedia.org/wiki/Al-Rajhi_Bank accessed 3 November 2017.

Al-Ramahi A, 'Sulh: A Crucial Part of Islamic Arbitration' (2008) LSE Legal Studies Working Paper 12/2008 https://papers.ssrn.com/sol3/papers.cfm?abstract_id=1153659 accessed 20 February 2018.

Al-Tamimi, 'Islamic Finance: A UAE Legal Perspective' (Dubai Chamber, 2018) http://web.dubaichamber.ae/LibPublic/Islamic%20finance%20a%20UAE%20legal%20perspective.pdf accessed 30 July 2018.

Al-Zuhayli W, *Al-Fiqh Al-Islam WaAdilatuh* (Juz' 6 Dar al-Fikr 1996).

ASEAN Law Association, 'Kuala Lumpur Court Mediation Centre: Court-Annexed Mediation' www.aseanlawassociation.org/11GAdocs/workshop5-malaysia.pdf accessed 26 August 2018.

Asian International Arbitration Centre, 'i-Arbitration' www.aiac.world/arbitration/i-arbitration accessed 26 August 2018.

Australia National Alternative Dispute Resolution Advisory Council (NADRAC), 'Legislating for Alternative Dispute Resolution, A Guide for Government Policymakers and Legal Drafters' (2006) www.ag.gov.au/LegalSystem/AlternateDisputeResolution/Documents/NADRAC%20Publications/Legislating%20for%20Alternative%20Dispute%20Resolution.PDF accessed 16 February 2018.

Azahari F, 'Islamic Banking: Perspectives on Recent Case Development' (2009) 1 MLJ xci.

Baamir A Y, *Shariah Law in Commercial and Banking Arbitration: Law and Practice in Saudi Arabia* (Ashgate Publishing Limited 2010) 213.

Backer H S A, *International Arbitration: With Commentary to Malaysian Arbitration Act 2005* (Janab (M) Sdn Bhd 2016).

Bälz K, 'Sharia Risk?: How Islamic Finance Has Transformed Islamic Contract Law' (2008) Islamic Legal Studies Program Harvard Law School.

Baamir A and Bantekas I, 'Saudi Law as *Lex Arbitri*: Evaluation of Saudi Arbitration Law and Judicial Practice', (2009) vol. 25 (2) *Arbitration International* 239–270.

Bank Negara Malaysia Shariah Resolutions in Islamic Finance (2nd ed, Bank Negara Malaysia 2010) www.bnm.gov.my/microsite/fs/sac/shariah_resolutions_2nd_edition_EN.pdf accessed 7 July 2017.

Bano S, 'Islamic Family Arbitration, Justice and Human Rights in Britain' (2007) *Law, Social Justice & Global Development.*

Bano S, 'In Pursuit of Religious and Legal Diversity' *Ecclesiastical Law Journal* (2008).

Bassens D, Derudder B and Witlox F, 'Searching for the Mecca of Finance: Islamic Financial Services and the World City Network' [2010] Area 42, no. 1, 35–46.

BBC, 'Sharia Law in UK is Unavoidable' http://news.bbc.co.uk/2/hi/uk_news/7232661.stm accessed 14 November 2017.

BBC, 'Sharia Law Could have UK Role' http://news.bbc.co.uk/2/hi/uk_news/7488790.stm accessed 14 November 2017.

Bello SA, *et al.*, 'Jurisdiction of Courts Over Islamic Banking in Nigeria and Malaysia', (2015) 1 (3) *Journal of Islam, Law and Judiciary* 70.

Bernstein H and Zekoll J, 'The Gentleman's Agreement in Legal Theory and in Modern Practice: United States' [1998] 46 Am. J. Comp. L. Supp. 87.

'Bill stages – *Arbitration and Mediation Services (Equality) Bill*' [HL] 2014–15. http://services.parliament.uk/bills/2014-15/arbitrationandmediationservicesequality/stages.html accessed 20 November 2017.

Blake S, Browne J and Sime S, *A Practical Approach to Alternative Dispute Resolution* (Oxford University Press 2011).

Blanke G, 'DIFC introduces Arbitration Institute' (*Kluwer Arbitration Blog*, 4 June 2014) http://arbitrationblog.kluwerarbitration.com/2014/06/04/difc-introduces-arbitration-institute/ accessed 30 July 2018.

Boisard M A, 'On the Probable Influence of Islam on Western Public and International Law' (1980) 11 International Journal of Middle East Studies 429.

Bond S R, 'How to Draft an Arbitration Clause' [1989] 6(2) J of Intl Arb.

Boyle S B, *What is a Theocracy* (Crabtree Publishing Company 2013) 48.

Brougher C, 'Application of Religious Law in U.S. Courts: Selected Legal Issues' (2011) Congressional Research Service.

Brown H J and Marriot A, *ADR Principles and Practice* (3rd edn, Sweet & Maxwell 2011).

Campbell C, *Legal Aspects of Doing Business in the Middle East* (Yorkhill Law Publishing 2009).

Cavanagh G, 'Regulatory Aspects of Islamic Banking in the United States' (Lecture) [2011] (4th U. California Berkeley Islamic Finance Forum, Berkeley School of Law).

Cavendish M, *World and Its Peoples: The Arabian Peninsula* (Marshall Cavendish Corporation 2007) 1584.

Central Bank of Malaysia, 'Financial Ombudsman Scheme Concept Paper (29 August 2014)', www.bnm.gov.my/guidelines/10_business_conduct/5_financial_ombudsman_scheme.pdf accessed 4 March 2018.

Chance C, 'A Guide to Doing Business in the Kingdom of Saudi Arabia' https://financial-marketstoolkit.cliffordchance.com/content/micro-facm/en/financial-markets-resources/resources-by-type/guides/doing-business-in-the-kingdom-of-saudi-arabia/_jcr_content/parsys/download/file.res/.pdf accessed 23 November 2017.

Chayes A, 'The Role of the Judge in Public Law Litigation' [1975] 89 Harv L Rev 1281.

Chiu S, 'Islamic Finance in the United States: A Small but Growing Industry' [2005] no 214 Chicago Fed Letter.

Choudhury M A, 'Development of Islamic Economic and Social Thought,' in Hassan M K and Lewis M K (eds), *Handbook of Islamic Banking* (Edward Elgar Publishing Ltd 2007) 443.

Choy C Y, Hee T F, and Siang C O S, 'Court-Annexed Mediation Practice in Malaysia: What the Future Holds' (2016) 1 *University of Bologna Law Review* 271.

Chuah J, 'Recent Case, *Shamil Bank of Bahrain EC v Beximco*' (2004) 10 J Intl Maritme L 126.

Cole R A, 'The Public Policy Exception to the New York Convention on the Recognition and Enforcement of Arbitral Awards' (1985–86) 1(2) Ohio St J on Disp Resol 365.

Colón J C, 'Choice of law and Islamic Finance' (2011) 46 Texas Intl LJ 412.

Colón J C, 'Improving Dispute Resolution for Muslims in the United States', (International Conference on Dispute Resolution 2017: Modern Trends in Effective Dispute Resolution, International Islamic University of Malaysia, August 2017) https://ssrn.com/abstract=3007811 accessed 7 July 2017.

Cotton T and Rothfus K, 'Repeal The CFPB's Anti-Consumer Ban on Mandatory Arbitration Clauses' www.forbes.com/sites/realspin/2017/07/25/repeal-the-cfpbs-anti-consumer-ban-on-mandatory-arbitration-clauses/#7ac953347fb0 accessed 16 February 2018.

Cusairi R M, 'The Application of Islamic Shari`ah to the Muslim Minority Living in the UK: A Comparative Study on Family Mediation Between English Law and Faith-Based Med-Arb at Shari'ah Councils' (PhD thesis, Glasgow Caledonian University 2013).

Daily Mail, 'Islamic Sharia Courts in Britain are Now Legally Binding' www.dailymail.co.uk/news/article-1055764/Islamic-sharia-courts-Britain-legally-binding.html accessed 1 November 2017.

Davidson J and Wood C, 'A Conflict Resolution Model' (2004) 43 *Theory into Practice Conflict Resolution and Peer Mediation* 6.

Davis K A, 'Judicial Estoppel and Inconsistent Positions of Law Applied to Fact and Pure Law' [2003] 89 Cornell L R 192.

Dubai International Financial Centre, 'About DIFC' (*DIFC*, July 2018) www.difc.ae/about accessed 30 July 2018.

El-Gamal M A, *Islamic Finance Law, Economics and Practice* (Cambridge University Press 2006) 221.

Elliot F, 'The Saudi Board of Grievances' (2014) 11 *International Quarterly*, www.fenwickelliott.com/research-insight/newsletters/international-quarterly/11/saudi-board-grievances accessed 20 November 2017.

Encyclopaedia Britannica, 'Theocracy Political System' www.britannica.com/topic/theocracy accessed 3 June 2018.

Esposito J L and Shahin E E D (ed.), *The Oxford Handbook of Islam and Politics* (Oxford University Press 2013).

Faruqi HS, *Faruqi's Law Dictionary: English-Arabic* (Librairie Du Liban 1991).

Fitch: Islamic Banking is Dominant in Saudi Arabia, Reuters 2 February, 2016, www.reuters.com/article/idUSFit947384 accessed 3 November 2017.

Foster N H D, 'Encounters Between Legal Systems: Recent Cases Concerning Islamic Commercial Law in Secular Courts' (2006) 68 *Amicus Curiae* 2.

Gaffney J, 'A new seat is born: Abu Dhabi Global Market issues a UNCITRAL-based Arbitration law' (*Al-Tamimi & Co.*, February 2016) www.tamimi.com/law-update-articles/a-new-seat-is-born-abu-dhabi-global-market-issues-a-uncitral-based-arbitration-law/ accessed 30 July 2018.

Garner J, 'A Critical Perspective on the Principles of Islamic Finance Focusing on Sharia Compliance and Arbitrage' *The New Jurist* (25 March 2016) http://newjurist.com/islamic-finance-principles.html accessed 7 July 2017.

Gemmell A J, 'Commercial Arbitration in the Islamic Middle East' (2006) 5 Santa Clara J Intl L 169.

Government of Dubai, 'Service Guide' (*Government of Dubai*, July 2018) www.dubaicourts.gov.ae/portal/page/portal/dc/Gess_service_info?_piref292_597916_292_597889_597889.service_code=1595 accessed 30 July 2018.

Griffiths A, 'Ideological Combat and Social Observations: Recent Debate About Legal Pluralism' (1998) *Journal of Legal Pluralism and Unofficial Law* 28.

Griffiths D, 'Sharia Compliant DIP Financing: Coming Soon, to a Bankruptcy Court Near You, Bankruptcy Blog' (2013) https://business-finance-restructuring.weil.com/dip-financing/sharia-compliant-dip-financing-coming-soon-to-a-bankruptcy-court-near-you/ accessed 7 July 2017.

Halim A H A, Interview with Dr Mahdi Zahraa, Reader in Law, Glasgow School for Business and Society, Glasgow Caledonian University (Glasgow, 11 May 2015).

Haltom R, 'Islamic Banking, American Regulation' [2014] 2nd quarter Econ Focus 15–19 www.richmondfed.org/~/media/richmondfedorg/publications/research/econ_focus/2014/q2/pdf/feature1.pdf accessed 10 October 2017.

Hamid S A B, *International Arbitration with Commentary to Malaysian Arbitration Act 2005* (Janab (M) Sdn Bhd 2016) 443–467.

Hamid M I A and Mohammad N A N, 'Cross-Culture Jurisprudential Influence on Mediation in Malaysia' (2016) 4 MLJ xli.

Hamid T A and Trakic A, 'Enforceability of Islamic Financial Contracts in Secular Jurisdictions: Malaysian Law as the Law of Reference and Malaysian Courts as the Forum for Settlement of Disputes' (2012) 33 *ISRA Research Paper* 1–34.

Hasan Z and Asutay M, 'An Analysis of the Courts' Decisions on Islamic Finance Disputes' (2011) 3 *ISRA International Journal of Islamic Finance* 41.

Horigan D P, 'The New Adventures of the Common Law' [2009] Pace Int'l L Rev vi.

Hoyle M, 'Specific Issues in Islamic Dispute Resolution' (2009) 75 Arbitration 219.

Hoyle M, 'Topic in Focus: Demystifying UAE Arbitration Law' (2013) www.lexology.com/library/detail.aspx?g=fc4ff6d6-cafb-4063-8dc1-f20fc1544c9e accessed 25 September 2017.

Huntington S P, *The Clash of Civilizations and the Remaking of World Order* (Simon & Schuster 1996).

H R Abdul-Nasser and Umar Oseni 'Dispute Resolution in the Islamic Banking Industry of Tanzania: Learning from other Jurisdictions' (2016) vol. 9 (1) *International Journal of Islamic and Middle Eastern Finance and Management* 125.

ICD-Thomson Reuters (Islamic Finance Development Report 2017) www.icd-ps.org/ accessed 30 May 2018.

Ilias S, 'Islamic Finance: Overview and Policy Concerns' [2008] Congressional Research Service (Order Code RS22931) CRS-1-CRS-2.

International Arbitration Law Network and Resources, '74 Jurisdictions Have Adopted the UNCITRAL Model Law to Date' http://internationalarbitrationlaw.com/74-jurisdictions-have-adopted-the-uncitral-model-law-to-date/ accessed 29 December 2017.

International Chamber of Commerce (ICC), 'Commission Report on Financial Institutions and International Arbitration (Report) 2016)' https://cdn.iccwbo.org/content/uploads/sites/3/2016/11/ICC-Financial-Institutions-and-International-Arbitration-ICC-Arbitration-ADR-Commission-Report.pdf accessed 18 November 2017.

International Islamic Center for Reconciliation and Mediation, 'Establishment' www.iicra.com accessed 4 March 2018.

International Islamic Mediation and Arbitration Centre, 'About Us: Establishment' www.arabcci.org/IMAC accessed 4 March 2018.

International Islamic Mediation and Arbitration Centre, 'FAQs: Arbitration' www.arabcci.org/IMAC_faqs.htm accessed 4 March 2018.

International Monetary Fund, 'Islamic Finance and the Role of the IMF' (International Monetary Fund, February 2017) www.imf.org/external/themes/islamicfnance accessed 14 June 2018.

International Swaps and Derivatives Association, 'ISDA/IIFM Tahawwut Master Agreement Clarification Summary' www.iifm.net/sites/default/files/TMA%20clarification%20summary_0.pdf accessed 15 November 2017.

Iqbal M and Molyneux P, *Thirty Years of Islamic Banking: History, Performance and Prospects* (Palgrave Macmillan Ltd 2005) 190.

Irani G E, 'Islamic Mediation Techniques for Middle East Conflicts' (1999) 3 Middle East Review of International Affairs 1.

Islamic Center of International Reconciliation and Arbitration (IICRA), 'About IICRA' (*IICRA*, July 2018) www.iicra.com/iicra/en/page/details/page_id/ee37cbdbcdad1a37ec1e4247382903ff accessed 30 July 2018.

Islamic Finance Country Index 2017 (Global Islamic Finance Report 2017) www.gifr.net/publications/gifr2017/ifci.pdf accessed 4 September 2018.

Islamic Financial Services Board, 'Islamic Financial Services Industry Stability Report' (Islamic Financial Services Board, 2018) www.ifsb.org/docs/IFSI%20Stability%20Report%202016%20(final).pdf accessed 15 June 2018.

Issa N and Stull J, 'Saudi Arabia, Steady Growth Amidst New Regulations' in Sasikala Thiagaraja *et al.* (eds), *The Islamic Finance Handbook: A Practitioner's Guide to the Global Markets* (John Wiley & Sons Pte Ltd) 256.

Jabbar S F A, 'Dispute Resolution in Islamic Finance: Malaysia's Financial Ombudsman Scheme' (2016) 37 *Company Lawyer* 130.

Jabbar S F A, 'Islamic Finance and Dispute Resolution' (2014) 35 *Company Lawyer* 65.

Jabbar S F A, 'Islamic Finance: Fundamental Principles and Key Financial Institutions' (2009) 30 *Company Lawyer* 23.

Jabbar S F A, 'The Islamic Financial Services Industry: Shari'ah Board's Governance Framework' (2013) 34 *Company Lawyer* 297.

James A R, 'Comment: Because Arbitration Can Be Beneficial, It Should Never Have to Be Mandatory: Making A Case Against Compelled Arbitration Based Upon Pre-Dispute Agreements to Arbitrate in Consumer and Employee Adhesion Contracts' (2016) 62 *Loyola Law Review* 531.

JAMS Mediation Services, 'Mediators Ethics Guidelines' www.jamsadr.com/mediators-ethics/ accessed 31 October 2017.

Jehle G, 'Innovation, Arbitrage, and Ethics: The Role of Lawyers in the Development of a New Transnational Islamic Finance Law' (2016) 104 Georgetown LJ 1345.

Johnston K, Camelino G and Rizzo R, 'A Return to Traditional Dispute Resolution' *Canadian Forum on Civil Justice* (2000).

Kabir Hassan H M and Lewis M K (eds), *Handbook of Islamic Banking* (Elgar Original Reference 2007).

Kamali M H, *Principles of Islamic Jurisprudence* (2nd edn, Ilmiah Publishers 2009) 283–296.

Kamali M H, *Principles of Islamic Jurisprudence*, (The Islamic Texts Society 2003) 22–258.

Keshavjee M M, 'Alternative Dispute Resolution – Its Resonance in Muslim Thought and Future Directions' (Ismaili Centre Lecture Series, London, 2 April 2002) https://iis.ac.uk/alternative-dispute-resolution-its-resonance-muslim-thought-and-future-directions accessed 20 February 2018.

Khan A A, 'United Arab Emirates' (*The Law Reviews*, July 2018) https://thelawreviews.co.uk/edition/the-islamic-finance-and-markets-review-edition-2/1150803/united-arab-emirates accessed 30 July 2018.

Khan A A, 'United Arab Emirates' (*The Law Reviews*, November 2017) https://thelawreviews.co.uk/edition/the-islamic-finance-and-markets-review-edition-2/1150803/united-arab-emirates accessed 30 July 2018.

Khan M M and Bhatti M S, 'Islamic Banking and Finance: On Its Way to Globalization' (2008) 34 *Managerial Finance* 708–725.

King and Spalding, 'Recent Legal Development in Saudi Arabia' www.lexology.com/library/detail.aspx?g=84306b89-e5a2-424d-89c2-2574e7ceeb62 accessed 20 November 2017.

Kingdom of Saudi Arabia www.britannica.com/place/Saudi-Arabia/The-Kingdom-of-Saudi-Arabia, accessed 30 September 2017.

Kutty F, 'Shari'a Factor in International Commercial Arbitration' (2006) 28 Loyola Intl & Comparative L Review 565.

Lawrence J, Morton P and Khan H, 'Dispute Resolution in Islamic Finance', (Global Islamic Finance Report, April 2012) http://klgates.com/files/Publication/0b2f56b0-d738-4217-85ee-6670f2101659/Presentation/PublicationAttachment/3e2c3cd0-43fd-4ef4-ac96-700e33340e6a/Dispute_Resolution_in_Islamic_Finance.pdf accessed 20 February 2018.

Lawrence J, Morton P R and Khan H S, 'Resolving Islamic Finance Dispute' *Legal Insight*, September 2013 www.klgates.com/resolving-islamic-finance-disputes-09-19-2013/ accessed 3 November 2017.

Lerodiaconou M J, 'Conciliation, Mediation and Federal Human Rights Complaints: Are Rights Compromised?' [January 2005], Centre for Employment and Labour Relations Law, Working Paper no. 32, 3–28.

Lukito R, 'Religious ADR: Mediation in Islamic Family Law Tradition' (2006) *Al-Jami'ah*.

Lye K C, 'Panel Discussion and Question and Answer Session' (Workshop on Dispute Resolution and Insolvency in Islamic Finance: Problems and Solutions, National University of Singapore, September 2013) 44–45.

MacCuish A and Dandekar S, 'United Arab Emirates: Applicability and Legal Entitlement to Interest under UAE Law' (*Mondaq*, 9 August 2016) www.mondaq.com/x/517384/Contract+Law/Applicability+And+Legal+Entitlement+To+Interest+Under+UAE+Law accessed 30 July 2018.

Madawi A R, *A Most Masculine State: Gender, Politics and Religion in Saudi Arabia* (Cambridge University Press 2013) 333.

Malaysia International Financial Centre in Collaboration with Islamic Corporation for the Development of the Private Sector (Islamic Finance in Asia: Reaching New Heights Report 2017), www.mifc.com/index.php?ch=28&pg=72&ac=188&bb=uploadpdf accessed 30 May 2017.

Malaysia Syariah Judiciary Department, 'Court Procedure According to the Level of Appellate Court' (In Malay) www.esyariah.gov.my/portal/page/portal/Portal%20E-Syariah%20BM/Portal%20E-Syariah%20Prosedur%20Mahkamah/Portal%20E-Syariah%20Prosedur%20Mahk.%20Tinggi/Portal%20E-Syariah%20Prosedur%20Mahk.%20Rayuan accessed 23 February 2018.

Maret R E, 'Mind the Gap: The Equality Bill and Sharia Arbitration in the United Kingdom' (2013) 36(1) *Boston College International and Comparative Law Review*.

McMillen M J T, 'Islamic Capital Markets for United States Parties: Overview and Select Shariʿah Governance Elements' in Inside the Minds: Financial Services Enforcement and Compliance (Aspatore 2013).

Merriam Webster Online Dictionary, 'Definition of Mediation' www.merriam-webster.com/dictionary/mediation accessed 14 November 2017.

Metcalf A M, 'United States' [2016] The Islamic Finance and Markets Review (1st edn).

McMillen Michael J T, 'An Introduction to Shariʿah Considerations in Bankruptcy and Insolvency Contexts and Islamic Finance's First Bankruptcy (East Cameron)' [2010] http://ssrn.com/abstract=1826246 accessed 20 October 2017.

Michaels R, 'Non-State Law in the Hague Principles on Choice of Law in International Contracts' https://ssrn.com/abstract=2386186 accessed 7 July 2017 (forthcoming).

Mirza M, Living Apart Together: British Muslims and the Paradox of Multiculturalism (2007) 5 www.policyexchange.org.uk/wp-content/uploads/2016/09/living-apart-together-jan-07.pdf accessed 1 November 2017.

Mohamad T A H and Trakic A, 'Critical Appraisal of the Companies' Obligations to Pay Zakat in the Malaysian Context' (2013) 10 ICCLR 375.

Mohamad T A H and Trakic A, 'The Adjudication of Shari'ah Issues in Islamic Finance Contracts: Guidance from Malaysia' (2015) 26 JBFLP 39.

Mohamad T A H and Trakic A, 'The Shari'ah Advisory Council's Role in Resolving Islamic Banking Disputes in Malaysia: A Model to Follow?' in Adnan Trakic and Hanifah Haydar Ali Tajuddin (eds), *Islamic Banking and Finance: Principles, Instruments and Operations* (2nd edn, Malaysian Current Law Journal 2016) 520.

Mohamad T A H, 'Interlink/interface between Common Law System and Shariah Rules and Principles and Effective Dispute Resolution Mechanism' (28–29 September 2009) www.tunabdulhamid.my accessed on 5 June 2018.

Mohammed A, *Understanding Islamic Finance* (John Wiley & Sons Ltd 2007) 516.

Mohammed R, 'Hot trend in 2017: Rise of Islamic banks on Main St. USA' (CNBC, 2 December 2016) www.cnbc.com/2016/12/02/under-the-radar-islamic-banks-rise-in-th.html accessed 9 October 2017.

Mohd Nor M Z, Mohamad A M and Yaacob H, 'The Development of Islamic Finance in Malaysia' in Adnan Trakic and Hanifah Haydar Ali Tajuddin (eds), *Islamic Banking and Finance: Principles, Instruments and Operations* (2nd edn, Malaysian Current Law Journal 2016) 601–617.

Molyneux P and Iqbal M, *Islamic Banking and Financial Services in the Arab World* (Palgrave Macmillan 2005) 336.

Motani H, 'Workshop on IIFM Standards Session: Islamic Hedging Standards' (September 2017) www.iifm.net/sites/default/files/Session%201%20-%20Hedging%20Legal%20Aspects%20by%20Habib%20Motani.pdf accessed 15 November 2017.

Muslim Arbitral Tribunal, History (2015) www.matribunal.com accessed 1 November 2017.

Nadar A, 'Islamic Finance and Dispute Resolution: Part 1' (2009) 23 Arab Law Quarterly 1.

Nomoto S, 'An Early Isma'ili-Shi'i Thought on the Messianic Figure (the Qa'in) according to al-Razi (d. *c.*322/933–4)' (2009) 44 Orient 19.

Nor M Z, 'Settling Islamic Finance Disputes: The Case of Malaysia and Saudi Arabia' in Vernon Valentine, *et al.*, (eds), *Mixed Legal Systems, East and West* (Routledge Taylor & Francis Group 2016) 299.

Olson W, *The Litigation Explosion: What Happened When America Unleashed the Law Suit* (Truman Tally Books 1991).

Ombudsman for Financial Services Annual Report 2017, 3. www.ofs.org.my/file/files/OFS-AR2017-lowres.pdf accessed 13 August 2018.

Ombudsman for Financial Services, 'Background' www.ofs.org.my/en/background accessed 4 March 2018.

Ortolani P and Warwas B, 'Arbitration in Southern Europe: Insights from A Large-Scale Empirical Study' (2015) 26 American Review of International Arbitration 187.

Oseni U A and Ahmad A U F, 'Towards a Global Hub: The Legal Framework for Dispute Resolution in Malaysia's Islamic Finance Industry' (2016) 58 *International Journal of Law and Management* 48.

Oseni U A, 'A Review of Malaysia as a Choice Jurisdiction for Dispute Resolution in the Global Islamic Finance Industry' in Backer H S A (ed.), *International Arbitration: With Commentary to Malaysian Arbitration Act 2005* (Janab (M) Sdn Bhd 2016).

Oseni U A, 'Dispute Resolution in Islamic Banking and Finance: Current Trends and Future Perspectives' (International Conference on Islamic Financial Services: Emerging Opportunities for Law/Economic Reforms of the Developing Nations, Nigeria, October 2009).

Oseni U A, 'Islamic Finance Arbitration: Integrating Classical and Modern Legal Frameworks', in Adnan Trakic and Hanifah Haydar Ali Tajuddin (eds), *Islamic Banking and Finance: Principles, Instruments and Operations*, (2nd edn, Malaysian Current Law Journal 2016) 549–568.

Othman A, 'And Amicable Settlement is Best: *Sulh* and Dispute Resolution in Islamic Law' (2007) *Arab Law Quarterly* 64, 65.

Othman A, 'Islamic Finance Dispute Resolution in Malaysia' Workshop on Dispute Resolution and Insolvency in Islamic Finance: Problems and Solutions, 19 September 2013, National University of Singapore, 13–26.

Otto J M, *Sharia Incorporated: A Comparative Overview of the Legal Systems of Twelve Muslim Countries in Past and Present* (Leiden University Press 2010) 676.

Oxford Islamic Studies Online, 'Fard Kifayah' www.oxfordislamicstudies.com/article/opr/t125/e625 accessed 3 November 2017.

Oxford Reference, 'Procedure' *The Oxford International Encyclopedia of Legal History*. Oxford University Press, 2009 www.oxfordreference.com/ accessed 1 November 2017.

Paldi C, 'Dubai as the Dispute Resolution Center for the Islamic Finance Industry', (30 December 2010) www.jdsupra.com/legalnews/dubai-as-the-dispute-resolution-center-f-54362/ accessed 20 February 2018.

Paldi C, 'The Dubai World Islamic Finance Arbitration Center and the Dubai World Islamic Finance Arbitration Center Jurisprudence Office as the Dispute Resolution Center and Mechanism for the Islamic Finance Industry: Issues and a Proposed Framework', *Master Dissertation in Islamic Finance*, Durham University, 2013, 1–57.

Palmer M and Roberts S A, *Dispute Processes: ADR and the Primary Forms of Decision Making* (Butterworths 1998).

Paul A, *Evidence: Practice and Procedure* (2003) Malayan Law Journal 448.

Pickl V, 'Islamic Roots of Ombudsman System' (1997) 6 *The Ombudsman Journal* 101.

Price Waterhouse Coopers, 'Corporate Choices in International Arbitration: Industry Perspectives' www.pwc.com/gx/en/arbitration-dispute-resolution/assets/pwc-international-arbitration-study.pdf accessed 21 February 2018.

PRIME Finance, 'History' https://primefinancedisputes.org/page/history accessed 3 March 2018.

PRIME Finance, 'Media Coverage' https://primefinancedisputes.org/page/media-coverage accessed 3 March 2018.

Prospect Magazine, 'Sense on Sharia' www.prospectmagazine.co.uk/2008/02/senseon sharia/ accessed 15 November 2017.

Public Works and Government Services Canada, 'Alternative Dispute Resolution (ADR) and Litigation: Key Features and Considerations' http://studylib.net/doc/18733895/alternative-dispute-resolution-adr-and-litigation-key- accessed 20 February 2018.

Rahman F, 'ADGM Arbitration Centre Aims to Resolve Disputes of all Parties' (Guld News, 13 September 2017) https://gulfnews.com/business/economy/adgm-arbitration-centre-aims-to-resolve-disputes-of-all-parties-1.2089785 accessed 30 July 2018.

Ramadan T, *The Messenger: The Meanings of the Life of Muhammad (*Allen Lane 2007).

Ras Al Khaimah Centre of Reconciliation and Commercial Arbitration, 'Articles of Association' (*Rak Chamber*, July 2018) www.rakchamber.ae/data/upload/mainE.pdf accessed 30 July 2018.

Rashid S K, 'Alternative Dispute Resolution in the Context of Islamic Law' (2004) 7 *The Vindobona Journal of International Commercial Law and Arbitration* 95.

Rashid S K, 'Peculiarities and Religious Underlining of ADR in Islamic Law' (Conference on Mediation in the Asia Pacific: Constraints and Challenges, Kuala Lumpur, 16–18 June 2008).

Rau A S, 'The Agreement to Arbitrate and the "Applicable Law"' (2017) University of Texas Law Public Law Research Paper No. 644.

Re: Murabaha Financing Facility/Islamic Home Finance Product, NYSBL 96(1), NYS DFS – Banking Interpretations (27 August 2001) www.dfs.ny.gov/legal/interpret/lo010827.htm accessed 5 December 2017.

Re: Net Lease and Purchase Agreement, NYSBL 96(1), NYS DFS – Banking Interpretations (12 April 1999) www.dfs.ny.gov/legal/interpret/lo990412.htm accessed 5 December 2017.

Redfern A *et al.*, *Law and Practice of International Commercial Arbitration* (4th edn, Sweet & Maxwell 2004).

Restatement (Second) of the Conflicts of Laws § 187 (Am Law Inst 1971).

Ribeiro J and Lee J, 'Overview of UNCITRAL Texts on International Commercial Arbitration in Islamic Law Influenced Jurisdictions (ILIJ)' (2015) 46 VUWLR 139.
Rider B, 'Islamic Financial Law: Back to Basics' in IFSB, *The Changing Landscape of Islamic Finance: Imminent Challenges and Future Directions* (IFSB 2010).
Robbers G, *Encyclopedia of World Constitutions* (Infobase Publishing 2007) vol. 1, 1168.
Royal Embassy of Saudi Arabia Washington DC, 'About Saudi Arabia: Facts and Figures' www.saudiembassy.net/about/country-information/facts_and_figures/ accessed 30 September 2017.
SAC Resolution on *Condition for Validity of Bai' Inah Contract* (16th meeting dated 11 November 2000 and 82nd meeting dated 17 February 2009) www.sacbnm.org/wp-content/uploads/2018/03/72.E.pdf accessed 7 August 2018.
Sadiqi M A, 'Islamic Dispute Resolution in the Shade of the American Court House' (October 2010) www.amjaonline.org/en/academic-research/cat_view/6-islamic-arbitration-guidelines-and-procedures-2010 accessed 20 February 2018.
Said A A, and Funk N C, *Peace and Conflict Resolution in Islam: Precept and Practice* (University Press of America 2001).
Said E, 'The Clash of Ignorance' (2001) 273 The Nation 11.
Saleh S, *Commercial Arbitration in the Arab Middle East: A Study in Shari'a and Statute Law* (Graham & Trotman Limited 1984).
Saleh S, *Commercial Arbitration in the Arab Middle East: Shari'ah, Syria, Lebanon and Egypt* (2nd edn, Heart Publishing 2006) 290–325.
Satkunasingam E, 'Jurisdiction over Islamic Banking in Malaysia: Challenges of Maintaining the Status Quo' in Adnan Trakic and Hanifah Haydar Ali Tajuddin (eds), *Islamic Banking and Finance: Principles, Instruments and Operations* (2nd edn, Malaysian Current Law Journal 2016) 783–798.
Saudi Arabian Monetary Authority (SAMA), Historical Preview www.sama.gov.sa/en-US/About/Pages/SAMAHistory.aspx accessed 3 November 2017.
Schwing M A, 'The KLRCA I-Arbitration Rules: A Shari'a-Compliant Solution to the Problems with Islamic Finance Dispute Resolution in Singapore and Malaysia?' (2017) 34 *Journal of International Arbitration* 425.
Shaharuddin A, 'The Bay' al-'Inah Controversy in Malaysian Islamic Banking' (2012) 26 *Arab Law Quarterly* 499.
Shapiro M, 'Islam and Appeal' (1980) 68 *California Law Review* 350.
Sharjah International Commercial Arbitration Centre, 'Official Page' (*Tahkeem*, July 2018) www.tahkeem.ae/en accessed 30 July 2018.
Shen NM, 'Malaya Remains Lead in Islamic Finance' (*The Malaysian Reserve*, 5 April 2018) https://themalaysianreserve.com/2018/04/05/malaysia-remains-lead-in-islamic-finance/ accessed 30 May 2018.
Speller D and Hornyold-Strickland F, 'International Arbitration in the Finance Sector: Room to Grow?' (Commercial Dispute Resolution, 8 March 2017) www.cdr-news.com/categories/arbitration-and-adr/featured/7122-international-arbitration-in-the-finance-sector-room-to-grow accessed 21 February 2018.
Strong M and Himber R, 'The Legal Autonomy of the Dubai International Financial Centre: A Scalable Strategy for Global Free-Market Reforms' [2009] 29 *Economic Affairs* 36–41.
Taimiyyah I, *Al-Hisbah fi al-Islam wa Wazifat al Hukkam al-Islamiyyah* (*Hisbah in Islam and Duties of Islamic Officials*) (Madinah University n.d.).
Tain V, 'Malaysia: Undisputed Leader?' http://islamicfinancenews.com/glossary/tawarruq accessed 7 July 2017.

Telegraph, 'What Can sharia Courts do in Britain' www.telegraph.co.uk/news/newstopics/lawreports/joshuarozenberg/2957692/What-can-sharia-courts-do-in-Britain.html accessed 1 November 2017.

Teslik L H, 'The U.S. Financial Regulatory System' (Council on Foreign Relations, 4 October 2008) www.cfr.org/backgrounder/us-financial-regulatory-system accessed 9 October 2017.

Tevendale C, '*Jivraj* – It's Back and This Time it's at the European Commission' (28 September 2012) *Kluwer Arbitration Blog* http://kluwerarbitrationblog.com/2012/09/28/jivraj-its-back-and-this-time-its-at-the-european-commission/ accessed 20 December 2017.

The Noble Qur'an: English Translation of the Meanings and Commentary (King Fahd Complex for the Printing of the Holy Qur'an 2009).

Thomas A, 'Methods of Islamic Home Finance in the United States' (2001) Shape Knowledge Services http://consultshape.com/wp-content/uploads/methods2017.pdf accessed 10 October 2017.

Thomas L C, 'Developing Commercial Law Through the Courts: Rebalancing the Relationship Between the Courts and Arbitration', The Bailii Lecture, 9 March 2016, available at https://aberdeenunilaw.files.wordpress.com/2016/05/lcj-speech-bailli-lecture-201603091.pdf accessed 24 July 2018.

Townsend S, 'ADGM Signs Accord with Ras Al Khaimah on Dispute Cases' (The National, 16 November 2017) www.thenational.ae/business/economy/adgm-signs-accord-with-ras-al-khaimah-on-dispute-cases-1.676341 accessed 30 July 2018.

Trakic A, 'The Adjudication of Shari'ah Issues in Islamic Financial Contracts: Is Malaysian Islamic Finance Litigation a Solution?' (2013) 29 *Humanomics* 260.

Tyser C R, Demetriades D G and Effendi I H, *The Mejelle: Being an English Translation of Majallah El-Ahkam-I-Adliya and a Complete Code on Islamic Civil Law* (The Other Press 2001).

UK Civil Mediation Council, 'What is Mediation?' www.civilmediation.org/about-mediation/29/what-is-mediation accessed 14 November 2017.

United Kingdom, *Parliamentary Debates*, House of Lords, 19 October 2012, Column 1683, (*Baroness Cox*) www.publications.parliament.uk/pa/ld201213/ldhansrd/text/121019-0001.htm#12101923000438 accessed 15 November 2017.

United Nations, 'World Population Prospects (2017 Revision), 2017' https://esa.un.org/unpd/wpp/publications/Files/WPP2017_KeyFindings.pdf accessed 16 June 2018.

United Nations, 'A Guide to UNCITRAL, Basic facts about the United Nations Commission on International Trade Law' www.uncitral.org/pdf/english/texts/general/12-57491-Guide-to-UNCITRAL-e.pdf accessed 15 November 2017.

United Nations, 'Case Law on UNCITRAL Texts (CLOUT)' www.uncitral.org/clout/index.jspx?lng=en#legislativeText accessed 15 November 2017.

United Nations, 'Convention on the Recognition and Enforcement of Foreign Arbitral Awards (New York, 1958) (The (New York Convention")' www.uncitral.org/uncitral/en/uncitral_texts/arbitration/NYConvention.html accessed 20 November 2017.

United Nations, 'Digests' www.uncitral.org/uncitral/en/case_law/digests.html accessed 15 November 2017.

United Nations, 'General Assembly Resolution 40/72 (11 December 1985)' www.un.org/en/ga/search/view_doc.asp?symbol=A/RES/40/72 accessed 15 November 2017.

United Nations, 'General Assembly Resolution 61/33 (4 December 2006)' www.un.org/en/ga/search/view_doc.asp?symbol=A/RES/61/33&Lang=E accessed 15 November 2017.

United Nations, 'Official Records of the General Assembly, Fortieth Session, Supplement No. 17 (A/40/17), annex I' www.uncitral.org/pdf/english/texts/arbitration/NY-conv/New-York-Convention-E.pdf accessed 15 November 2017.

United Nations, 'Official Records of the General Assembly, Sixty-first Session, Supplement No. 17 (A/61/17)' http://unctad.org/en/Docs/a61d17_en.pdf accessed 15 November 2017.

United Nations, 'Treaty Series 330/4739 (7 June 1959)' https://treaties.un.org/pages/showDetails.aspx?objid=080000028002a36b accessed 15 November 2017.

United Nations, 'UNCITRAL Model Law on International Commercial Arbitration 1985 with amendments as adopted in 2006' www.uncitral.org/pdf/english/texts/arbitration/ml-arb/07-86998_Ebook.pdf accessed 15 November 2017.

United Nations, 'UNCITRAL Model Law on International Commercial Arbitration (1985), with amendments as adopted in 2006' www.uncitral.org/uncitral/en/uncitral_texts/arbitration/1985Model_arbitration.html accessed 29 December 2017.

United Nations, 'UNCITRAL Technical Notes on Online Dispute Resolution (2016)' www.uncitral.org/uncitral/en/uncitral_texts/odr/2016Technical_notes.html accessed 18 November 2017.

US Consumer Financial Protection Bureau, 'CFPB Issues Rule to Ban Companies from Using Arbitration Clauses to Deny Groups of People Their Day in Court' www.consumerfinance.gov/about-us/newsroom/cfpb-issues-rule-ban-companies-using-arbitration-clauses-deny-groups-people-their-day-court/ accessed 16 February 2018.

Vogel J H, 'Current Status of Islamic finance in the United States' [2012] no 27 Cayman Financial Review Magazine B43 http://caymanianfinancialreview.cay.newsmemory.com/?date=20120404&goTo=B43 accessed 9 October 2017.

Vogel J H, 'United States' [2016] Getting the Deal Through: Islamic Finance & Markets 51.

Warde I, *Islamic Finance in the Global Economy* (Edinburgh University Press 2010) 252.

Whitman R, 'Incorporation by Reference in Commercial Contracts' (1961) 21 Maryland L Review 1.

Wilson P W and Graham D, *Saudi Arabia: The Coming Storm* (M E Sharpe Inc 1994) 384.

Woolf H, *Access to Justice: Final Report to the Lord Chancellor on the Civil Justice System in England and Wales* (Her Majesty's Stationery Office 1996).

World Bank, World Bank National Accounts data and OECD National Accounts data files, 2016 https://data.worldbank.org/indicator/NY.GDP.MKTP.CD accessed 16 June 2018.

World Population Review http://worldpopulationreview.com/countries/saudi-arabia-population/ 30 September 2017.

Yaacob A M (ed.), *Sistem Kehakiman Islam* (IKIM 2001).

Yaacob H, *Alternative Dispute Resolution (ADR): Expanding Options in Local and Cross Border Islamic Finance Cases*, (Kuala Lumpur, ISRA, 2012), 53.

Yaakob H, 'Arbitration – Consistent with the Spirit of Islamic Banking? The Benefits and Challenges of Arbitrating in Islamic Banking and Finance Disputes' (Asia Pacific Regional Arbitration Group Conference, Kuala Lumpur, 9–10 July 2011).

Yacoob H, Muhammad M and Smolo E, 'International Convention for Islamic Finance: Towards Standardization' (2011) 29 *ISRA Research Paper* 1–58.

Yaqubi N, DeLorenzo Y T and Shleibak A, 'Fatwa: SHAPE Profit Sharing Deposit (Letter)' (July 2005) Shape Financial.

Yasin N M, 'Legal Aspects of Islamic Banking: Malaysian Experience' in Salman Syed Ali and Ausaf Ahmed (eds), *Islamic Banking and Finance: Fundamentals and Contemporary Issues* (Islamic Research and Training Institution 2007) 225.

Yatim H, 'Nine-member Bench to Rule if Shariah Council Decision Binds Civil Court' (*Malaysiakini*, 27 August 2018) www.malaysiakini.com/news/440593 accessed 28 August 2018.

Yildirim Y, 'The Medina Charter: A Historical Case of Conflict Resolution' (2009) *Islamic and Christian-Muslim Relations*.

Zahid A and Ali H M, 'Shariah as a Choice of Law in International Islamic Finance Contracts: Shamil Bank of Bahrain Case Revisited' (2013) 27 US-China L Review 10.

Zahid A and Ali H M, 'Texas Enacts 'Anti-Sharia' Law' www.breitbart.com/texas/2017/06/16/texas-enacts-anti-sharia-law/ accessed 7 July 2017.

Zakaria A Z, 'Speech by Tan Sri Arifin bin Zakaria, Chief Justice of Malaysia, at the Opening of the Legal Year 2012 (14 Jan 2014)' www.malaysianbar.org.my/speeches/speech_by_tan_sri_arifin_bin_zakaria_chief_justice_of_malaysia_at_the_opening_of_the_legal_year_2012_14_jan_2012.html accessed 13 August 2018.

Zanki N K K, 'Codification of Islamic Law Premises of History and Debates of Contemporary Muslim Scholars' (2014) 4 *International Journal of Humanities and Social Sciences* 127.

Zyp V L, 'Islamic Finance in the United States: Product Development and Regulatory Adoption' (Masters of Arts thesis, Georgetown University 2009).

Zyp V L, 'Fast Answers: No Action Letters' (23 March 2017) US Securities and Exchange Commission www.sec.gov/fast-answers/answersnoactionhtm.html accessed 3 January 2018.

Zyp V L, 'Securities law history' Wex (Legal Information Institute at the Cornell Law School) www.law.cornell.edu/wex/securities_law_history accessed 2 January 2018.

Index

AAOIFI *see* Accounting and Auditing Organization for Islamic Financial Institutions
Ab Halim, Asma Hakimah ix, 30, 30–44, 160
Abdulaziz, King (known as Ibn Saud) 132
Abu Dhabi 28, 134, 137, 149, 171; and Dubai 137–138; Executive Council 142
Abu Dhabi Global Market *see* ADGM
Abu Dhabi Law No. 4 of 2013 142
Accounting and Auditing Organization for Islamic Financial Institutions 11, 16, 141
ADGM 142–143, 146, 149–151, 153, 155–156, 163, 168, 173, 181, 183; arbitration centre 150; and Chairman Ahmad Al Sayegh 149; courts 142, 149–151, 153, 156; Courts Procedure Rules 149; laws 152; registration authorities 142
ADR *see* alternative dispute resolution
Affin Bank Bhd v Zulkifli Abdullah 34
agreements 2, 8–11, 14–20, 24–25, 39–40, 47, 62–63, 82–87, 96, 110–111, 118–120, 128–130, 151, 162–163, 165–166; to arbitrate 20, 36, 49, 51, 61, 85–86, 111; commercial 35, 38, 111; cross-border 159; for loans 91
Ahmed, Pervaiz K 1, 6, 158–167
AIAC *see* Asian International Arbitration Centre
AIAC i-Arbitration Rules 2018 (Malaysia) 113, 119, 162, 168
Ajman (Emirate) 137
All Malaysia Reports 19
alternative dispute resolution 1–3, 6, 36, 43, 45, 51–53, 58–60, 64–65, 107, 148, 150, 155, 174, 181, 184
Amiri Decree No. 6, 2009 145
Arab-Malaysian Finance Bhd v Taman Ihsan Jaya Sdn Bhd & Ors 34, 100, 104, 171
Arab-Malaysian Merchant Bank Bhd v Silver Concept Sdn Bhd [2006] 8 CLJ 9 105
arbitral awards 22, 28, 35–36, 39–40, 44, 51, 85, 94, 110, 112, 129–130, 149, 163, 175; cross-border 39; domestic 129, 147; enforcement of 86, 149; non-domestic 49; recognition of 20, 27, 36, 49, 85, 110, 130, 147, 152, 167, 170, 183; Shari'ah compliant 111
arbitral tribunal 20, 22, 28, 36, 63, 113
arbitrate 21–23, 37–38, 51, 86, 112, 150, 178; according to the law 112; agreement to 20, 36, 49, 51, 61, 85–86, 111
arbitration 2–3, 20–22, 35–40, 42–46, 48–52, 54–55, 110–114, 128–130, 134–135, 143, 145, 148–151, 155–156, 159–168, 176–178; agreements 36, 49, 51, 61, 85–86; awards 22–23, 37, 112, 118; binding 55; bodies 36, 161; decisions 3, 36–37; impartial 23; of Islamic finance disputes 63, 161; key features and foundations of 35; mandatory 51; place of 20–21; practice of 37, 148; proceedings 21, 36, 40; process 40, 61, 130, 145; religious 22; and reconciliation centres 59, 153; rules 63, 67, 112, 129, 145, 148, 156; uses of 6, 37, 50, 166
Arbitration Act 1996 (UK) 59, 61, 161
Arbitration and Mediation Services (Equality Bill) 61, 66
Arbitration Centre 149, 163
arbitration clauses 2, 20, 27, 39, 47, 50–51, 111, 113, 174, 184; contractual 21, 35; mandatory 39–40, 51, 160, 166, 175

Arbitration Regulations 2015 149–150
arbitration tribunals 111–112
arbitrators 3, 18–22, 28, 35, 37–40, 42, 46, 55, 101, 109–114, 116, 129–130, 145, 162–165, 167; neutral 35; panel of 3, 35, 110, 113; professional 153; qualified 38, 44, 160; selection of 21, 35, 46, 111–112
Asian International Arbitration Centre 5, 38, 50, 63, 67, 112–113, 162, 173
Australia National Alternative Dispute Resolution Advisory Council 51
awards 20–23, 28, 36, 38, 40, 49, 85–86, 94, 110–112, 114, 129–130, 145, 147, 149–152, 156; domestic 36, 40, 49, 51; foreign arbitral 36, 49, 51, 85, 110, 130, 147, 151–152, 167, 170, 183; international 40; resolution's 152

Bahrain Islamic Bank 136
baitulmal (revenue generation) 97
Bank Islam Malaysia 101, 136, 172
Bank Islam Malaysia Berhad v Adnan bin Omar 97
Bank Islam Malaysia Berhad v Lim Kok Hoe & Anor 100, 105
Bank Kerjasama Malaysia Rakyat Bhd v PSC Naval Dockyard 16, 19
Bank Kerjasama Rakyat Malaysia Bhd 106, 115n22
Bank Kerjasama Rakyat Malaysia Bhd v Emcee Corp Sdn Bhd 34
Bank Kerjasama Rakyat Malaysia Bhd v MME Reality & Management Sdn Bhd 106, 115n22
Bank Negara Malaysia 27, 95, 98–101, 103, 109, 174
Bank Negara Malaysia Shari'ah Advisory Council 18
banking interest *see* interest
Bano, Samia 60–61
Basic Law 1992 (Saudi Arabia) 12, 121, 125, 128
Benson, John 1–6, 158, 160, 162, 164, 166–167
Beth Din (House of Judgment) 57, 60
Bhatti, Maria ix, 54–64, 141, 161, 178
BIM *see* Bank Islam Malaysia
Blake, Susan 45, 47, 51–52
Blanke, Gordon 148
BNM *see* Bank Negara Malaysia
Board of Grievances Law 1982 122, 126–127, 134, 168
Britain 57–59, 65–66, 134, 174–175, 183; and the legal system 57–58, 60, 161; and Muslims 57, 60, 65, 179
'Broad Murabahah Requirements' 106
'Broad Shariah Principles' 106

Caliph 32, 64
Capital Market Authority 124
cases 17–19, 48, 68, 73, 83, 158, 183; *Affin Bank Bhd v Zulkifli Abdullah* 34; *Arab-Malaysian Merchant Bank Bhd v Silver Concept Sdn Bhd* [2006] 8 CLJ 9 105; *Bank Islam Malaysia Berhad v Adnan bin Omar* 97; *Bank Islam Malaysia Berhad v Lim Kok Hoe & Anor* 100, 105; *Bank Kerjasama Malaysia Rakyat Bhd v PSC Naval Dockyard* 16, 19; *Bank Kerjasama Rakyat Malaysia Bhd v Emcee Corp Sdn Bhd* 34; *Bank Kerjasama Rakyat Malaysia Bhd v MME Reality & Management Sdn Bhd* 106, 115n22; *Central Bank of Malaysia Act 2009* (Malaysia) 7, 18–20, 96, 98–100, 162; *In re East Cameron Partners, LP, 'Order on Def [s'] Rule 12 Motions,' Bankruptcy Case No 08–51207; Adv Proc No 08–5041 (Bankruptcy Court, WDLa 2009) (unpublished order 17 April 2009)* 82, 85, 92–93, 171; *Malayan Banking Bhd v Marilyn Ho Siok* 34; *National Group for Communications & Computers v Lucent Technologies International* 12, 17, 77; *Semenyih Jaya Sdn Bhd v Pentadbir Tanah Daerah Hulu Langat* 103; *United Islamic Society v Masjed Abubakr Al-Seddiq* 81–82
CBD *see* Committee of Banking Disputes
CBMA 98–102, 104–107, 113, 116
Central Bank of Malaysia 44, 162
Central Bank of Malaysia Act 1958 99
Central Bank of Malaysia Act 2009 7, 18–20, 96, 98–100, 162
choices of law 5, 7–12, 14, 20–25, 27–28, 60, 62–64, 67–68, 77–79, 108–112, 114, 154, 158–160, 164, 175; in arbitration 20; in Islamic disputes 4, 14, 96, 107; in Islamic finance 8–9, 11, 13, 15, 17, 19, 21, 23, 25, 27, 29, 160; in the US and UK 4, 14, 96, 107
CIBAFI *see* Council for Islamic Banks and Financial Institutions
Circuit of Appeal (Saudi Arabia) 127
civil courts 34, 59, 79, 91, 96–98, 100, 105, 115, 117, 144, 147, 150–151, 153, 162, 164; federal 143; judges 98, 162

Civil Procedure Rules 45
CMA *see* Capital Market Authority
Colón, Julio C ix, 8–23, 68–87, 159–161
commercial agreements 35, 38, 111
commercial arbitration ix, 11, 25, 49, 111–112, 134, 145, 154–155, 162, 176, 181–182
Commission Report on Financial Institutions and International Arbitration 2016 38
Committee of Banking Disputes 127–128
contracts 8–16, 18, 20–21, 23–24, 26–28, 33–34, 38–39, 62, 77–80, 112–114, 129, 139, 143–144, 147–148, 159–160; commercial 26, 144, 184; conventional non-Shari'ah compliant 160; financial 4, 160; *ijarah* 69; international 11, 24, 48; Islamic banking 100; law of 74–75; master *wakala* 15–16; and the parties 2, 9, 33, 35, 39, 138; self-sufficient (*contrat sans loi*) 11; traditional 14
Convention on Judicial Assistance, Recognition and Enforcement of Judgments in Civil and Commercial Matters 1992 130
Convention on Judicial Assistance in Civil and Commercial Matters 2004 152
Council for Islamic Banks and Financial Institutions 38
courts 4–7, 10, 12–19, 32–35, 50–52, 77–87, 96–110, 115–116, 125–126, 130–131, 137–138, 143–145, 147, 149–153, 158–166; of appeal 33, 39, 59, 100, 138; local 137–138; lower 15, 105, 126
CPR *see* Civil Procedure Rules
creditors 83, 139
cross-border 33–34, 36, 39, 44, 114, 159–160, 162, 164; agreements 159; arbitration awards 39; enforcement of arbitral awards 39, 44, 160; enforcement of Shari'ah arbitral awards 44; enforcement of Shari'ah contracts 160; Islamic financial transactions 1, 34
The Current Law Journal 19

damages 17, 19, 38, 75, 77, 79; expectation of 13, 17, 78; monetary 127; speculative 15
debtors 83, 85
debts 71, 83, 88–89, 139, 144
decisions 3, 13–15, 17–19, 21–23, 30–35, 37, 44–46, 57–59, 78–81, 103–107, 110–111, 126–128, 147, 150–152, 161–163; administrative 104; arbitral 55, 130, 163; arbitrator's 110; binding 30, 55; final 3, 46, 55, 59, 103, 144; judicial 17, 31, 101, 113; procedural 79
Declaratory Judgment Act 84–85, 94
deposits 69, 72–73, 88, 90; consumer 69; initial 88; *mudaraba* 89; sharing 87
DIAC *see* Dubai International Arbitration Centre
DIFC 142, 146–150, 153, 155–156, 163, 174–175, 182; and ADGM courts 142–143, 146, 150–151, 163; and ADGM laws 152, 163; Arbitration Institute 146, 148, 156, 174; and the Court of Appeal 147; and the Court of First Instance 147; courts 146–151, 153, 156; laws and regulations 147
dispute resolution ix–xi, 23, 29–31, 44, 46–47, 51, 54–57, 64–65, 117–119, 126, 144–146, 163, 166–167, 177–178, 180; channels 153; clauses 20, 56; interactions between Islamic and Western 56; international 22; in Islamic finance 1–6; mechanisms 1–3, 5–6, 30–31, 33, 35, 37–39, 41, 43, 45, 47, 49, 53–54, 95, 158–161, 164–166; procedures 6, 160
Dispute Resolution Authority 142, 146, 148
dispute settlements 2, 38, 130–131, 159–160; issues surrounding 159; judicial mechanism 127, 130; procedures 160; processes 162
disputing parties 5, 30, 32–34, 37, 39, 41–42, 107, 110, 112, 120, 144–145, 148, 150–153, 167
DRA *see* Dispute Resolution Authority
Dubai ix, 47, 137–138, 142, 144–147, 155, 176, 181; onshore courts of 147, 151
Dubai Chamber of Commerce and Industry 145–146, 155, 169, 173
Dubai International Arbitration Centre 129, 145–146, 156
Dubai International Financial Centre *see* DIFC
Dubai Law No. 12 (2004) 147
Dubai Law No. 12 (2004) (UAE) 147
Dubai Law No 16 (2011) (UAE) 147

El-Farra v Sayyed 226 SW3d 792 (2006) 171
emirates 137–138, 143, 154; Abu Dhabi 28, 134, 137, 149, 171; Ajman 137; Dubai ix, 47, 137–138, 142, 144–147,

155, 176, 181; Fujairah 137; Ra's Al Khaimah 137, 144–145, 149, 155–156, 181, 183; Sharjah 137–138, 145; Ummal-Qawain 137
enforcement 20, 22, 27–28, 36, 39–40, 49, 85–86, 94, 110–112, 114, 128, 130, 150–152, 167, 170; agencies 69; cross-border 39, 160; of foreign arbitral award in KSA 130; language favouring 86; legal 3; order 151; power 55; and recognition 28, 36, 49, 94, 110–111, 145, 175; and regulatory authority 70
England 9, 14–15, 21, 43, 45, 52, 59–60, 62, 184; and the Appellate Court 10, 62; court decisions 33; and the courts 21, 33–34, 96, 117; *see also* United Kingdom
equality (principle of) 56, 66, 174
Equality Act 2010 (UK) 61
Equality Bill (UK) 61, 66

FDIC *see* Federal Deposit Insurance Corporation
Federal Arbitration Act 22, 85
Federal Constitution 96–97, 102–103, 115–117, 168
Federal Court 16, 69, 74, 77, 92, 101–104, 106, 108, 118, 138; decisions 5, 104; nine-member Malaysian 162
Federal Decree No. 15 (2013) (UAE) 142
Federal Decree No. 35 (2004) (UAE) 142, 146
Federal Deposit Insurance Act (USA) 68–69, 72
Federal Deposit Insurance Corporation 68, 72–73, 81, 87
federal government 85, 146; central 137; dispersing relief funds 87
federal law 5, 89, 99, 102, 138–142, 144, 146, 148, 151, 153–157, 169
Federal List 96–97, 102, 115
Federal Rules of Civil Procedure (USA) 77, 84–85, 91, 93, 148, 169
Federal Supreme Court 137–138
FIDReC *see* Financial Industry Disputes Resolution Centre
finance ix–xi, 45, 47, 68–69, 96, 98, 114–116, 121–123, 125–127, 133, 136–137, 140–142, 144–145, 155, 178–180; adjudication of Shari'ah issues in Islamic 26, 117, 179; alternative 15; arbitration in Islamic 38, 68; contracts in Islamic 18; development of Islamic 100, 114, 160, 180; dispute resolution in Islamic 3, 6, 17, 20–21, 33, 53, 68, 111, 125–126, 145, 158–159, 161, 163–165, 167, 177; practice of Islamic 123, 130; underlying nature of Islamic 96, 162–163
Financial Industry Disputes Resolution Centre 44
financial institutions ix, 1–3, 9, 38, 50–51, 69–73, 80, 88, 123–125, 133, 136, 140–141, 163–164, 166, 177; conventional 141, 163; foreign 125; unnamed 71
Financial Institutions and International Arbitration 38
Financial Mediation Bureau 44, 109
Financial Ombudsman Service (Australia) 44
Financial Ombudsman Service (United Kingdom) 44
Financial Service Providers 44
financial systems 98, 120–121
financial transactions 33–35, 38, 139
financing 16, 71–72, 74, 106, 123, 128, 130; activities 124, 133; banks 122; debtor-in-possession 16; facilities 87, 106; instalment sales 87; *murabahah* home 74; residential 92; transactions 124
First Amendment (USA) 79–81, 91
First Instance Circuit (Saudi Arabia) 127
fitrah (Islamic religious revenue) 97
foreign arbitral awards 36, 49, 51, 85, 110, 130, 147, 151–152, 167, 170, 183
fraud 75–77, 152
FSPs *see* Financial Service Providers
Fujairah 137
funds 16, 68, 70, 73, 83, 87–88, 92, 95, 123–124, 130–131; administration 131; equity investment 88; Islamic investment 87, 95, 123, 130; mutual 68, 73, 76, 87, 123–124; regime 123
Funk, Nathan C 56

Gaffney, John 149
Gandhi, Indira 104
GCC *see* Gulf Cooperation Council
General Council of Islamic Banks and Financial Institutions 38, 145
government 60, 68, 77, 101, 103, 120, 122, 127, 131, 134, 145, 153, 161, 163, 166; of Canada 45, 181; of Dubai 155, 176; interference 80; local xi, 137; of Malaysia 50, 95; multicultural 57; municipal 87; of Saudi Arabia 127

grievances 40, 122, 126–127, 134, 168, 175
Griffiths, David 57
Gulf Cooperation Council 1, 123, 125, 157

Hague Principles 11–12, 16, 24–26, 160, 179
hakam 37–38, 55
Hasan, Rusni 136–153
hisbah (ombudsman) 43, 53
home ownership 68, 81

ICC *see* International Chamber of Commerce
IDB *see* Islamic Development Bank
IFIs *see* Islamic financial institutions
IFSA see *Islamic Financial Services Act 2013* (Malaysia)
IFSB *see* Islamic Financial Services Board
IICRA *see* International Islamic Center for Reconciliation and Arbitration
ijarah contracts 69
IMAC *see* International Islamic Mediation and Arbitration Centre
In re East Cameron Partners, LP, 'Order on Def [s'] Rule 12 Motions,' Bankruptcy Case No 08–51207; Adv Proc No 08–5041 (Bankruptcy Court, WDLa 2009) (unpublished order 17 April 2009) 82, 85, 92–93, 171
institutions ix, 1, 4, 19, 42–43, 50, 68, 75–76, 97, 109, 115–116, 124, 162, 166; arbitral 38; arbitration 129, 163; commercial 38; independent non-profit 38; Islamic banking 4, 123; Islamic financial ix, 1–3, 16, 18, 95–101, 107, 109, 113–114, 116, 133, 136, 140–141, 159, 161, 166; licensed 116; religious 80
interest 15, 17, 20, 22, 24, 70–71, 73, 80–81, 87–88, 90, 92–93, 122–123, 132–133, 139, 154; credited 73; delay of 139; given 152; involving 122; legalese 119; ownership 24; provisions 122; religious 122; royalty 83–84
international arbitration 7, 21, 27, 36, 38, 50–51, 112, 118–119, 129, 134, 163–164, 174, 176–177, 180–182
International Chamber of Commerce 21, 38, 50, 129, 163, 177
International Islamic Center for Reconciliation and Arbitration 38, 145, 155–156, 163, 177
International Islamic Mediation and Arbitration Centre 42
International Swaps and Derivatives Association 39, 50, 177
The Investment Dar 33
ISDA *see* International Swaps and Derivatives Association
Islam 31–32, 41–43, 53–56, 62, 65, 109, 111, 119, 121, 133–134, 136, 165–166, 174, 176, 182; arbitration 111; assets under management 1, 95; religion of 100, 105, 116; teaching of 165–166
Islamic banking ix–x, 24, 28, 47, 50, 87–88, 95, 115, 117, 119, 123, 132–133, 140, 174–178, 184–185; accounts for nearly a quarter of Malaysia's banking sector 18; adopted by major worldwide institutions 136; institutions 4, 123
Islamic Banking Act 1983 (Malaysia) 18
Islamic Banking Services Act 2013 (Malaysia) 99, 101
Islamic banks 1, 18, 50, 63, 72, 75–76, 87, 100, 119, 123–124, 132–133, 136, 139–141, 144–145, 148; chartered 73; foreign 140–141; resolving disputes 146
Islamic capital markets x, 47, 88, 95, 123, 179
Islamic civil law 37, 46, 183
Islamic conflict intervention principles 44
Islamic contract law 38
Islamic Development Bank 38, 123, 133, 140, 145
Islamic dispute resolution processes 44–45, 50, 54–55, 57, 59, 61, 63–65, 67, 176, 182
Islamic family and personal law disputes 161
Islamic finance x, 4, 6–7, 19, 25–27, 46–47, 53, 87–89, 93, 114, 118, 155, 159, 173–182, 184–185; and arbitration of disputes in Malaysia 113; and dispute resolution in Saudi Arabia 121, 123, 125–127, 129, 131, 133, 135; and settlement of Islamic finance disputes 120–131
Islamic financial arrangements 14–15
Islamic financial assets 1
Islamic financial businesses 99
Islamic financial disputes 42, 44
Islamic financial elements 98
Islamic financial facilities 51
Islamic financial institutions ix, 1–3, 16, 18, 95–101, 107, 109, 113–114, 116, 133, 136, 140–141, 159, 161, 166
Islamic financial products 19, 124, 158

Islamic financial providers 4
Islamic Financial Services Act 2013 18, 26, 96, 99, 116, 168
Islamic Financial Services Board 4, 6, 47, 141, 177, 182
Islamic financial transactions 1, 33–35, 39, 63
Islamic insurance 123–124
Islamic insurance providers 50
Islamic Investment Company 33, 96, 147, 172
Islamic investment funds 87, 95, 123, 130
Islamic istisna' contract (for manufacture) 38
Islamic jurisdictions 79, 160
Islamic jurisprudence 2, 28, 51, 54, 98, 100, 105, 109, 111, 118, 132, 178
Islamic jurists 31–32, 55–56, 63, 105
Islamic law 3–4, 7–8, 13–15, 31, 41–42, 45–46, 55, 64–65, 97–100, 105, 121–122, 129–130, 159, 165–166, 180–181
Islamic legal framework 54, 68, 98, 122, 136
Islamic mediation and arbitration 42, 161, 165
Islamic religious revenue 97
Islamic school of legal thought 138
Islamic Shari'ah 21, 38
Islamic Shari'ah Law 140
Islamic traditional courts 59

Jabbar, Siti Faridah Abdul 30, 44
judges 8–11, 13, 17–21, 30–35, 45–46, 100, 103–108, 110, 121–122, 126–128, 144, 147, 149–151, 154–155, 162–165; district court 13; federal 17; learned 104–106; lower court 126; mediating 108, 118; secular court 159; sitting 144, 147, 153; trial court 13–14, 77–78
judgments 31, 33–34, 37, 41, 46, 104–106, 115, 128, 130, 138, 143, 145, 147, 149–152, 156; court 36; default 164; final 74, 147; local 123
judicial bodies 127–128
judicial principles 121, 131
judiciary 3, 5, 103, 105, 108, 133–134, 137, 168, 174
jurisdictions 4–5, 10–11, 14–18, 21–23, 36, 39–41, 47–48, 79–82, 96–97, 115, 125–127, 129–130, 133, 147, 166; exclusive 96–97; exercise 85, 94; local 36; non-Shari'ah 9; particular 8, 12, 120, 166; secular 7, 77, 159–162, 176
justice 31–32, 42–43, 55–56, 60, 64, 86, 102, 105, 121, 126–127, 137, 144, 146, 158–159; administration 120; and the arbitration procedure to ensure fair dealing and 37; and the Islam emphasis (to all parties) on the act of doing 31; natural 152

Khalid, Waleed 101–102
Khan, Amjad Ali 141, 144
Kingdom of Saudi Arabia *see* Saudi Arabia
KLCMC *see* Kuala Lumpur Court Mediation Centre
KLRCA *see* Kuala Lumpur Regional Centre for Arbitration
Kuala Lumpur 98
Kuala Lumpur Court Complex 108
Kuala Lumpur Court Mediation Centre 52, 107, 173
Kuala Lumpur Regional Centre for Arbitration 7, 38, 50, 67, 112, 119
Kuala Lumpur Stock Exchange Islamic Index 75
Kuwait 21, 27, 38, 137, 152, 172

Land Acquisition Act 1960 (Malaysia) 103–104
language 10, 20, 76, 84, 86, 113, 129, 144; of the arbitration 22; contractual 81; plain 84; recommended 22; in which proceedings are conducted 35
law ix–xi, 4–5, 7–30, 33–38, 42–43, 64–65, 67–69, 74–83, 94–100, 114–115, 117–126, 128–134, 151, 158–165, 174–176; and choices in Islamic finance 8–9, 11, 13, 15, 17, 19, 21, 23, 25, 27, 29, 160; civil ix, 47, 143, 146, 151–153, 173; clauses 8–9, 11–12, 15, 21, 159; distinct 62, 68; governing 5, 10, 20, 23, 33, 36, 77, 111, 113, 117, 119, 121, 159; international 8, 22, 53, 86, 174; non-Islamic 12, 14–16, 18; rules of 11, 26; secular arbitration 57; securities 69–70, 73; sharia 57, 59, 62, 92
law courts 12, 43, 68, 144
Law of Arbitration 2012 21, 128–129, 135, 162, 168
Law of Commercial Agency 1962 21
lawsuits 3, 74, 76, 79
LCIA *see* London Court of International Arbitration
legal framework x, 4, 6, 26, 59, 68–69, 95, 117–118, 123, 180; global 38; Islamic 54, 68, 98, 122, 136

legal pluralism 58, 65, 176
legal principles 8, 28, 30
legal services xi, 48, 142–143, 146, 149
legal systems 5, 7, 19, 57–58, 60, 121–122, 125, 131–132, 134, 136, 142–144, 148, 166, 176, 180; civil 137, 142, 144; mixed 132, 143, 153, 180
legislation 51, 102, 124, 137–138, 142, 149–150, 162, 164, 166–167; primary 142; principal source of 138; secondary 142
litigation 1–3, 6, 8–9, 14–16, 30–31, 33–35, 44–46, 96, 107–110, 113–114, 125–126, 143, 159–160, 162, 164–167; alternatives to 107, 164–165; costs 22, 50; dispute resolution approaches 158; in Islamic finance 33; of Islamic financial disputes 44; in Islamic law 31; proceedings 144; process 30–32, 63, 108, 143, 150; securities enforcement 73
loans 17, 24, 75, 80, 83–85, 92–93, 139; agreements 91; contracts 139, 154
London Court of International Arbitration 129, 148, 163
Louisiana Commercial Code 84
Louisiana law 83, 85
Lucent Technologies International 12–13, 17, 77–78, 91, 172

MAAS *see* Masjed Abubakr Al-Seddiq
Majallah Al-Ahkam Al'Adliyyah (a compilation of Islamic civil law) 37
Malayan Banking Bhd v Marilyn Ho Siok 34
Malayan Law Journal 19
Malaysia ix–xi, 4–7, 18–19, 26, 47, 50–53, 95–99, 103, 107, 109, 113–119, 136, 160–165, 174–176, 179–180; *AIAC i-Arbitration Rules 2018* 113, 119, 162, 168; *Arbitration Act 2005* 51n112, 168; and the basis in Islamic law supporting the various dispute settling processes 165; and case law 1, 19; and the *Central Bank of Malaysia Act 2009* 7, 18–20, 96, 98–100, 162; and conventional finance laws 95; and the dispute resolution mechanism for Islamic finance 5; and the *Islamic Financial Services Act 2013* 18, 20; *National Land Code* 98, 115; *Penal Code* 97; and the possibility of becoming a forum for settlement of international Islamic finance disputes 113; ranked first in terms of Islamic finance leadership 95; recognized as the most developed Islamic finance market globally 95
Malaysian Court of Appeal 51
Malaysian Islamic finance regulations 20
Malaysian judiciary 20, 164
Malaysian law ix, 18–19, 113
Malaysian Law Review Appellate Courts 19
Malaysian Law Review High Court 19
Masjed Abubakr Al-Seddiq 81–82
MAT *see* Muslim Arbitration Tribunal
mazhabs 105, 111
mechanisms 2–3, 7, 31, 33, 36, 44, 107, 114, 136, 158, 160, 164, 181; appropriate dispute resolution 2; appropriate Shari'ah compliant dispute resolution 2; available dispute resolutions 1, 3, 5–7, 44, 115, 129, 143, 165–166, 179; for dispute settling 159; exploring alternative dispute resolution 2, 125, 165; unofficial dispute resolution 58
mediation 2–3, 30–31, 38, 40–44, 50–56, 60–61, 63–65, 107–110, 113–114, 117–118, 148–149, 151, 160, 163–166, 176–177; advantages of 41, 52; and arbitration 2, 6, 96, 107, 114, 160, 164–165; centres 108; conventional 41; court-ordered 108; evaluative 41, 52; facilitative 41; forums 43; in Islamic law 41; judge-led 109, 118; non-binding 55; outcomes 108–109; private nature of 43–44; proceedings 43; processes 41–42, 56, 108; rules 148, 156; services in Islamic finance 42, 61, 66, 169, 174; transformative 41
mediators 40–42, 55–56, 108–109, 118, 153; external 108–109; impartiality of 118
'Medina Charter' 56
mediation 114, 164–165
mediators 164–165
misrepresentations 75–77, 90
Model Law 36, 40, 48, 51
Mohamad, Tun Abdul Hamid 98, 115–117
mortgages 70–71, 80–81, 83–84, 89, 123
motions 15–16, 79, 83, 85, 93, 171; Appellants' 86; granting of Sukuk Certificateholders' 84; pretrial 74
Muamalat Court 98
Mubadalatul Arbaah (Profit Rate Swap) Agreement 39
Muhammad, Prophet 12–13, 28, 31, 37, 42–43, 46, 55–56, 63–64, 120–121

muhtasib (ombudsman) 43
Muneeza, Aishath 120–131
murabahah 39, 62, 69, 72–73, 80, 96; financing transactions (equivalent to a real estate mortgage transaction) 71; invalid contracts 33; sale contracts (mark-up) 33, 39, 69, 87
Muslim Arbitration Tribunal 57–59, 61, 64, 161
Muslims 31, 42, 57, 60–62, 64, 96–97, 104–105, 112, 115, 136, 161, 175; communities 58; and the conduct of mediations and arbitrations within the British legal system 58; "dangerous" 60–61; jurisdictions 34; new immigrants in the West 57; and the oneness of Allah 32; parties 97; prefer to live under British law 57
Mustapha, Zakariya 120–131

NADRAC *see* National Alternative Dispute Resolution Advisory Council (Australia)
National Alternative Dispute Resolution Advisory Council (Australia) 51, 174
National Bank Act (USA) 68–71, 88
national courts 11, 20, 39
National Group for Communications & Computers v Lucent Technologies International 12, 17, 77
National Land Code (Malaysia) 98, 115
national securities exchanges 76
'Net Lease Agreement' 70–71, 73, 90, 181
New York 14, 16, 23, 73–74, 77, 81; bankruptcy court 8; law 74, 77, 91
New York Convention 20, 22, 28, 36, 39–40, 49, 51, 85, 94, 110–112, 145, 147, 151, 163, 167
New York Department of Financial Services 73–74, 90, 181
Nigeria x, 45, 133, 174, 180
NYDFS *see* New York Department of Financial Services

OCC *see* Office of Comptroller of the Currency
Office of Comptroller of the Currency 68, 70–74, 80, 89, 92
OFS *see* Ombudsman for Financial Services (Malaysia)
Ombudsman for Financial Services (Malaysia) 44, 53, 109–110, 180
ORRI *see* Overriding Royalty Interest
outcomes 2, 55, 81, 109–110, 113–114, 158, 163, 165–166; acceptable 158; effective dispute resolution 164; final 107, 110; through mediation 108–109; ultimate 102–103; win-win 109
Overriding Royalty Interest 82–84
ownership 80, 82, 92; bank's 92; home 68, 81; transferring 83

parties 1–6, 8–11, 13–17, 19–22, 24–28, 30–33, 35–42, 77–79, 82–87, 102–103, 107–114, 127–130, 143–145, 147–149, 163–167; deciding to deal with Islamic banks 63; deciding to dismiss the arbitrator 37; mitigating against the use of Shari'ah-related defences being used during litigation 15; stipulating that the arbitrator must be Muslim and male 61
Penal Code (Malaysia) 97, 146
petitions 74, 81–82, 90, 171
plaintiffs 75, 78–79, 97, 101, 106, 143–144
Practice Direction on Mediation (Malaysia) 107, 117–118
pre-Islamic Arabia 37, 54
precedent 17, 31, 127, 131; not followed by Saudi Arabia judges 17; judicial 18, 34, 131
primary sources of Shari'ah law 17, 20, 42, 46, 78, 105, 143
principles 7–13, 28–29, 32–33, 42, 56, 62–63, 75, 78–79, 87, 114–116, 118, 121–122, 138, 140–141, 178–180; fundamental 46, 59, 177; Islamic conflict intervention 44; Islamic legal 1, 58; mudarabah 105; neutral 82, 92; Shari'ah 5–6, 17, 22, 28, 38, 60, 78–79, 99, 160–161
Procedural Rules Before the Board of Grievances 1989 168
profit sharing deposits 72, 89, 184
Prophet Muhammad 12–13, 28, 31, 37, 42–43, 46, 55–56, 63–64, 120–121
PSD *see* profit sharing deposits
public policy 22, 28, 39–40, 61, 80, 86, 94, 112, 130, 152, 154; considerations 23; defence 39; exceptions 86, 94, 175

Qadhi (judge in a litigation) 31–32, 37–38
Qur'an 13, 17, 31, 37, 41–43, 78, 121, 165

Al-Rajhi Bank 123
Ramadan, Tariq 62
Ras Al Khaimah Centre of Reconciliation and Commercial Arbitration 137, 144–145, 149, 155–156, 181, 183

rate of return 139, 145
real estate 69, 71, 81, 88–89, 123
reconciliation 38, 40, 42, 49–50, 55–56, 58, 143, 145, 151, 153, 155, 163, 165, 177, 181; centres 153; process 143–144; use of the term 143
Reconciliation and Settlement Committee 144
regulations 10, 17–18, 20, 68–69, 73–74, 82, 96, 99, 121–125, 127, 133, 146–147, 149, 156, 168–170; common law-based 142; existing US 87; financial x; new 123, 132, 177
religious arbitration 22
religious law 12, 28, 77, 131, 161, 174
resolution process 19, 21, 27–28, 31, 40, 42–43, 46, 48, 106–107, 125, 134, 151–152, 161–162, 165, 167; adjudicative dispute 35; annexed dispute 143–144; formal dispute 59; organizational initiated dispute 145; private dispute 63
Rome Convention on the Law Applicable to Contractual Obligations 1998 9–10, 24, 160
Royal Decrees 120–122, 124, 126–128, 132
royalty interests 83–84
RSC *see* Reconciliation and Settlement Committee

SABIC *see* Saudi Basic Industries Corporation
SAC *see* Shari'ah Advisory Council
Said, Suzana Muhamad 30–44
SAMA *see* Saudi Arabian Monetary Authority
Saudi Arabia 4–6, 12–14, 17, 20, 22–23, 77–78, 119–135, 152, 158, 160, 162–164, 173–174, 176–180, 182, 184; arbitration in 129, 135, 173; authorities 128, 131, 134; *Basic Law 1992* 12, 121, 125, 128; *Board of Grievances Law 1982* 122, 126–127, 134, 168; courts 79, 130; judges 13, 17; Law 13–14, 18, 79, 121–122, 125, 129–130, 132, 134, 174; *Law of Arbitration 2012* 21, 128–129, 135, 162, 168; *Law of Commercial Agency 1962* 21; legal system of 13–14, 130, 132; legislators 122; and Malaysia 136; and Shari'ah Law 129
Saudi Arabian Monetary Authority 124, 127, 133, 182
Saudi Basic Industries Corporation 13–14, 17, 25–26, 78–79, 91, 172
SC *see* Shari'ah Committee
SDA *see* International Swaps and Derivatives Association
Semenyih Jaya Sdn Bhd v Pentadbir Tanah Daerah Hulu Langat 103
services 30, 35, 44, 61, 75, 95, 99, 108, 121, 123, 140–141, 155, 176; dispensing arbitration 148; investment 140–141
settlement 2, 4–5, 40–42, 44–45, 94–96, 108, 120–121, 124–126, 131, 134, 136, 139, 143–144, 146–147, 159–160; agreement 108; forum 120; forum for 7, 113, 122, 176; negotiated 41; peaceful 55; procedures 120
Shamil Bank of Bahrain EC 9–10, 15, 23–25, 62–63, 66–67, 78, 81, 91–92, 96, 117, 147, 157, 160, 175
Shapiro, M 32
Shari'ah 1–2, 4–6, 8–13, 20–23, 26–29, 31–35, 37–39, 58–64, 99–102, 109–113, 118–126, 128–131, 138–143, 148, 158–166; arbitration process 61; aspects of Islamic finance contracts 1; award violating 130; based defences 14; based disputes 63; based sources of jurisprudence 14, 22; influenced jurisdictions 14, 86; inspired defence 15; and Islamic financial transactions 35, 109–110; misconceptions surrounding 61; recognized 38; referencing as the governing contract 8
Shari'ah Advisory Council 5, 18, 26, 34, 47, 64, 75, 98–107, 109, 113, 116, 118, 162–163, 165
Shari'ah Board 35, 75–76
Shari'ah Committee ix, 18, 99, 101, 116, 147
Shari'ah compliance 1, 9, 95–96, 101, 104, 106, 112–114, 118, 131, 140–141, 152–153, 162–163; and contractual language regarding 81; in Islamic finance disputes 163; of Islamic finance practice 125; issues 101; resolution to Islamic finance disputes 145, 148, 153
Shari'ah compliant 2, 9, 63, 101, 103–104, 107, 111–112, 114, 167; aspects of Islamic financial transactions 34; contracts 159; decisions for Islamic finance disputes 153; investments 69; student loans 80; transactions 86, 125
Shari'ah Councils 58–59, 61–64, 161, 175
Shari'ah Court of Appeal 126
Shari'ah Court of First Instance 126
Shari'ah courts 34–35, 47, 54, 58, 60–61, 64, 96–98, 115, 125–127, 129, 134, 162,

168; conducting mediations and arbitrations 58; hierarchy of 32, 126; and Shari'ah Councils 58–59, 61–64, 161, 175
Shari'ah expert witnesses 9, 100, 113, 118, 162
Shari'ah law 58–59, 62–63, 132, 134, 158, 162, 167, 174; clauses 63; flexible 64; and Islamic jurists 63
Shari'ah principles 5–6, 17, 22, 28, 38, 60, 78–79, 99, 160–161
Shari'ah questions 98–99, 103–104, 106–107, 110, 113, 163, 165; to be considered 102; and courts having full autonomy to adjudicate and make rules on 104; in Islamic finance disputes 101, 106, 162; in the Malaysian courts 96; meriting referral to the SAC for its ruling 102; referred to it by a court or arbitrator 99; and the SAC making rulings on 101
Shari'ah scholars 11, 35, 98, 105, 109, 128, 141, 149, 153, 163, 165
Shari'ah Supervision Authority 141
Sharjah 137–138, 145
Sharjah International Commercial Arbitration Centre 144–145, 155, 182
Siddiqui, Mona 62
Singapore 44
state courts 12, 40–41, 85, 108
state jurisdictions 73
statutes 17–18, 68–71, 104, 117, 168–170
statutes and regulations: *Abu Dhabi Law No. 4 of 2013* (UAE) 142; *AIAC i-Arbitration Rules 2018* (Malaysia) 113, 119, 162, 168; *Amiri Decree No. 6, 2009* (UAE) 145; *Amiri Decree No. 17, 2008* (UEA) 145; *Arbitration Act 1996* (UK) 59, 61, 161; *Arbitration and Mediation Services* (Equality Bill) (UK) 61, 66; *Arbitration Regulations 2015* (UAE) 149–150; *Basic Law 1992* (Saudi Arabia) 12, 121, 125, 128; *Board of Grievances Law 1982* 122, 126–127, 134, 168; *Central Bank of Malaysia Act 1958* 99; *Central Bank of Malaysia Act 2009* 7, 18–20, 96, 98–100, 162; *Civil Code* (UAE) 139–140, 154–155, 169; *Dubai Law No. 12 (2004)* 147; *Dubai Law No 16 (2011)* 147; *Dubai Law No 16 (2011)* (UAE) 147; *Equality Act 2010* (UK) 61; *Equality Bill* (UK) 61, 66; *Federal Deposit Insurance Act* USA 68–69, 72; *Federal Rules of Civil Procedure* (USA) 77, 84–85, 91, 93, 148, 169; *Islamic Banking Act 1983* (Malaysia) 18; *Islamic Banking Services Act 2013* (Malaysia) 99, 101; *Islamic Financial Services Act 2013* (Malaysia) 18, 20; *Land Acquisition Act 1960* (Malaysia) 103–104; *National Bank Act* (US) 68–71, 88; *National Land Code* (Malaysia) 98, 115; *Penal Code* (Malaysia) 97, 146; *Rome Convention on the Law Applicable to Contractual Obligations 1998* 9–10, 24, 160; *Syariah Criminal Offences (Federal Territories) Act 1997* 168; *Trust Indenture Act 1939* (USA) 69; *Truth in Lending Act* (USA) 68
Stevens, John 73
Syariah Criminal Offences (Federal Territories) Act 1997 168

Tahawwut Master Agreement 39, 50, 177
tahkim (arbitration) 37, 54–55, 59, 63, 165
tawsit (mediation) 41, 52
terrorism 57
Texas Islamic Court 86
Texas Supreme Court 22
Thomas, Lord (Chief Justice) 52
TID *see* The Investment Dar
TMA *see* Tahawwut Master Agreement
Trakic, Adnan xi, 1–2, 4, 6–7, 26, 95, 95–118, 158, 158–167, 176, 179–180, 182–183
transactions 1–2, 4–5, 16, 24, 33–34, 70–71, 81, 83–86, 90, 92, 98, 122, 124–125, 131, 133; commercial 138–139; *gharar* 13; *ijarah* sale-leaseback 90, 92; principal securities 72
trial courts 14, 17, 79, 86, 92, 126; decisions 13; lower 126
trials 14, 19, 31, 45, 74, 81, 108
Trust Indenture Act 1939 (USA) 69
Truth in Lending Act (USA) 68

UAE 4–6, 38, 136–155, 157–158, 160, 163–164, 168–170, 173, 178–179; *Abu Dhabi Law No. 4 of 2013* 142; *Amiri Decree No. 6, 2009* 145; *Amiri Decree No. 17, 2008* 145; *Arbitration Regulations 2015* 149–150; Central Bank 140; *Commercial Code* 139, 155, 169; courts 144, 151, 163; *Dubai Law No. 12 (2004)* 147; *Dubai Law No 16 (2011)* 147; existing laws of 140; *Federal Decree No. 15 (2013)* 142;

UAE *continued*
Federal Decree No. 35 (2004) 142, 146; Federal Supreme Court 139; Government 154, 163; Islamic banking and finance industry 153; Islamic finance disputes in Saudi Arabia 121, 123, 125, 127, 129, 131, 133, 135; *Penal Code* 146
UBK *see* United Bank of Kuwait
UIS *see* United Islamic Society
UK *see* United Kingdom
Ummal-Qawain (Emirate) 137
United Bank of Kuwait 70–71
United Islamic Society 81–82, 92, 172
United Islamic Society v Masjed Abubakr Al-Seddiq 81–82
United Kingdom 4, 6, 8, 44–45, 49, 54–55, 57–67, 81, 158, 160–161, 169, 171, 174–175, 179, 183; *Arbitration Act 1996* 59, 61, 161; *Arbitration and Mediation Services* (Equality Bill) 61, 66; *Equality Act 2010* 61
United Nations 4, 36, 48–49, 183–184
United Nations Commission on International Trade Law 36, 48, 63, 155–156, 170, 183
United States *see* US
US 4, 11–12, 16–17, 22, 24, 68–69, 71–73, 75, 77–81, 83, 85–93, 158, 160–161, 169, 172; arbitration 85; Bankruptcy Code 16; courts 12, 14, 28, 77, 81–82, 86–87; dispute resolution processes 161; Supreme Court 79

Walid Al-Samaani (Supreme Judicial Council) 131
waqf (religious term) 81–82
wasitah (mediation) 41, 52
wasta (mediation) 41, 55
Western countries 57, 142; dispute resolution processes 54, 56; and Islamic dispute resolution mechanisms 56; legal structures 57
Williams, Rowan 60

zakat (Islamic religious revenue) 97, 115

For Product Safety Concerns and Information please contact our EU representative GPSR@taylorandfrancis.com Taylor & Francis Verlag GmbH, Kaufingerstraße 24, 80331 München, Germany

Printed and bound by CPI Group (UK) Ltd, Croydon, CR0 4YY
01/05/2025
01858416-0003